ACTING LESSONS FOR TEACHERS

Using Performance Skills in the Classroom

Second Edition

Robert T. Tauber and Cathy Sargent Mester

Westport, Connecticut
London

Library of Congress Cataloging-in-Publication Data

Tauber, Robert T.
   Acting lessons for teachers : using performance skills in the classroom / Robert T.
Tauber and Cathy Sargent Mester. — 2nd ed.
      p.   cm.
   Includes bibliographical references and index.
   ISBN 0–275–99192–X (alk. paper)—0–275–99204–7 (pbk.)
   1. Teachers—Training of. 2. Acting—Study and teaching. 3. Communication in
education. I. Mester, Cathy Sargent. II. Title.
LB1732.T38   2007
370.71—dc22   2006021057

British Library Cataloguing in Publication Data is available.

Library of Congress Catalog Card Number: 2006021057
ISBN: 0–275–99192–X
      0–275–99204–7 (pbk.)

First published in 2007

Praeger Publishers, 88 Post Road West, Westport, CT 06881
An imprint of Greenwood Publishing Group, Inc.
www.praeger.com

Printed in the United States of America

The paper used in this book complies with the
Permanent Paper Standard issued by the National
Information Standards Organization (Z39.48–1984).

10   9   8   7   6   5   4   3   2   1

CONTENTS

ILLUSTRATIONS

ACKNOWLEDGMENTS

Robert T. Tauber

First and foremost, I wish to thank my wife, Cecelia. The truth is that no simple acknowledgment could ever be enough. Her own enthusiastic teaching, for over thirty years, modeled much of what is presented in this text. I could have written this book just by watching her teach. Cissie was a pro at using performance skills to engage students. Our discussions on the content of this text, as well as on endless other education topics, has kept my pedagogical spirits glowing. I thank her for that! I also want to thank my coauthor, Cathy Sargent Mester, and my secretary (before I retired), Wendy Kallgren. Cathy helped make the ideas happen; Wendy helped make the final product happen. Finally, I want to thank those teachers who used the first edition of this text and, as a result, justified this second edition.

Cathy Sargent Mester

This book is the result, for me, of inspiration from the new generation of teachers who come to the task with such energy, dedication, and creativity. They face new and daunting challenges in the classroom, but never stop working to meet those challenges and help the children learn. I thank them all, but especially my own daughter and son-in-law, Cari and John Russell, who make me believe that good education is still possible. Great thanks also go to my own mentor and coauthor, Robert T. Tauber, for his unselfish and energized devotion to this project.

PREFACE

We love teaching. Both your authors and you, the readers, love the classroom experience. We accept that the students don't always learn as much or as readily as we might have hoped, and we accept that we might not have executed a planned lesson as smoothly as we had hoped. But we still love the excitement of the first day, the thrill of seeing a student learn, and the satisfaction of a project well done.

Loving the experience as we do, we are always trying to do it better. That is what this book is all about: helping dedicated teachers develop new and better strategies to meet the unending need for stronger students. Whether you teach at the elementary, secondary, community college, or university level, you will find ideas and methods here that suit your classroom. Beginning teachers and graduate teaching assistants will be inspired to "act" the part of a confident, experienced teacher, and those with more years in the classroom will be supported in expanding the "roles" in their repertoire.

In this second edition, we have brought the ideas and pedagogical principles of the first edition into the twenty-first century by including new chapters covering instructional technology and classroom entrances and exits. In addition, each chapter has been revised to include the conclusions from recent pedagogical research and the experiences of award-winning K–12 teachers.

Read, experiment, enjoy!

PART 1

Background

CHAPTER

Teacher Enthusiasm: A Pedagogical Necessity

Nothing great was ever accomplished without enthusiasm!
—Ralph Waldo Emerson

INTRODUCTION

As new or veteran teachers, we are all constantly struggling with the same goal: helping more students to learn more. A number of factors have been identified as contributing to the differences in student learning, explaining why some students grasp all of the material, some grasp only certain parts of it, and, sadly, some grasp very little. As we look at those factors, it is readily apparent that most relate to differences in the students that exist from the moment they enter our classroom—factors such as basic intelligence, family background, learning style, and so on. The proactive teacher trying to improve student learning cannot change such factors. So it is easy to become discouraged.

However, one factor *is* within our control, and that is teacher style. Differences in teachers' communicative styles do impact the degree to which students learn and learn meaningfully. This is something all teachers *can* learn and use to accomplish that universal teaching goal. By adopting some creative verbal and nonverbal techniques, we can help more students learn more in all levels and types of educational settings. The techniques we recommend are found in the world of the actor.

OUR GOAL

To waken interest and kindle enthusiasm is the sure way to teach easily and successfully.
—Tryon Edwards

We should explain the title for this book, *Acting Lessons for Teachers*. In actuality, there are few if any of the "lessons" that you might expect to experience in an Acting 101 class. Most theater or acting classes would have students run through, often with fellow students, a series of exercises with descriptive names such as "space walks," "zip zap zop," "positive affirmations," "gibberish," "woosh," and "alien visitor." Certainly these experiences would be fun, informative, and confidence building. Stanislavski's book (1936), *An Actor Prepares*, probably would be required reading.

What we attempt to do, instead, is to convince readers that there is an acting–teaching parallel that, once recognized (and we will help you do this) and adopted, will improve their effectiveness as classroom teachers. Teachers will have more fun teaching, and students will be more engaged and learn more. We plan to accomplish this by helping readers recognize the lessons to be learned from the world of actors and actresses and the stage and cinema environment that make up their world.

We point out specific lessons to be learned from the actor's world. These lessons focus on animation in voice, animation in body, space utilization, humor, role-playing, props, and suspense and surprise, as well as creative entrances and exits. Lessons in these specific acting skills for teachers are accompanied by a continuous recognition of the importance of teachers' enthusiasm and passion. We offer many stage and cinema examples with which the reader can identify, and we then suggest classroom counterparts. We encourage the reader to brainstorm even more classroom applications—the more the better.

Having made this distinction between a typical introduction to acting class and the goal of our text, we do offer several Acting 101–type exercises, mainly in Chapter 13, the "Behind the Scenes" chapter. But, our focus is on extracting lessons from the actor's world and then showing how they can be applied to the teacher's world. This is what separates our text from others that have words such as "acting" and "performing" in their titles.

TEACHER ENTHUSIASM: ITS RELATIONSHIP TO PEDAGOGY

Enthusiasm is the greatest asset in the world. It beats money, power and influence.

—Henry Chester

It is Wednesday morning, 9 AM. Faculty and staff have gathered for an in-service program. Some teachers have a cup of coffee; others have coffee and doughnuts. The stage is set for a morning of "in-servicing!" The workshop leader welcomes the educators and asks them to read a series of quotations handwritten in large print on poster board that he tapes, one at a time, to the walls of the classroom. Two sides of the room are needed to display the eight or nine quotations. Participants then are asked to determine the message that is common in all of the displayed quotations. The task is not difficult.

Among the quotations hung on the wall are the following:

- "Enthusiasm is the key to being a successful teacher" (Soenksen 1992).
- "Effective teachers motivate their students with an enthusiastic style of teaching" (Brophy and Good 1986).
- "One of the five delivery characteristics associated with effective teaching is the projection of enthusiasm for the subject matter" (Goulden 1991).
- "A great teacher qua teacher—as opposed to scholar or ethical exemplar or authority figure—has intensity and communicates it enthusiastically" (Hanning 1984).
- "The outstanding feature of effective teaching is the ability to communicate effectively. Put another way, a good teacher is a good talker—one who exemplifies enthusiasm for his or her work" (Schwartz 1980).
- "One of twelve affinity-seeking strategies used by teachers that is associated with competence and motivation is dynamism—physically indicating to students that one is dynamic, active, and enthusiastic" (Frymier and Thompson 1992).
- "What constitutes masterful teaching? A factor found prominent in most studies is the instructor's ability to stimulate enthusiasm for the subject, a skill frequently related to the teacher's personal enthusiasm" (Lowman 1984).
- "A teacher who is not able to convey enthusiasm for his or her subject (even though he may feel it inwardly) labors under a great handicap. Students are unwilling to accept a teacher who cannot transmit to them something of the excitement of his or her field" (Jordan 1982).
- "Students who received enthusiastically delivered presentations reported greater intrinsic motivation" (Patrick, Hisley, and Kempler 2000).

A great teacher is not just someone who is approachable as a person, although this is not an uncommon characteristic of a great teacher. A great teacher also isn't simply a scholar—one who knows a lot—although knowing a lot about one's field certainly can contribute to greatness. What one knows must be communicated. Jordan (1982, 124) reminds us that "the Teacher as Scholar is *important*, that the Teacher as Person is *crucial*, and that the Teacher as Communicator is *indispensable*" (italics added for emphasis). Teacher enthusiasm, the common factor in the displayed quotations, is fundamental to effective communication.

The workshop leader continues by stating that teacher enthusiasm is a pedagogical necessity. Cautious, but slightly nervous, participants agree. One participant, though, volunteers that classrooms do not just contain teachers; they contain students, too. Therefore, one might argue—in fact, one should argue—that enthusiastic teaching is of little value unless effective student learning takes place. Measures of effective learning consist of heightened student interest, positive student attitude, more on-task student behavior, and greater student achievement, among other factors.

We would argue that effective actors, too, must communicate what they know. But, unlike teachers, actors have long recognized the need to develop specific skills, especially means and methods of expression, to enhance their communication. The bulk of this book is devoted to helping teachers develop acting skills that can help them communicate better.

TEACHER ENTHUSIASM: ITS RELATIONSHIP TO STUDENT ACHIEVEMENT

Enthusiasm is the mother of effort, and without it nothing great was ever achieved.

—Ralph Waldo Emerson

At this point, the workshop leader asks those gathered to read the remaining quotations, prepared as handwritten signs that he also tapes, one at a time, on the remaining two walls of the classroom. Among the quotations displayed are the following:

- "Teachers' enthusiasm has been found to be related [positively] to student achievement gains" (Rosenshine and Furst 1973).
- "Children taught at a high level of enthusiasm were more attentive, interested, and responsive" (Burts et al. 1985).
- "Student rating scores were significantly higher for expressive [enthusiastic] than for nonexpressive lectures" (Meier and Feldhusen 1979).
- "Research has shown correlational and causal links between teacher enthusiasm and student achievement" (Gillett 1980).
- "Teachers who received enthusiasm training had students who demonstrated a more positive attitude toward reading" (Streeter 1986).
- "Educators trained in how to enhance their enthusiasm had students whose on-task time was significantly greater than for non-trained teachers" (Bettencourt, Gillett, and Hull 1983).
- "Teachers receiving training in how to be more enthusiastic had LD students who scored substantially higher on post-tests and exhibited more acceptable classroom behaviors" (Brigham 1991).
- "Teacher enthusiasm is correlated with increased student attentiveness and, hence, increased student achievement" (Murphy and Walls 1994).
- "Students repeatedly indicate that they learn more from those who evince enthusiasm and concern for the quality of teaching, even though they may frequently complain about their own required extra effort" (Browne and Keeley 1985).
- "Teacher enthusiasm can have a profound effect on students. Teaching enthusiastically can yield twice the achievement and significantly lessen behavior problems" (Brigham, Scruggs, and Mastropieri 1992).
- "Teacher enthusiasm is an important factor in affecting student learning" (Pilla 1997).
- "Educator enthusiasm is correlated with students' course achievement and their motivation to further learn. Motivated students, in turn, motivate teachers to

show still more enthusiasm. A positive cycle, benefiting both teachers and students, is created" (Murray 1997).

The connection between teacher enthusiasm and desired student learning outcomes is clear. Researchers document it; practitioners testify to it. Teacher enthusiasm is one means to the end of greater student achievement.

Another point that emerges from these quotations is that teacher enthusiasm is a quality associated with effective teaching across all disciplines, all grade levels, and all categories of students. Teacher enthusiasm is as important in English as it is in physics, as important in social studies as it is in mathematics. "Regardless of content, the college classroom does not have to be agonizingly dull" (Welsz 1990, 74). The same point applies to all classrooms.

Figure 1.1, titled "Teacher Enthusiasm and Student Achievement," depicts the catalyst role that enthusiasm plays in holding students' attention, generating students' interest, and developing students' positive attitudes toward learning. Highly enthusiastic teachers are highly expressive in vocal delivery, gestures, body movement, and overall energy level. All of these are crucial ingredients that, in turn, contribute to greater student achievement.

In addition to producing greater student achievement, highly expressive (enthusiastic) teachers tend to have students who attribute their higher student achievement to "their own attributes—namely, ability and effort" (Perry 1985, 44). Given that the attributions of "ability" and "effort" are internal—within students' own power to influence—one would expect students who develop such attributes to experience still greater achievement in the future. After all, these students perceive the world, now, as more controllable. A circle, then, of greater student achievement credited to ability and effort leading to more student achievement has been created—all influenced by enthusiastic teachers.

Eison (1990) believes that in the classroom, a teacher's enthusiasm is often contagious; so too is his or her lack of enthusiasm. He believes that "enthusiasm and energy can carry the day" (p. 24). Who has not personally experienced the infectious enthusiasm generated by singers in an outdoor concert (e.g., the Beach Boys, Jimmy Buffett, or Bob Seger), by a well-performed Nutcracker Suite, or by a stirring symphony and its conductor? That same infectious enthusiasm can exist in classrooms.

McKeachie, a recognized name in the field of pedagogy, claims that probably no one characteristic is more important in education than a teacher's enthusiasm and energy (1986). Jackson and Murray (1997) offer supporting evidence in their book, *What Students Really Think of Professors*, where they found evidence to back up the obvious—students want more "umph," more enthusiasm, from their teachers. Lowman (1984) argues that a factor found prominently in most research on teaching effectiveness is the instructor's ability to stimulate enthusiasm for the subject. As reported in *The Penn State Teacher II*, one thing that remains constant in any discussion of good teaching is enthusiasm. "Enthusiasm is compelling and infectious. Lack of enthusiasm is also infectious, but it is deadly" (Enerson et al. 1997, 14).

Figure 1.1
Teacher Enthusiasm and Student Achievement

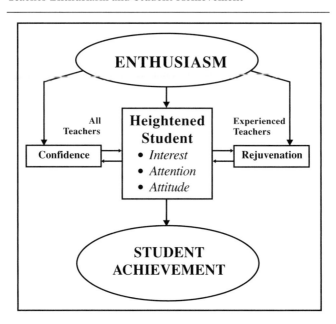

Sincere enthusiasm helps create, as well as maintain, a good learning environ-ment (Campbell 1981). Faculty are encouraged to find a balance between heightened enthusiasm and periods of calm (Brookfield and Preskill 1999). Teacher enthusiasm has a positive impact—greater student achievement—on kindergarten youngsters, college students, and all those in between. The evi-dence is overwhelming in favor of teacher enthusiasm!

"LET'S KICK IT UP A NOTCH!"

Enthusiasm is contagious. Be a carrier.

—Susan Rabin

Perhaps Chef Emeril has it right when he says to his studio and television audi-ence, "Let's kick it up a notch!" Maybe teacher enthusiasm is not enough; perhaps we should hold out for teacher passion! Mariska Hargitay, the star who plays Olivia on *Law and Order: SVU*, was shown (March 2006) on the cover of *LIFE* magazine leaning on the shoulder of her favorite teacher—Sister Margaret. Of her favorite teacher, Mariska says, "There's no way I would be the actor I am without Sister Margaret. Her passion lit a fire in me." According to Day (2004), passion should be center stage for good teaching. Our passion, in turn, can help students keep that passion with which they came into this world (Fried 2001). The notion has been affirmed and confirmed since ancient times, in fact. We find it in the writings of the ancient philosopher Plutarch, who wrote, "The mind is not a vessel to be filled, but a fire to be ignited."

Is passion too high a goal? Not according to Fried, the author of the often-cited book *The Passionate Teacher: A Practical Guide* (2001). Fried argues that "the passion that accompanies our attention to subjects, issues, and children is not just something we offer our students. It is also a gift we grant ourselves: a way of honoring our life's work, our profession" (19). Therefore, passion benefits both students who are in it for the short run and faculty who are in it for the long run—twenty or thirty years! Although some passionate teachers may naturally show that attribute, others have to be encouraged to reveal the passion that drove them initially into the teaching profession.

The prestigious 2005 Lilly South Conference on College and University Teaching had as its theme *Teaching So Everyone Learns*. This included a focus on finding the "core of our passion." In some teachers that "core" may be deeply buried, but we believe that it exists in all of us. We believe that this book can help readers find and release the passion within their core. Passion is not something that is reserved for the young, those just entering the teaching profession, idealistic and ready to make their mark. Passion also is something for the seasoned educator. McTaggart (2003), after forty-two years of teaching first grade, reports in her book, *From the Teacher's Desk*, that for her, teaching is not simply a profession; teaching is a passion! She autographs her books, "A teacher has a profession; a good teacher has a passion. Be passionate!" (McTaggart 2005).

In addition to reading and then attempting to master the lessons in this text, the reader can enhance his or her passion for teaching by watching passionate teachers teach, passionate preachers preach, and passionate sales people sell. What is it that they do? How do they use their voices, their bodies, and their environs to convey their passion? Readers also can scour their own lives for times and events when they were most passionate, whether in a teaching situation or not. Here the reader draws upon his or her own emotions and vivid memories. The suggestions in this paragraph are all a form of Konstantin Stanislavski's Method Acting technique, one that Travers and Dillon (1975) would recommend for use in training teachers as performing artists.

One of the authors uses the Method Acting technique when he prepares to teach a portion of his graduate course, Democracy and Schooling. An assigned reading in the course is the classic *Harvard Educational Review* (Rist 1970) article "Student social class and teacher expectations: The self-fulfilling prophecy in ghetto education." In this article a kindergarten teacher begins the school year by placing her students at three tables throughout the room. The students who, among other characteristics, looked and smelled most like her—in other words, students who had the financial means to reflect her middle-class values—were placed at the table closest to her. The other students were placed at the remaining two tables—both farther away from the teacher.

Immediately the teacher began treating her students differently based on the expectations she held for them, expectations formed on subjective attributes. The teacher's differential treatment was clear to the research observer by the end of the first two weeks. By the end of the year, her students had achieved just as she had expected—those at the table closest to her had excelled; those at the table farthest away from her had not excelled. The kindergarten teacher's end-of-the-year evaluations became part of the students' permanent record and followed them into first grade. Acting on this "evidence" of achievement (or lack thereof), the first grade teacher continued the differential treatment of the children. The sad part, the part that brings tears to these authors' eyes, is that each child's academic future was determined the moment he or she entered the kindergarten classroom and was placed at one table or another. The children at the table farthest away from the kindergarten teacher never had a chance! What if one of these kids was yours?

If you are a teacher or professor, you should err on the side of passionate teaching (Gravois 2005). Lai (2005) summarizes his article, "Passionate Teaching," by stating that a passionate teacher teaches with his heart, inspires passion in others, energizes others, and helps them reach their goals. Passionate teaching makes a real difference in students' lives; "passionate teaching is the foundation of sound teaching" (1). One of the nice things about teacher passion—besides keeping students awake and attentive—is that it has a tendency to rub off on students. In turn, more passionate students can further fuel the passion in teachers. The process is reciprocal and nonreflexive as we build on another's enthusiasm and passion for the subject matter and for the learning process.

TEACHER EVALUATIONS

Passion is energy. Feel the power that comes from focusing on what excites you.

—Oprah Winfrey

It is possible for the opening night of a play to be the last night of that play. It also is possible for the production to run months or years. It often depends upon the reviews the play, and in particular, the actors and actresses, receive. Savvy consumers read these reviews and then act accordingly. The same goes for movies. Before spending their hard-earned money on a movie, most people read the critics' reviews and check how many stars the movie has been awarded.

Well, teachers are reviewed and rated too. In addition to the informal, often word-of-mouth evaluations of student critics, most teachers are evaluated formally by administrators and supervisors. A teacher's professional career can hang in the balance. These supervisors often use standardized forms. Whether the form is being used to assess K–12 teachers or university faculty, one of the most common categories evaluated is that of "enthusiasm." Typically the category falls under a broader label of "Professional Skills." Sample category wordings include "Shows enthusiasm," "Demonstrates enthusiasm for teaching," or "Demonstrates personal enthusiasm for the subject and learner." The reviewer checks off the degree—Observable Strength / Satisfactory / Needs Improvement—to which enthusiasm has been observed.

Can you imagine how the character Mr. Cantwell, the biology teacher on the television program *The Wonder Years*, would have been evaluated on the category of enthusiasm? When he stood behind the overhead projector and in a slow monotone voice tried to teach, the class all yawned and quickly got glassy-eyed. They were bored because their teacher was boring. He inspired no one. Mr. Cantwell obviously had not read this book!

SUMMARY

If you are not fired with enthusiasm, you will be fired with enthusiasm.
—Vince Lombardi

A teacher's zest for teaching, like an actor's zeal for acting, is revealed in his or her displayed enthusiasm. It is obvious in his or her expressiveness. Weimer (1993), in her book *Improving Your Classroom Teaching*, devotes an entire chapter to the importance of enthusiasm. Early in the chapter she boldly declares, "Enthusiasm: Do It!" She states that one should not try to be enthusiastic. Teachers should instead focus upon things that will convey their enthusiasm to the class. Teachers need to create an enthusiasm for the subject matter (Lubawy 2003). Like Oppenheimer (2004), we agree.

In thinking about the parallel between acting and teaching and about the common denominator, enthusiasm, other "e" words come to mind. Among them are expressing, exhilarating, exciting, enlightening, enthralling, and, for that matter, even entertaining. A stage production or movie described this way would signal a dramatic or cinematic success. It would be a credit to the actors. A classroom characterized this way similarly would be a "hit" and a credit to the teacher. Exactly how teachers or professors are supposed to convey their enthusiasm—their passion—is the emphasis of the book you are reading.

Enthusiasm and passion do not have to take one single form, and they do not always include being loud, having grand hand gestures, or running around the classroom. But they do require that teachers raise their awareness of their own way of being passionate about their material and then graft it into their teaching persona (Carroll 2002). And, says Carroll, on those days when you don't feel all that excited about the material that you are teaching, at least *act* like you are excited. Put on your best performance! You may very well be convincing—to your students and maybe even to yourself.

SEARCH FOR MORE ON ENTHUSIASM AND PASSION

Enthusiasm is the most important thing in life.
—Tennessee Williams

An Education Resources Information Center (http://www.eric.ed.gov/) search for the terms "Enthusiasm" or "Passion" and at least one other acting-lessons term reveals numerous citations. All of them, because they are announced in ERIC, have applications to education settings.

An ERIC search for the term "enthusiasm" with a variety of education-related terms reveals the following number of citations: "enthusiasm" plus "teaching": 716,000; plus "elementary education": 8,330; plus "secondary education": 26,400; plus "student achievement": 15,800; and plus "student interest": 7,150. An ERIC search for the term "passion" with a variety of education-related terms reveals the following number of citations: "passion" plus "teaching": 879,000; plus "elementary education": 9,610; plus "secondary education": 18,700; plus "student achievement": 8,790; and plus "student interest": 2,960. Two more searches include the following: "passionate" plus "teachers": 193,000; and "passionate" plus "teaching": 318,000. The number of citations located is staggering!

In addition to exploring ERIC, you should consider searching other databases as well for books, articles, and programs related to the enhancement of enthusiasm and passion in the classroom. You also are encouraged to search the Web using many of the ERIC descriptors suggested in the previous paragraph.

CHAPTER 2

Boosting Teacher Enthusiasm: A Craftsperson's Toolbox

It is not who you are but what you do that conveys enthusiasm.

—Anonymous

INTRODUCTION

Craftspersons craft things, and they use the tools of their trade to do it. Without their tools they are lost. Aspiring craftsmen are apprentices who are introduced to and instructed in the use of the tools of their trade by master craftsmen or journeymen. The process is the same whether one is talking about masons, plumbers, and electricians or actors, actresses, and teachers. It is the skilled use of one's tools that separates the master from the apprentice. Different craftspersons, such as masons and carpenters, might use the same tool (i.e., using a level to plumb a wall), but for different ultimate reasons. Likewise, actors and teachers share many of the same tools even though their ultimate goals differ.

BOOSTING TEACHER EFFECTIVENESS THROUGH PERFORMING

The point of Chapter 1 was that more enthusiastic teachers are perceived as more effective teachers. Teacher enthusiasm (and the perceived competence that it conveys), in turn, often leads to greater student achievement. The question, now, is how can teachers become more enthusiastic? As the quotation at the beginning of this chapter says, "It is not who you are but what you do that conveys enthusiasm."

Years ago, one of the authors supervised student teachers. Prior to entering the classroom for the first time, many of these student teachers had bouts of severe anxiety—they had the actor's version of stage fright. In an effort to calm their nerves, the author reassuringly offered this profound statement: "Don't worry. Just go in there, and be yourself." In hindsight, this was terrible advice to give because many of these student teachers were, in fact, rather anxious people. If they went into the classroom and "remained themselves," they would have been anxious teachers. We can't imagine a director telling stage-frightened actors to just go on stage and "be themselves."

According to Hanning (1984, 33), "You [teachers] don't have a 'self' to be when you start out as a teacher; that is you don't have a teacher-self. You have to develop one, and you do that by acting a part, by performing a role . . . as you would (in) a theatre." Hanning (2005) stands by his 1984 proclamation. New teachers, in particular, have a wonderful opportunity to define themselves and their teaching by using their passion to connect their teaching and their students. Carroll (2002) offers support for this position when he states that one must develop a teaching persona when one deals with students, a persona that is different from the one used with colleagues and friends. Teachers can use their teacher-self or persona to present their subject matter in much the same way effective salespersons and performing artists do. Teachers can enhance their versatility by using the same tools of the trade as performing artists.

At first glance, performing a role—acting a part—may appear out of place to some educators. It shouldn't. In both cases, a group of persons (students or theatergoers) perceive themselves as passive participants in an interaction led by a dominant other. Successful teaching is a performance, and the sooner we make peace with that fact, the better (Carroll 2002). Teaching in the classroom is not unlike acting on the stage or in the cinema. In both the theater and the classroom, the character on stage must hold the attention of the listeners by using a variety of captivating devices. Teachers have the additional burden of having to hold the attention of their audiences 180 days a year! That "stage" can be frightening.

Ask new teachers, and even some seasoned teachers, how they feel when entering the classroom for the first time. It is not uncommon for them to feel illprepared, inadequate, anxious, and apprehensive, wondering what they will do if they forget their lines and fearful that everyone in the audience will see them as phonies. Physiologically, their bodies send them strong messages, too—sweaty palms, knees like rubber, soaked armpits, churning stomach, shallowness of breath, and increased heart rate. It is a wonder that these teachers have the courage to step across that classroom threshold. Yet, Burns and Woods (1992) "believe that a certain level of anxiety and tension are necessary concomitants to performance" (55). Although the descriptors listed earlier in this paragraph are often associated with feelings experienced by **new** teachers, actually the list is a description of how actors and actresses describe the feeling of *stage fright!* It is clear that teaching and acting have parallel emotions.

According to Lowman (1984, 11), "classrooms are fundamentally arenas in which the teacher is the focal point, just as the actor or orator is on a stage—teaching is undeniably a performing art." He further argues that, like other performers, teachers must convey a strong stage presence, often using overt enthusiasm, animation, and humor to accomplish this goal. Rubin (1985, 100), too, argues that "teaching was [and is] a performing art" and supports this belief by including chapters titled "The Classroom as Theatre," "Teacher as Actor," and "Lesson Staging."

Rubin (1985) states that school, like drama, is meant to be experienced directly. When a student who has missed a class asks, "What did we do in class yesterday?" his or her teacher often is at a loss to offer an appropriate response. Although the teacher might like to say, "Gee, you really lucked out. We didn't do a thing in that class," more often he or she responds by saying something to the effect of, "You had to be there in order to understand what happened in yesterday's class." A missed session might be described, but the real spirit of the event is missed.

Teachers act the role of teachers—a role that can, and does, vary from school to school and classroom to classroom. The classroom teacher is on stage. "The acting or performing dimension of the teaching act is highly relevant to a large portion of the teacher's role. Verve, color, humor, creativity, surprise, and even 'hamming' have characterized most great teachers" (Baughman 1979, 27).

Despite the parallel between the two professions, very little has been written about how teachers might employ techniques used by actors to develop Hanning's concept of teacher-self. Nor has much been written about theatrical or acting devices for holding the audience's attention that might be suited to that same goal in the classroom. This book attempts to address this void.

This chapter outlines a number of specific things teachers can do—most with a foundation in drama—in order to appear more enthusiastic. If educators *act* enthusiastic as teachers, over a period of time they may, in fact, *become* more enthusiastic.

One need only look at the world of drama in order to see people regularly acting as someone or something they most often are not in real life. Actors constantly are developing their acting-selves in a manner similar to Hanning's recommendation that teachers develop their teaching-selves. Actors use acting skills. More successful actors more successfully use these performance skills. Teachers, too, can—and should—use these same skills.

A CRAFTSPERSON'S TOOLBOX

Knowledge is power and enthusiasm pulls the switch.

—Steven Droke

We envision a teacher's performance skills, his or her teaching strategies, as analogous to the tools carried by any craftsperson, including actors. This analogy is supported by Rubin (1985, 15) when he explains that the artistry part of teaching consists of "master craftsmanship." In our toolbox we present skills that should be part of all teacher training—preservice or in-service—programs. According to Showalter (2003, 17), these skills should, among other things, address "developing a speaking voice that has range, force, and direction; a presence that uses the dynamics of physical movement to lend conviction to inner strengths and imagination; and the dramatic abilities that can fashion scenes, build climaxes, manage stage props."

In the craftsperson's toolbox there are two categories of tools. Some tools are used more frequently and so are kept ever-handy in the top tray. Other tools, used less frequently, are stored in the bottom of the craftsperson's toolbox.

Such a variety of tools enables the knowledgeable craftsperson to have the right tool handy to accomplish the desired task. Without the right tools, always kept sharp, and the knowledge of how to use them, a craftsperson would be limited in his or her effectiveness. The same holds true for teachers.

THE CRAFTSPERSON HIMSELF OR HERSELF
Subject-Matter Mastery

Although having the right tool for the job helps, a prerequisite to this is possessing the knowledge to use that tool in the first place. Tools do not operate themselves. But, even prior to knowing *how* to use a tool, one needs to know *what* tool from those available should be used in a given situation. It reminds us of students trying to solve problems in a physics course. The mathematics used in physics normally is not the stumbling block. The real difficulty for students is deciding (knowing) what formula of the many available best applies to the circumstances of the present problem. It takes knowledge to make these intelligent decisions.

Actors must know their lines before they can expect to deliver them effectively. Teachers must know their subject matter before they can expect to teach it effectively. One of the major conclusions from Bain (2004) is that "outstanding teachers know their subjects extremely well" (15).

Subject-matter mastery is the first acting/teaching skill that we will address. Because even the anticipation of having to deliver subject matter to a student audience can create feelings of anxiety, we agree with Burns and Wood (1992) when they say that the best advice for nervous actors is to overprepare! This holds true for teachers, too. Teachers should start their overpreparation with a goal of mastering their subject matter.

In our craftsperson analogy, subject-matter mastery is not something viewed as a tool to be carried in the toolbox. Subject-matter mastery is carried in the craftsperson's head—always ready, constantly used. Without the proper mastery of content knowledge, the delivery, no matter how exciting, becomes, as Shakespeare wrote, "full of sound and fury, signifying nothing" (*Macbeth*, Act V, Scene 5). More recently, Spencer Tracy is reported to have offered this advice to an aspiring actor: "know your lines and don't bump into the furniture." Bain declares, "Without exception, outstanding teachers know their subject matter extremely well" (2004, 15). Effective use of acting skills is a complement to, not a substitute for, subject-matter mastery. Teachers must know their material.

In an often-cited experiment (Naftulin et al. 1973), a professional actor, introduced to a conference audience as Dr. Myron L. Fox, PhD ("The Dr. Fox Effect"), presented an enthusiastic lecture that not only contained little content but also used double-talk and irrelevant and contradictory examples (Perry 1985). "Dr. Fox" presented his lecture to three separate audiences with the same results. The audiences highly rated the lecture, citing that, among other things, it stimulated their thinking. No one detected that it all was a hoax (Clark 2005). Several in the audience even claimed to have read some of his work.

Is it possible, then, to secure and hold the attention of an audience but, in the end, deliver little in the way of content? At first glance, the Dr. Fox experiments would have us answer "yes." But, some, such as Bain (2004), have argued that these experiments are misleading in that Dr. Fox's audiences were never asked the key question of whether or not they had actually *learned* anything from his lectures! Teachers who lack subject-matter expertise may be able to use acting skills, in the famous words of Abraham Lincoln, "to fool some of the people all the time and all the people some of the time," but those who lack subject-matter knowledge will not be able to fool "all the people all of the time."

The evidence is clear: enthusiastic teachers, those who are expressive in their manner and method and who demonstrate mastery of their subject matter, do earn higher student evaluations. But, some might ask, at what expense to student learning? The answer is: at *no* expense to learning. Research confirms that these same expressive teachers generally have students who exhibit higher achievement (Abrami, Leventhal, and Perry 1982). Where you find informed, enthusiastic teachers, you find greater student achievement. These teachers are delivering the goods—the requisite content!

THE CRAFTSPERSON'S TOP-TRAY TOOLS

Through both research and interviews with award-winning faculty, we have identified three acting/teaching skills that, because of their routine use by teachers, can be visualized as "top-tray" tools. They are

1. animation in voice,
2. animation in body, and
3. creative use of classroom space.

The justification for including these three skills as top-tray tools (skills) is presented in separate chapters that follow. For now, suffice it to say that it would be unheard of for actors to ignore the importance of vocal animation (e.g., pitch, volume, voice quality, and rate) in their attempts to hold an audience's attention and to get their message across. Should teachers be any less concerned about their effective use of voice? Actors take lessons and practice-practice-practice these skills. Should teachers, too, work at improving the impact of such a resource?

In like manner, no successful actor could, or would, overlook the importance of physical animation and effective use of space. The power of body language, perhaps even more convincing than verbal language, is not lost on the successful actor. Nor is the value of one's physical placement within the stage setting. Teachers, too, should be sensitive to their physical animation and use of space.

THE CRAFTSPERSON'S OTHER TOOLS

Our research and interviews with award-winning faculty have led to the identification of four acting/teaching skills that are most effective when used less routinely in the classroom. These skills include

1. humor,
2. role-playing,
3. use of props, and
4. suspense and surprise.

All the tools are useful in both direct and interactive instruction. Although they may be incorporated anywhere in a day's lesson, they are particularly beneficial in the opening and closing of a class and in facilitating classroom management. You will find details of these applications in later chapters.

Once again, successful actors work long and hard at perfecting each of these skills. With respect to role-playing, no doubt some actors feel more comfortable in some roles than in others. Yet, through a combination of sweat and talent, most are able to carry out many roles in a convincing manner. We believe that teachers, too, can convincingly take on various roles.

Like actors, teachers can hone their skills in the use of props, can make better use of subject matter–related humor (e.g., pun, short story, joke, riddle), and can create attention-getting suspense and surprise. Not only *can* teachers use all of these acting-related tools; we argue that they *must* use these tools. These tools, in conjunction with the educators' top-tray tools, can help teachers deliver their message more effectively.

ACTING SKILLS, TEACHER ENTHUSIASM, AND STUDENT ACHIEVEMENT

Act enthusiastic and you will be enthusiastic.

—Dale Carnegie

With the introduction of the toolbox analogy and the tools (skills) contained within the toolbox, it is now time to expand the "Teacher Enthusiasm and Student Achievement" diagram presented in Chapter 1. We can now add the specific acting/teaching skills contained within the toolbox to the diagram, as in Figure 2.1.

The educational foundations for teachers' use of acting skills is laid in Chapter 3, followed by a series of chapters introducing specific acting skills and relating how they can, and do, apply to the classroom.

Figure 2.1
Acting Skills, Teacher Enthusiasm, and Student Achievement

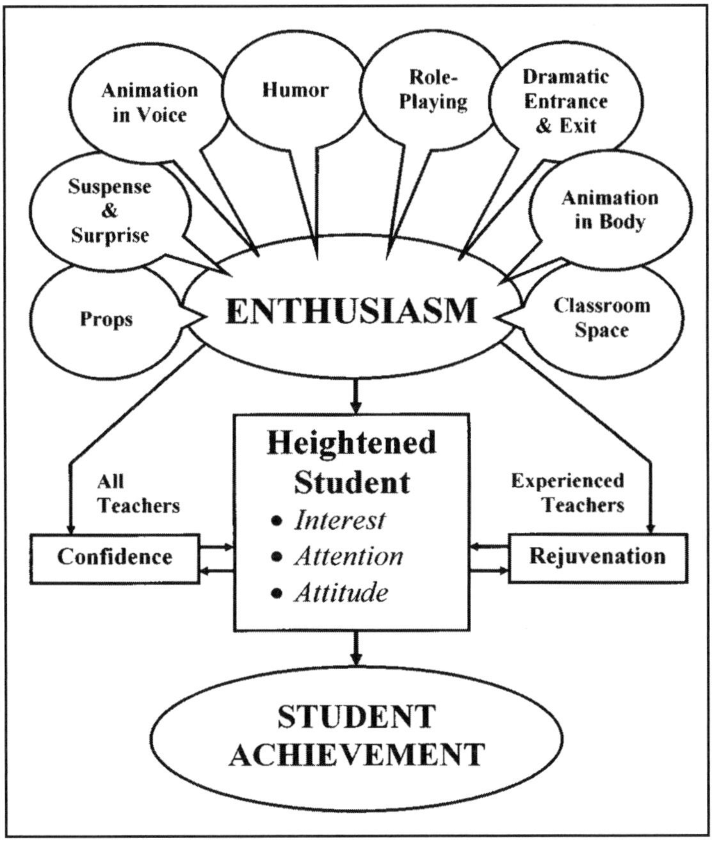

ENTHUSIASM RATING CHART

How enthusiastic are you in the classroom? A rough indication of your enthusiasm level can be estimated by referring to the "Enthusiasm Rating Chart" by Collins (1981), reproduced in Figure 2.2. One could simply examine the categories, for example, "vocal delivery" through "overall energy level," and the descriptors that are used to rate oneself as low, medium, or high, in order to get a rough estimate of one's enthusiasm. Although it is a bit more intimidating, one could also ask a colleague to peer-review a class using this same chart as a basis for data collection. Repeated measurements, across several classes, should be taken before any definitive judgment is made.

Is it OK for teachers to incorporate the characteristics typified by the descriptors under the "high" column? Is it OK for teachers to move from excited speech to a whisper, to use demonstrative gestures, to change facial expression suddenly, to use unpredictable body movements? We argue, yes!

Figure 2.2
Enthusiasm Rating Chart

Categories	Low	Medium	High
Vocal Delivery	Monotone, minimum inflections, little variation in speech; poor articulation.	Pleasant variations in pitch, volume, and speed; good articulation.	Great and sudden changes from rapid, excited speech to a whisper; varied tone and pitch.
Eyes	Looked dull or bored; seldom opened eyes wide or raised eye-brows; avoids eye contact; often maintains a blank stare.	Appeared interested; occasionally lighting up, shining, opening wide.	Characterized as dancing, snapping, shining, lighting up, opening wide, eyebrows raised; maintains eye contact.
Gestures	Seldom moved arms out toward person or object; never used sweeping movements; kept arms at side or folded, rigid.	Often pointed; occasional sweeping motion using body, head, arms, hands, and face; maintained steady pace of gesturing.	Quick and demonstrative movements of body, head, arms, hands, and face.
Body Movements	Seldom moved from one spot, or from sitting to standing position; sometimes "paces" nervously.	Moved freely, slowly, and steadily.	Large body movements, swung around, walked rapidly, changed pace; unpredictable and energetic; natural body movements.

Categories	Low	Medium	High
Facial Expression	Appeared deadpan, expressionless or frowned; little smiling; lips closed.	Agreeable; smiled frequently; looked pleased, happy, or sad if situation called for.	Appeared vibrant, demonstrative; showed many expressions; broad smile; quick changes in expression.
Word Selection	Mostly nouns, few adjectives; simple or trite expressions.	Some descriptors or adjectives or repetition of the same ones.	Highly descriptive, many adjectives, great variety.
Acceptance of Ideas & Feelings	Little indication of acceptance or encouragement; may ignore students' feelings or ideas.	Accepted ideas and feelings; praised or clarified; some variations in response.	Quick to accept, praise, encourage, or clarify; many variations in response.
Overall Energy Level	Lethargic; appears inactive, dull or sluggish.	Appeared energetic and demonstrative sometimes, but mostly maintained an even level.	Exuberant; high degree of energy and vitality; highly demonstrative.

Chart courtesy of Mary Lynn Collins. (Adapted from *Practical Applications of Research, PHI DELTA KAPPA Newsletter, June* 1981.)

SUMMARY

Nothing is as important as passion. No matter what you want to do with your life, be passionate.

—Jon Bon Jovi

When surveyed, students often point out that the "worst teachers" share a common characteristic—they are boring! Clearly, teachers who are aspiring to be judged as the "best teachers" should work, and work hard, at not being boring. Given the physics principle that two things cannot occupy the same place at the same time, one cannot be perceived as enthusiastic and, at the same time, be perceived as boring. This book is all about boosting teacher enthusiasm—even passion—something that the authors know can contribute to creating more exciting, interesting, and engaging classrooms where student achievement is heightened. For those who believe that enthusiastic teaching somehow sacrifices truth and scholarship, consider what Eble has to say. He asserts, "I have never encountered any evidence that a dull and stodgy presentation necessarily carries with it an extra measure of truth and virtue" (Showalter 2003, 16).

The bottom line here is that we have two forces operating—delivery and subject matter. These can be combined in a two-by-two matrix, generating only four possible combinations. The combinations are as follows:

1. An instructor can lack enthusiasm (i.e., be boring) and not know the subject matter.
2. An instructor can lack enthusiasm (i.e., be boring) and know the subject matter.
3. An instructor can be enthusiastic and not know the subject matter.
4. An instructor can be enthusiastic and know the subject matter.

Which of these four, and only four, choices would you choose for yourself, for teachers in your school, and for teachers of your own children (if you have any)? The pedagogical literature clearly supports the last choice. We also believe that this last combination, enthusiasm and knowledge of subject matter, best serves learners. Patricia Graham, former Dean of Harvard Graduate School of Education, agrees. She asserts, "You can have academic mastery with no passion, and that is not effective . . . it is extremely rare to have passion for an academic subject and not have a degree of mastery" (Graham 1999). During Graham's tenure in the mid-1980s, a teacher-training program at Harvard was started; it was titled the "passion program" because they "wished to attract persons who had a passion for their subject and therefore wished to express their passion by acquainting others with the subject so they might develop a passion for it as well" (Graham 2005).

The authors are not saying that teachers should entertain students just for the sake of entertainment. However, we do say that teachers should incorporate some of the proven components of entertainment that lead to greater perceived teacher enthusiasm. For the authors, it is very satisfying to see some of these educators begin to recognize—even begin to champion—the value of enthusiasm.

All we ask is that readers *act* as professionals. What does it mean to be a professional? Recall that a professional is someone who regularly turns to a recognized body of knowledge in order to make decisions. As you read this text, you will find that it is full of sound references, many from books and refereed journal articles from your field and from ours. Let these references help you make up your mind regarding the need for teacher enthusiasm and for incorporating the skills that we will present.

Lest anyone think otherwise, the authors of this book push the value of enthusiasm as a valuable pedagogical tool to be used *in conjunction with* one's mastery of subject matter! One can enhance the other. One, specifically enthusiasm, is not a substitute for the other. We ask that the readers beware of those who would too quickly dismiss the value of teacher enthusiasm.

Clearly, teachers' perceived enthusiasm can be enhanced through the judicious use of the skills outlined in this chapter, which until now may have been seen only as relating to the acting world. These skills, whether used by teachers or by actors, are simply a means to an end. They are the tools of one's craft. The more of these acting tools that teachers have at their disposal, and the better they are able to use them, the more effective these teachers will be in the classroom.

If they like you, they didn't applaud—they just let you live!

—Bob Hope

CHAPTER

Educational Foundations for Teachers as Actors

All the world's a stage,
And all the men and women merely players:
They have their exits and their entrances;
And one man in his time plays many parts.
                              —Shakespeare, *As You Like It*

INTRODUCTION

Although, as Rubin (1985) argues, all the world may *not* be a stage, acting is part and parcel of everyday life. Everyone plays a role—many roles, in fact: parent, child, sibling, colleague, coach, neighbor, friend, and teacher. Acting, then, for most of us, is not used to deceive, but to stimulate, convince, and instruct.

Although many readers may be more interested in the how-to chapters to come, little of what follows would be of any use to educators if it were not based upon firm pedagogical grounds. Educators are, and should be, held accountable for what they do in today's classrooms. Being accountable means, at a bare minimum, understanding *why* one uses the teaching strategies one does.

Teachers, like other professionals, have access to a unique body of knowledge they draw upon in order to do their job. It is not good enough simply to use teaching techniques that work; one must also know *why* they work. Without understanding *why*, teachers stop being professionals, and teaching stops being a profession. This chapter is designed to review the educational foundations for the use of theatrical devices as teaching strategies.

When we think of theater, we think of acting and the goals of entertainment, whereas in our classrooms we think of teaching and the goal of informing. Because these two goals are often deemed incompatible, entertainment has been a dirty word to many instructors. More than once we have overheard a teacher, with a scowling face, proclaim with some vehemence in class these following statements:

Figure 3.1
Scowling Face

- "I'm paid to educate them, not entertain them!"
- "What do you want me to be, some kind of cheerleader?"
- "If I wanted to be a clown, I would have joined the circus."
- "I will not 'Oprah' my course, no matter what you say."
- "I'm not going to sacrifice scholarship by entertaining students."
- "Teachers who entertain students are just trying to get higher student ratings."
- "I see entertaining as just pandering to students!"

The fact these instructors fail to realize is that if they expect to educate their students, they must, in some form or another, first attract and hold their attention—just as an actor must do with an audience.

EDUCATIONAL FOUNDATIONS FOR TEACHERS AS ACTORS: THEORISTS SPEAK

All teachers want their students to value what is taught. According to the taxonomy for the affective domain of learning (Krathwohl, Bloom, and Masia 1956), receiving is a prerequisite to valuing. Therefore, before students can possibly have a commitment to something (value it), they must first be willing to give controlled or selected attention to it, both physically and mentally.

If we expect students to absorb the material presented and discussed in class, we must cultivate their attention by offering the material in an interesting and captivating way. This is, essentially, the goal of entertainment—entertainment is a means to an end.

According to Jerome Bruner, a renowned cognitive psychologist, such attention and interest can be generated through the use of "dramatizing devices," including the development of a dramatic personality on the part of the teacher (1960, 82–83). These strategies support his fourth major theme in *The Process of Education* (1960), the consideration of how students' interest in learning can be stimulated.

Other cognitive psychologists use a three-part information-processing model to depict how learners recognize, transform, store, and retrieve information. The three parts include: sensory register, short-term (working) memory, and long-term memory. Simply put, information available in the sensory register will be lost if not attended to! It follows, then, that information (e.g., concepts, principles) will not reach one's short-term or long-term memory unless attended to. "Therefore, the first thing a successful teacher must do is to get students to attend to important material" (Dembo 1988, 343). Getting students to focus their attention on the task at hand is a necessary, if not sufficient, condition for learning to take place.

Similarly, Albert Bandura (1986), a name synonymous with the study of modeling, notes that securing students' attention is first among four important elements involved in observational learning. Whether one is demonstrating a process in a chemistry lab, elaborating upon a Shakespearian play in a literature class, or showing the contrast between the letters "b" and "d" in a first-grade classroom, little or no learning will take place unless the teacher is able to hold students' attention.

For youngsters, natural attention-getters (and holders) are those persons whom they perceive to be attractive, popular, successful, and interesting. We should not be surprised, then, at the ease with which film stars, rock stars, and sports figures appear to command the attention of young people by their very presence. These stars are effective models because they are able to secure the first element of observational learning—attention. Hence the "big bucks" they are paid to endorse products from sneakers to stereos.

How are educators to compete with such natural attention-getters? For those teachers who are not startlingly good-looking or who may be trying to teach the Crimean War in college history the day after the team has won the NCAA championship, is there hope? Yes, there is! Effective entertainment skills can be the great equalizer as teachers compete for getting (and holding) students' attention.

Clearly, the theorists offer sound educational foundations for teachers' use of acting skills as an enthusiasm-generating strategy to secure, as well as to hold, students' attention. No other single strategy seems to have the potential for generating perceived teacher enthusiasm—a characteristic shown to be associated with teacher effectiveness and student achievement.

EDUCATIONAL FOUNDATIONS FOR TEACHERS AS ACTORS: PRACTITIONERS SPEAK

Practitioners—in particular, award-winning teachers—concur. In the research conducted prior to writing this book, we contacted award-winning professors and K–12 teachers in various disciplines and asked them to comment on their use of acting skills in the classroom. Their testimonials, which are included in Appendix 2, Testimonials from Award-Winning K–12 Teachers and Professors, testify to the value of teachers' incorporation of acting skills in their classrooms.

An English teacher agrees that acting skills "can be useful in engaging students in the course and focusing their attention on the major ideas or problems of a discipline" (Carroll, testimony 4). Another English teacher, with twenty years of experience, readily attests to the usefulness of acting skills as an "aid in maintaining both the vibrancy and quality of learning" (Harrison, testimony 8).

A biology teacher, although admitting that she has had no formal training in acting techniques, has "become increasingly aware of their [acting skills'] importance to the quality and effectiveness" of her teaching (Grimnes, testimony 6). Another biology teacher claims that "good teaching sweeps people away and involves them in the mood of the acting production. It is the ability to involve an audience that a teacher must master if he/she is to be completely successful in teaching" (Light, testimony 10).

An instructor of theater and dance writes that acting skills "will help a teacher create classes with drama: classes that generate interest, sustain suspense, and leave students with a feeling that something important has been achieved" (Hall, testimony 7). According to a philosophy teacher, "students considering secondary-school teaching need to become very outgoing and spontaneous in their delivery. While instruction is never coextensive with entertainment, nonetheless, to learn how to work an audience should not be downplayed" (Lisska, testimony 11).

The world of drama pervades a history teacher's comments when he says that he has spent a decade learning his craft "in an environment conducive to the development of educational acting skills and the awareness of the classroom as a stage upon which the instructor may combine aspects of the lecturer and the performer" (Mahoney, testimony 12). A psychology instructor, although admitting that his acting experience outside of the classroom has been limited, has "learned how to act, and how to teach, on the same stage." His use of acting skills has not limited his responsibility to teach content: "they simply enhance the content and make it a part of the student's reality" (McBrayer, testimony 13).

A marketing teacher acknowledges the importance of teaching up-to-date, well-organized material. The real challenge, she argues, is to "teach the material each time as if it's the first time. Every 'performance' must retain the excitement of opening night. For every member of the audience, after all, it is just that" (Rogers, testimony 15). In a response typical of those received from our award-winning teachers, a political science instructor starts off her testimony with, "I never thought of myself as an actor" (Steuernagel, testimony 19), and then goes on to enumerate teaching techniques that she believes she shares with fellow performers.

Our testimonials support Kelly and Kelly's (1982) interviews with, and observations of, award-winning teachers. Among other common elements, the teachers compared their teaching to a theatrical performance. Effective basic-education and higher-education teachers report that they "come alive" when they step in front of the class. At this point they feel they are on stage. When educators take on the teacher role, they are able to speak with a sense of confidence and enthusiasm that energizes both themselves and their students.

In a special issue of *Communication Education*, writers offered a series of "docustories" celebrating situations when teaching actually "worked." Immediately following these stories, four guest authors critiqued the stories, attempting to analyze common elements. One such element was performance. Conquergood (1983) sees successful teaching as a shift from informative to performative. Sprague (1993, 356) cites the common element of "teaching as assisted performance." Strine (1993, 374) sees teaching as crossing "comfort zones" where lessons are learned from performing.

Wulff (1993), an associate director of a center for instructional development, acknowledges how the various contributors' stories have influenced him. When faculty visiting his center ask, "What makes you successful in helping faculty with their teaching," his first inclination is to enumerate a series of reasons. Instead, now he says, "Let me tell you a story . . ." Storytelling is probably the oldest, and most enduring, of the performing arts! Puckett and Shaw (1988) offer ways to enhance the powerful skill of storytelling.

Worldwide, the message—the evidence—is the same. The dramatic style of teachers in many cultures emerges as one of the highest correlates of teacher effectiveness (Sallinen-Kuparinen et al. 1987). In Australia, for example, Holloway, Abbott-Chapman, and Hughes (1992) report that a common element among effective teachers was demonstrated through their enthusiastic—to the point of being highly dramatic—presentation of subject matter.

Successful practitioners everywhere, in every discipline, and at every grade level, agree: there is an educational foundation for using acting skills in the classroom.

THE PROFESSION'S RESPONSE, OR LACK THEREOF

Although there are strong educational foundations for teachers' use of acting skills in today's classrooms, too few teachers are prepared to do so. It is not their fault. They should not be blamed because they have not been trained. Today's teachers have not, by and large, had acting-skills training—whether in their current in-service programs or in their previous teacher training. Tomorrow's teachers, those still in training, fare no better. The situation is just as bad for university professors. Tompkins (1996) reflects, "I'm amazed that my fellow PhDs and I were let loose in the classroom with virtually no preparation for what we would encounter. . . . If only I'd known, if someone I respected had talked to me honestly about teaching, I might have been saved from a lot of pain" (Showalter 2003, 5–6).

In Australia, a bulletin board announcement at the University of Melbourne's School of Education shows that teachers-in-training themselves recognize the connection between drama (acting skills) and effective teaching. The announcement, "Using Drama Techniques Across the Curriculum," reads,

> Free up your teaching styles! Move away from chalk and talk! Drama is a powerful teaching strategy in any and all subject areas. Students will be enthused by experiential learning and your lessons will become more dynamic and interesting.

The three students advertising this noncredit elective, designed for non–drama method students, apparently felt the topic was not being stressed enough in their formal teacher training, and therefore, they were going to do something about it.

Travers (1979, 16) writes that the process of making your teacher-self "has been neglected by schools of education not because the matter seemed unimportant, but because the difficulties of providing training seemed insuperable." Almost three decades later, the task may be daunting but perhaps even more necessary. Teacher-training programs, whether at home or abroad, seem to overlook two crucial areas of skill development associated with making your teacher-self: speech communication and drama.

The first area overlooked in helping teachers develop their teacher-self is speech communication. Although not the specific focus of this book, many speech communication skills parallel those found useful in drama: animated voice, animated body, and space utilization, for example. It is astonishing that education majors—past and present—typically are required to take only one speech course, usually the same course taken by students majoring in agriculture, engineering, and liberal arts. One would think that potential teachers, in preparing for a field so reliant upon speaking, would be required to schedule more than one speech course. Such is not the case.

Part of the reluctance of schools of education to incorporate more speech communication courses in their teacher-education programs may spring from the attitude of educators (professors) themselves. In what could be viewed as an insult, if it were not so true, Nussbaum (1992, 177) comments, "Communication scholars have at least one advantage over education scholars: we read their literature. A quick look at the references of communication education articles indicates that our literature is influenced by the research findings in education. Education research rarely mentions any result from the communication discipline."

A concrete example of Nussbaum's damning assertion that educators ignore relevant topics in speech communication is the fact that the prestigious School of Education at the University of Melbourne recently canceled its education-library subscription to *Communication Education*, the official journal for the National Communication Association. An inquiry to the head librarian revealed that she was instructed to cancel those journals used infrequently by faculty and students. Could it be that educators judge speech communication to be of little value in teaching? We hope not.

The second overlooked skill necessary to develop one's teacher-self is drama. The situation for preservice teachers is even worse when it comes to their receiving training in drama than it is in the area of speech communication. Typically, education majors are required to schedule no acting or drama courses. Yet Hanning (1984, 33) claims that teachers regularly "must give a performance, of sorts, in order to communicate effectively with students." Sarason (1999), in his book, *Teaching as a Performing Art*, proposes that teacher-education candidates audition for their "part" in much the same way that actors and actresses are required to do. But, where are teachers supposed to learn how to perform?

Why the reluctance to incorporate speech communication and acting skill development in yesterday's, as well as today's, education training? The answer is fear! It has been our experience that methods teachers in higher education (one of the authors of this book was a "methods teacher"), those who teach preservice teachers how to teach, are uncomfortable at best, and downright scared at worst, of anything that has to do with speech communication. Timpson (1982, 4) claims that "while professors of education will lecture about the components and varieties of effective instruction, they do little to assist teachers in developing anything beyond an awareness of ideals. There is, in other words, no practical training in this area."

This "fear" of speech communication *and* drama (acting skills) carries over to building administrators in basic education, principals, for example—the very people who plan and sometimes themselves conduct in-service programs. What are we to do?

Some teacher-training institutions have tried to address this unmet need, although it typically occurs only if the faculty has someone on board who is comfortable with the field of drama. Rarely is such a course recommended across the board by a curriculum committee. Robert Keiper, an education professor with a drama background, has created such a course as part of his school's teacher-education program at Western Washington University. Rod Hart (UMASS at Amherst) and Joe Cosentino (Dutchess SUNY) have created similar courses at their respective institutions.

Unfortunately, little help can be expected from educational psychology texts, even though such resources are supposed to present the best application of psychology to educational settings. For instance, with regard to the acting skill of humor, in spite of the fact that a number of best-selling introductory textbooks in educational psychology "employ humorous cartoons and illustrations, apparently to gain and maintain student interest and attention to make educational points more effectively, none of these texts examines the place of humor in teaching" (Bryant et al. 1980, 512–13). An examination by the authors of more current educational psychology textbooks (e.g., Glover and Bruning 1990; Woolfolk 1993) reveals that Bryant's 1980 observations are still true.

SUMMARY

Both educational theorists and award-winning teachers testify to the instructional benefits of educators' use of acting skills. What we present here are recommendations based on decades of research that has sought to answer the elusive question "What can I do to help my students learn?" By your actions, you can show a fascination with the subject matter and a passion for helping students to understand it. That's the answer.

THE MASTER'S VOICE

For further discussion of the concepts and skills presented in this chapter, read the following paragraphs in Appendix 2, Testimonials from Award-Winning K–12 Teachers and College Professors: Baleja, 2; Borecky, 1, 5; Carroll, 1; Harrison, 1, 2; McBrayer, 6; Rogers (Martha), 1, 4; Steuernagel, 1.

PART 2

The Acting Lessons

CHAPTER

Animation in Body

Actions speak louder than words.

—Anonymous

INTRODUCTION

Actors and teachers alike have two sets of inherent tools for conveying ideas and information to audiences—their bodies and their voices. Both can be used to provide emphasis, distinguish among ideas, clarify, and create connotative meanings, thus complementing the verbal component of the message.

Our attention to our physical behavior in the classroom is especially warranted because this generation of students has been attuned since birth to the visual rather than the aural medium. Many teachers have been heard to complain that television has had such an impact that students cannot seem to pay attention to material unless it is presented in a visually stimulating manner. That reality is dealt with in this book as a challenge for teacher action rather than a cause for hand-wringing.

VALUE OF MODERATE ANIMATION

As is obvious from what has been said in earlier chapters about the value of enthusiasm, this book takes the position that a teacher who is moderately animated while presenting material will be somewhat more successful in getting that material across to the students. In the specific case of physical animation, we are referring to the use of facial expression, gesture, posture, and movement as nonverbal forms of expression that are found in the teacher's toolbox to convey enthusiasm. These four expressive elements will be referred to throughout this chapter.

Numerous researchers have raised questions about the relative value of teacher animation. In doing so, they have devised various experimental formats, asking teachers to act in a particular way or to imitate certain movements. Other studies have simply worked from a phenomenological basis and have analyzed the natural characteristics and unplanned behaviors of successful teachers. In both cases, the conclusions are similar: a teacher's nonverbal expression is positively linked to instructional effectiveness as long as that expressiveness is perceived as natural and is not excessive to the point of distraction (Andersen and Withrow 1987).

This perspective echoes the lesson learned by actors that careful, subtle physical expression complements the playwright's words, whereas excess or unnatural movement "steals the show." The actor has also learned that although some physical expression can be definitively planned in advance, the best is that which spontaneously reflects the actor's perception of the feelings and meaning of the words spoken. Such expressiveness is triply beneficial for the teacher, since it not only complements meaning but also contributes to the teacher's confidence and to the students' motivation.

Specifically, research conducted by Justen (1984) demonstrated that people trained in comfortable, expressive, physical movement were people who were able to speak with more confidence, thus developing better control of the total communication situation. This would seem to indicate that teachers who try to be more expressive will develop a certain amount of self-confidence as a fringe benefit.

Finally, several researchers whose work was summarized by Andersen (1986) concluded that a teacher's physical expressiveness positively impacts the students' affective domain. That is, the more expressive teachers (within reasonable bounds of moderation) are better liked by their students. Thus, the students are more motivated to learn.

So, we can see that, like actors, teachers should act with a moderate level of animation, as is appropriate to their own enjoyment of the subject matter and of the process of teaching and learning. Their reward will be enhanced instructional effectiveness resulting from their own increased confidence and their students' increased motivation. The all-important "bottom line" is that animated teachers have students who learn more!

PURPOSES SERVED BY PHYSICAL ANIMATION

When a teacher gestures, uses a variety of facial expressions, changes posture, and moves about the room, he or she does so in order to achieve one of several specific instructional purposes. Grant and Hennings (1971) defined those purposes as "Conducting, Acting and Wielding." This categorization is meant to include only those movements considered to be instructional rather than personal in nature ("personal" meaning such movements as smoothing the hair, stifling a sneeze, and so on).

Movements that have the purpose of conducting would include gestures, head nods, and other movements that encourage or organize student responses. The teacher's movements in this instance essentially regulate the pattern and direction of class conversation.

Acting movements are those that serve the more basic communication functions of amplifying and clarifying meaning. Included in this category would be a variety of facial expressions and descriptive gestures.

Wielding movements would include any use of the hands or body needed to deal with physical objects used to supplement the verbal message. Like actors, teachers could consider such objects "props." These are discussed in more depth elsewhere in this book.

Other scholars would, no doubt, add to this list of purposes served by animation. The one additional purpose mentioned in several instances is that of establishing a desired power relationship between teacher and students. That is, a particular movement or posture may be used to convey or reinforce the teacher as an "authority figure." Knapp's work (1971) went so far as to identify very specific power-related teacher behaviors, for example, standing with arms akimbo and squaring the shoulders. The point here is simply that although many teacher behaviors serve to fulfill very specific instructional goals related to the subject matter, other behaviors have the purpose of contributing to the teacher–student power relationship.

A fringe benefit of physical animation that some may consider among its purposes is that movement can help diminish a speaker's perceived nervousness. By gesturing or moving about the room, nervous energy is burned up in constructive ways. This may be especially beneficial to the beginning teacher or to anyone whose confidence is flagging.

RECOMMENDATIONS FOR PRODUCTIVE TEACHER ANIMATION

As we turn to actual recommendations growing out of the accumulated studies on teacher movement, we should again recall the specific categories of movement to be considered. The standard categories are facial expression (with special emphasis on eye contact), gestures, posture, and overall movement.

Facial Expression

Facial expression is a tool for all speakers that exemplifies the communication law, "One cannot *not* communicate." Our faces always convey some message to our listeners. The catch is that we are not always aware of what that message might be. As teachers, we would do well to sensitize ourselves to our own expressions so that our faces can be assisting the teaching process, not hindering it. For instance, are we smiling and nodding to encourage only certain or almost all students in the class? Has a grimace crossed our face before a student has finished replying? Do we show an interest in the material by speaking with eyes wide open and animation in our expression?

Smiling is one specific facial expression that contributes significantly to the creation of teacher immediacy and thus to student attention. Smiles tell students that we expect them to be interesting and that we are happy to have them in class. Smiles tell students that we enjoy the subject matter being discussed. This is not to suggest that we should fake a pleasant expression, but to encourage teachers to allow their own enjoyment of class to be evident. Research indicates that female teachers tend to smile more frequently than male teachers, but for both the rule is: "when you want to be considered likable and approachable, put on a smile" (Richmond 1992, quoted in Kougl 1997, 73).

Eye Contact

Eye contact is a sufficiently important feature of facial expression to merit individual attention. Via eye contact, we provide encouragement to our students, maintain their attention, show interest and concern, signal to the students, and portray our own confidence. Listeners tend to be quite sensitive to the initiation of eye contact. So by looking directly at a student whose interest appears to be wavering, we rekindle his or her attention. We might even use our eyes to convey that we want that student to respond to a question or to start taking notes. In other circumstances, our direct eye contact may be read as a statement of confidence and commitment. By looking directly at the students, we establish that we feel we have something important to say and trust the students to attend to it. Research conducted by Beebe (1980) confirms that reasonably consistent (not constant) eye contact between teacher and students resulted in greater attention and retention on the students' part (Cooper 2003, 104).

Sometimes when asked a challenging question, our natural tendency is to let our eyes wander from the questioner to dart left, right, or back and forth as we are thinking (Knapp and Hall 1992). Though a natural behavior, it should be minimized by teachers in order to hold the attention of the student and convey a respect for his or her contribution to the classroom dialogue.

Too often, as we must juggle notes, props, students' papers, and so on, we break that eye contact and thus momentarily sever the teacher–student bond. As Lowman (1984) points out, this is what actors call "losing the house," and it is nearly always fatal to anyone trying to build a sustained positive relationship between speaker and listeners. Hence, the recommendation to maintain positive eye contact with the students as much as possible is a suggestion for the good of one's entire career as a teacher.

In addition to nurturing a positive teacher–student relationship, eye contact opens the door to student learning. When the teacher holds the student visually, it is hard for the student not to listen to the teacher's words. Once a student looks away, intellectual involvement with the material has probably ceased (Penner 1984).

Gestures

Gestures include a nearly limitless range of hand and arm movements. In earlier times, we would have found textbooks recommending that teachers, like all speakers, should specifically plan each and every gesture ahead of time. Those earlier textbooks also would have suggested that specific gestures would always be interpreted in very specific, predictable ways. Fortunately, the theories underlying such assertions have long since been found to be faulty.

Instead of such prescriptive recommendations, we suggest that the best gestures for a teacher to use are those that are natural, purposeful, and nondistracting. Our enthusiasm for the subject matter and for the teaching act will typically show itself in gestures that reinforce, emphasize, encourage, and clarify. These might include, but not be limited to, jabbing the air, pointing to students or objects, contrasting one hand motion with another, or sweeping the air like an orchestra conductor. Arnold (1990) reports that one award-winning professor was famous for his repertoire of football referee signals that he used during class discussions. These gestures, which might seem extreme to some, were well received by the students. They believed that by his going to such extremes, he showed the degree to which he cared about their learning and his willingness to work hard to make it happen.

Fundamentally, gestures are good if they are positively communicative. That means that the gesture should complement the words spoken. The gesture may be a *descriptive* one that clarifies the physical properties of the subject being discussed; it may be an *emphatic* one that indicates the most important aspect of the words spoken; or it may be *signalic*, indicating something the listeners are to do relative to the words spoken.

Posture and Overall Movement

Posture and overall movement are expressive tools used less frequently than gestures and facial expressions. However, to a certain extent, a teacher's enthusiasm should occasionally reveal itself in the form of posture changes and overall movement. The best teachers certainly are often described as being "unable to contain themselves" because they find the material so interesting and, in some cases, exciting. Teachers have been known to leap in the air, for instance. This last action is not necessarily recommended for all of us. But certainly, if we feel so moved by a student's response or by the subject matter itself, we should allow ourselves to show that in a physical manner.

Posture also should be considered when establishing particular teacher–student power relationships. Generally, a person who is standing while others are sitting is an individual with relatively more power. Therefore, if the teacher wants to assert power, it may be wise to stand; on the other hand, if the teacher wants to establish an equality of power, it may be wise to sit.

One special moment in every class period in which total movement can be especially influential is at the beginning. As every actor knows, it is important to make a meaningful entrance. The same import is attached to a teacher's entrance. By our pace and posture at that precise moment, we essentially set the tone for the rest of the class period. We communicate eagerness, anger, dread, confidence, and enthusiasm, all in those few short strides from the doorway as the class begins. The recommendation here, as in the other areas of physical animation, is simply to be sensitive. Know what message your body may be conveying in those few moments, and ask yourself if that is your *intended* message for the class. See Chapter 12 for a more extended discussion of entrances and exits.

Photo 4.1
Meaningful Use of Gestures

Note that all of the previous recommendations are suggestions for behaviors that *may* be beneficial to the teacher aspiring to do a more successful job of holding the students' attention and motivating them. There are no hard-and-fast "rules," and every teacher's individuality will define his or her comfort with physical animation. But no one of us should dismiss active gesturing and expressiveness simply because it may make us a little uncomfortable initially. It is too valuable a tool to ignore.

BEHAVIORS TO AVOID

Although there are no strict rules about what to do in terms of physical movement, there are a few strict rules regarding what *not* to do. Some of our physical behaviors, committed out of habit, may actually be interfering with our efforts to create a positive learning environment.

As Dolle and Willems (1984) have observed, we may inadvertently be sending contradictory messages; that is, our words may be sending one message while our behaviors are conveying an opposite view. For instance, the teacher asks a student to speak ("The class is interested in your ideas") but then conspicuously checks the time ("Your answer isn't that interesting, after all") before the student has finished. The student receives a mixed message. The teacher's words expressed interest, yet his or her concurrent actions expressed disinterest. Typically, listeners put more faith in a speaker's nonverbal message than the verbal. Consequently, in our time-checking example, the students will have probably inferred that the teacher's interest in the student's response was not sincere. That is an interpretation from which the teacher–student relationship will be slow to recover. So rule number one: Don't use nonverbal behaviors whose meaning conflicts with your verbal choices.

In the same vein, teachers should not begin to walk (other than to write on the board) while a student is talking (Fisch 1991). In doing so, the teacher would be "walking on the other's line," to use theatrical parlance. As theatergoers, we may have seen a background actor commit such an error, and we called it upstaging. The problem is that the other listeners in the room will be attracted to the person in motion instead of to the person speaking. So when the teacher upstages the student, the teacher is essentially stealing the attention that the student has earned by participating. That will annoy not just the student who is trying to speak but all of his or her friends in the room as well. Such alienation is definitely something we want to avoid in teaching. Rule number two, then, is the following: Don't upstage the students.

Finally, a teacher should avoid any physical actions or behaviors that could be considered distracting. Pacing and coin-jingling are probably the two most common examples of this fault. Such behaviors serve none of the goals or purposes mentioned earlier and, by their repeated nature, only invite student mockery. Because the behaviors in this category are frequently subconscious habits, we may be unaware of doing them and of how annoying they have become for the students. It may be in our best interest occasionally to ask a trusted student whether there is anything about our classroom behavior that could be perceived as nervous habit or distraction in general. Then, of course, work to replace that bad habit with more constructive, purposeful behaviors. Rule number three: Do no distracting.

SUMMARY

A great Canadian professor, Richard Day of McMaster University, has been described in this fashion: "His performance is riveting. . . . He never stops moving, circling, stalking" (Johnson 1991). It is telling that the student commentator used a performance metaphor to describe Day's classroom animation. Reflected again is the concept that, to a certain extent, we teachers are performing artists. As such, it would behoove us to follow the actors' guidelines in regard to physical movement. We should allow ourselves to move enough to create character, convey meaning, share enthusiasm, and hold the listeners' attention, but not so much as to become a caricature.

THROUGH THE STUDENTS' EYES

When surveyed regarding the use of animation in body in the classroom, students offered real-life examples such as those that follow. Although each example refers to the use of animation in body in a particular subject area, the application to other disciplines is evident.

Talk about Gestures

Mr. S., my geography teacher, was very dramatic. He always used some interesting gyration of his body to emphasize a certain point that he wanted us to remember. Once he asked me a question about a geographical region, and I told him that I didn't know the answer. He immediately threw his tie over his shoulder, opened his eyes so wide that they were as big as saucers, and then grasped his chest as if he were having a heart attack. I'll never forget the answer that I didn't know—it was "The Gateway to the West."

English with a Flair

My English composition teacher used gesture and facial expression as a communicative form. No message about our work or the principles we were studying was ever conveyed with words alone. Her approach led to a more comfortable attitude toward learning for everyone in the class.

Jump in the Boat

My college choir director always gestures to get us to sing louder, softer, more intensely. He even went so far as to walk like he was following a boat down a river, and then he acted like he jumped into it. This was to illustrate that we must follow the music and jump in when it's our turn. Don't wait for the boat; follow it.

Creepy Crawly

My biology teacher was trying to get us to understand how a paramecium moves. Words didn't seem to be getting the point across, so she used her own body to demonstrate—creeping along just like a paramecium.

SEARCH FOR MORE ON ANIMATION IN BODY

An Education Resources Information Center (http://www.eric.ed.gov/) search for the term "animation in body" (or related term) and at least one other education-related term—an exercise that takes just seconds—reveals numerous citations. All of the cited sources, because they are announced in ERIC, have applications to education settings.

An ERIC search for the term "animation in body" (or related term) with a variety of education-related terms reveals the following number of citations: "physical," "animation," and "teachers": 289; "animated" and "teachers": 3,222; "movement" and "teaching": 3,555; "nonverbal communication": 3,228; "movement" and "teachers": 5,278; and "nonverbal" and "teacher effectiveness": 114.

In addition to exploring ERIC, you should consider searching other databases as well for books, articles, and programs related to the effective use of animation in body in the classroom. You also are encouraged to search the Web using many of the ERIC descriptors presented in the previous paragraph.

THE MASTER'S VOICE

For further discussion of the concepts and skills presented in this chapter, read the following paragraphs in Appendix 2, Testimonials from Award-Winning K–12 Teachers and College Professors: Baleja, 3, 4; Grimnes, 1–3, 5; Light, 2; Rogers (Martha), 3; Rotkin, 5; Steuernagel, 3.

CHAPTER

Animation in Voice

It is not enough to know what to say, but it is necessary to know how to say it.
—Aristotle

INTRODUCTION

The voice is an especially personal element in anyone's expressive repertoire. It reflects our character, background, personality, and moods. Using the voice to create and modify meaning should occur in a completely natural fashion for the speaker, with the particular expression growing out of—not overlaid on—the speaker's internal understanding and feeling for the ideas expressed.

Considerable research has been undertaken in an effort to determine whether a teacher's vocal expressiveness influences student learning. Results have varied considerably. Two overall conclusions seem to be firm, however: (1) a moderately inexpressive voice will not hinder learning (Knapp 1971); and (2) a moderately expressive voice correlates with more significant learning (Richmond, Gorham, and McCroskey 1987). So good vocal expression being potentially advantageous, the voice is certainly a subject worthy of consideration for the aspiring teacher.

VOCAL FITNESS

Actors, appreciative of the voice's potential, work to keep their voices healthy and flexible so that they can be responsive to moderate changes in emotion. Some actors do daily vocal exercises, some take voice lessons, and still others simply treat their voices with care so that the vocal folds will not be strained. Regular general exercise to maintain an overall level of fitness, well-balanced diets, and avoidance of abusive practices such as smoking are the basics of a sensible approach to maintaining vocal strength and flexibility. Teachers, being equally dependent professionally on their voices, should exercise similar care.

Specifically, if voices are to be healthy enough to achieve the projection and expressiveness necessary in the classroom, teachers should

- practice deep diaphragmatic breathing,
- maintain relaxed throat muscles,
- drink plenty of water and fruit juices,
- avoid smoking and inhaling others' smoke, and
- go silent when bothered by a sore throat.

There have been several instances in recent political campaigns when the candidates found themselves voiceless simply because they had tried to ask their voices to perform when strained. They were talking above the loud noise of crowds and airplanes, speaking in rooms with poor acoustics, and drinking too much coffee for too many days. They paid a high price in temporary vocal damage.

Teachers are equally susceptible to problems of vocal health, an "occupational hazard." We sometimes have to talk for six or eight hours in a day over the hum of instructional technology or the noise of children playing right outside the window. We sometimes get tense, and we drink coffee instead of water. We also commit the sin of pride in thinking that we need to be in school and conducting class even though we have a respiratory infection. The voice is far too delicate an instrument to bear this kind of abuse! More than that, it is far too important an instrument to place in such danger.

Why is this so? What is it about the human voice that makes it such an important tool for both actors and teachers? And what can we learn from actors about the care and use of this tool?

VOCAL VARIATIONS: PARALANGUAGE

Paralanguage is a term for the conglomerate of vocal variations that accompany oral verbal expression. Specifically, the elements of vocal pitch, speech rate, volume, and tonal quality are voice characteristics that are all capable of significant variation within any one individual.

Each of us has a certain vocal character that is identifiable as our own. In fact, recent developments in forensic science verify that each human voice is unique, possessing a distinct combination of variations within the four vocal characteristics. No one uses only one pitch level or degree of loudness or rate, of course. We might speak, for instance, an average of 175 words per minute, but that is not a constant speed. We may slow down to 100 words per minute when speaking about something very tragic or somber and speed up to 225 words per minute when sharing exciting news. It is the *pattern* of variations that is constant for an individual and thus makes that person's voice unique.

Every human being has a range of vocal variations comfortably within our own vocal repertoire. We use those variations consciously and subconsciously to provide shades of meaning to the words we speak. A relatively significant amount of variation in a teacher's paralanguage will convey the enthusiasm that is positively correlated with higher student evaluations of teachers (Murray 1985), more consistent student attention, and increased levels of comprehension.

SPONTANEOUS VARIATIONS

Most vocal variations are initiated subconsciously. As noted earlier, our voices should be responsive to variations in our thoughts and feelings. When conflict is building within the scene of a play, the actor does not need to be reminded to speak more loudly and with greater variations in pitch. That change in voice is going to happen as a direct result of the actor's sensitivity to the developing conflict—the actor will *feel* angry and tense, and thus the voice will *sound* angry and tense.

Similarly, as a teacher is presenting material found to be personally fascinating, no thought needs to be given to the idea of speaking with a higher pitch level, a faster rate, and a louder volume. Those vocal variations will likely occur simply because the teacher is so caught up in the material, and having a healthy voice capable of responding to changing emotional states, the teacher will experience vocal changes that convey that fascination. This is what was meant earlier in referring to variations that grow out of an involvement in our thoughts.

One of the authors has a new puppy whose antics are often quite comical. When telling someone about the puppy's efforts to walk through two-feet-deep snow, the author does not plan to speak faster and louder than usual. It just happens! Each of us probably has that level of enjoyment during some moments of our teaching. You find tales of the discovery of the new world so amazing. Your colleague can't get over the creativity in Maya Angelou's latest work. Another is completely thrilled that a struggling student has finally grasped the basics of long division. Our voices will naturally manifest that amazement, surprise, or thrill!

As teachers facing the challenge of holding the attention of easily distracted young people, it is especially important that we allow ourselves to use as much of our natural vocal range as possible to make our ideas captivating and their full connotative meaning clear. This is precisely what aspiring actors spend hours practicing—expanding their ability to use their full vocal range comfortably. We would do well to follow their example.

DELIBERATE VARIATIONS

In addition to the natural patterns of pitch, rate, volume, and quality changes, we may make some deliberate decisions in order to provide specific vocal emphasis to our ideas. Again, there is a parallel in acting, for the actor knows ahead of time that, during the performance, a particular inflection is going to be necessary to create a specific meaning at certain key points. Let us look at each of the four vocal characteristics to understand how and why such deliberate variations would be planned for the classroom.

Pitch

Pitch, the highness or lowness of the voice, has the capacity to reflect a great many emotions and connotations. Rising pitch at the end of a thought group, for instance, typically indicates incredulity or questioning. A lowered pitch, on the other hand, indicates finality or certainty. So if I were explaining an assignment to a class and stated the due date in a relatively lower pitch, the class would likely interpret this as a firm deadline. For example, "The term papers are due *on or before the 24th*" (with the italicized words spoken in a lower pitch). If a class had become somewhat lax in their homework responsibilities, I might want to plan deliberately to speak about the next assignment with such firmness and thus plan a particular pitch variation.

In a more routine vein, Andersen (1986) points out that pitch changes typically are perceived as signals indicating whose turn it is to speak—the teacher's or the students.' In addition to this classroom-management function, pitch changes may be used to encourage students. If a teacher asks, "Who can tell me what eight times twelve is?" with a pleasantly varied, higher pitch, it sends a signal that the teacher expects that students do know the answer. Such subtle establishment of positive expectations is likely to be rewarded with accurate student responses. So pitch changes can be deliberately used both to convey feelings and to manage the classroom conversation flow.

Volume

Volume changes can be used similarly to convey a particular urgency or commitment about a statement. It is the *change* in volume that calls attention to the accompanying thought, not the volume level per se. Just being loud is not necessarily more beneficial than being quiet. As a famous commercial line notes, "If you want to get someone's attention, whisper." By purposely changing volume— by speaking either louder or softer—a teacher, like a good actor, focuses the listeners' attention on the point thus spoken. You might want to plan to change volume deliberately to convey a particularly suspenseful moment in a history lesson or an especially dynamic point in a science experiment.

In addition to considering volume changes, we should note that an adequate general volume is a fundamental necessity for both the actor and the teacher. Especially since a reasonably strong voice is perceived as conveying confidence, self-assurance, and control (Anderson 1977), it is a tool particularly beneficial to the beginning teacher. The general guideline is that, except in cases of confidentiality or emphasis as noted previously, a sufficient volume should be maintained so as to make the speaker heard from anywhere in the room.

Keep in mind that a "strong" volume is characterized by diaphragmatically centered vocal power, not by tensing the throat muscles and screaming. You want a voice that carries well, not that causes students to shudder in ear-splitting pain.

Quality

Voice quality is achieved as the result of our typical resonance and pattern of vocal fold movement. Common examples are breathiness, raspiness, stridency, nasality, and mellowness. Again, each one of us has a recognizable personal quality most of the time but may achieve variations in response to changing emotions or the need to convey a specific feeling. Generally speaking, we as teachers should try to maintain a pleasant quality devoid of any annoying effects such as hypernasality or stridency. After all, students will be listening to that voice for hours on end!

Actors who find they have a tendency to produce an annoying vocal quality seek professional assistance from speech coaches in order to achieve a pleasant, unstrained voice. Likewise, teachers should listen to their voices on tape to determine whether the quality is pleasant enough for sustained attention.

Assuming that the basic quality has no distracting elements, voices should be capable of occasional quality variations. A teacher of literature, for example, may need to produce a more resonant, almost stentorian, tone when reading from some of Poe's work or a more breathy tone to read from Dickinson. These variations are achieved by modifying the resonating cavities (mouth, nose, and pharynx) or by changing the muscle tension on the vocal folds. Poet e. e. cummings' voice is famous for its high-pitched stridency. Yet, in performing public readings of his poetry, even cummings was able to temper that quality for more romantic phrases or for conveying less contentious ideas.

Rate

Rate, the final variable vocal characteristic, has arguably the greatest potential as an expressive tool for the actor and teacher. Rate can be varied by changing the overall speech speed (words per minute), by changing the duration of a single syllable or word, or by using pauses of various lengths.

Slower overall rate or duration might be purposefully selected when we need to be perceived as speaking more seriously or emphatically. On the other hand, we may deliberately speed up to convey enthusiasm, panic, or surprise. The actor will have considered the script and plotted specific rate changes to match the intended meaning of the lines. Although the teacher may not make such definitive plans, some advance attention to the lesson plan to determine which points could be emphasized by a simple rate change is appropriate. In addition, the other common teaching situation calling for a change in overall rate is when providing clarification for a student or students who have failed to understand a concept. In that case, a teacher should use a slow, deliberate speed while watching closely for feedback from the involved student(s). As with volume, it is the *change* in rate that catches the listener's attention and provides emphasis.

Sometimes the classroom message is delivered best by a well-placed pause between words. Actors have long used this technique. Perhaps the best-known "pauser" in the entertainment industry is Paul Harvey, who uses the pause to keep his radio audience in suspense waiting for the "rest of the story." Pauses do that—they build suspense. But in addition, the pause is a device for punctuating our thoughts by separating items in a list, setting off direct quotes, pointing to key words or phrases, and signaling a change in focus. Strategically placed pauses can sometimes have a more dramatic effect on listeners' attention and comprehension than words themselves. In fact, studies that have analyzed the effect of "teacher wait time"—the time following a question asked by the teacher—indicate that by carefully using pauses, we enhance the likelihood of students' learning (Tobin 1986). Wait at least three seconds before asking the question of a different student or providing the answer yourself.

Teacher speech rate also has been shown to have an indirect effect on student learning because of its effect on student attentiveness. Students are less likely to be noisy when the teacher speaks at a moderate and varied pace than when the teacher speaks at either a noticeably fast or slow, unchanging pace (Grobe, Pettibone, and Martin 1973). Because the students are less noisy, they are more attentive and susceptible to learning.

So, although the teacher, like the actor, should have a healthy, flexibly expressive voice capable of adapting to changes in mental orientation, persons in both roles are well advised also to plan a few deliberate modifications in vocal pitch, rate, volume, and quality.

CREATING CHARACTERS

For the elementary school teacher, creative, deliberate vocal changes can also be used to create characters. In reading to pre-readers, in particular, the teacher will want to read dialogue with different vocal quality or inflection for each character in the story. The differences clarify the plot and character interaction as well as help to hold student interest and attention. This can be done most easily by using different speech rates for the characters, though other vocal variations could be used as well. Br'er Rabbit would probably speak his lines much faster than Br'er Bear, for instance.

INFLUENCING CREDIBILITY

We have spoken about vocal changes as assisting clarity by placing emphasis and establishing relationships among ideas. But vocal expressiveness has another very important benefit to both the actor and the teacher: influencing credibility.

Although research indicates no direct causal link between a speaker's vocal expressiveness and listeners' retention or comprehension of messages, there is evidence that the speaker's expression does influence his or her perceived credibility, and that credibility subsequently does influence the listeners' comprehension and retention (Knapp 1971).

Such credibility is crucial to the success of both the actor and the teacher for both must be believable "characters" to the listeners. Although the communicative goal is not persuasion, credibility is still an issue. Theater critics, for instance, frequently refer to believability as a criterion for measuring the quality of an actor's portrayal—the audience must sense that they are listening to Hamlet, not Sir Laurence Olivier. Thus, in trying to develop the best combination of vocal cues, the actor is fixing on a manner of articulation that can be consistently sustained and will positively influence the listeners' perception of the speaker's credibility.

Teachers should also be cognizant of the need to establish credibility in the classroom. In order for students to be motivated to be attentive and purposeful, they must believe in the teacher's expertise, interest in the subject matter, and interest in them as students. That is credibility.

Therefore, the best kind of vocal expression is that which is natural, sounds unforced, and allows the teacher's true feelings about the subject matter and the learning process to be evident. This goal brings us back to an earlier point suggesting that a relatively relaxed physical state will allow the voice to reflect feelings and attitudes. When the students can pick up on subtle vocal suggestions (e.g., pitch, rate, volume, and quality changes that place emphasis,) they will believe that the teacher is knowledgeable and sincere. Consequently, they will be likely to remain relatively attentive, thus enhancing the possibilities of learning.

Credibility and thus overall impact are also enhanced by the speaker's ability to maintain vocal control. That is, a controlled voice free of unplanned, nonproductive extremes conveys to the listeners that the speaker is in control of his or her emotions and in control of the situation. A good actor knows to engage in vocal warm-up exercises prior to a vocally demanding performance so that his or her voice will not squeak or become hoarse during the performance and betray a sense of uneasiness. If such a slip should occur, the listeners become overly conscious that they are watching a performance and the characters are not real. Thus the play's credibility is damaged.

Teachers, too, need to maintain control within the performance that is a class. Voices can contribute to the ability to maintain discipline in the class because the voice is a barometer of emotions. The students will immediately sense that the teacher is "losing it" if his or her voice breaks when telling someone to sit down, for example. The teacher who can dole out disciplinary instructions in a calm, firm voice is much more worthy of the students' respect than the one who shrieks in angry frustration. That respect will have beneficial ramifications for the students' long-term learning as well as for the immediate quality of the classroom atmosphere. Such vocal control can be attained by performing warm-up exercises similar to those of the actor and by the simple process of taking a deep, cleansing breath before speaking in emotionally stressful circumstances such as disciplining (Anderson 1977). If the voice is in control, the teacher is in control.

SUMMARY

The human voice is an incredible resource of particularly remarkable value to teachers and actors. Like any resource, it must be treated with care in order to be appreciated fully. If teachers adopt vocal exercise regimens similar to those used by actors, they will find that their voices can be responsive to their feelings and that they can actually plan a few specific vocal variations to add clarity and emphasis to ideas. In addition, vocal expression contributes to the teacher's perceived credibility and control of the classroom situation, thus enhancing learning in the long term.

THROUGH THE STUDENTS' EYES

When surveyed regarding the use of voice animation in the classroom, students offered real-life examples such as those that follow. Although each example refers to vocal animation in a particular subject area, the application to other disciplines is evident.

The Three Witches

Mrs. H., my senior English teacher, would always read passages in different voices so that they fit the character she was quoting. For example, in the first scene of *Macbeth*, she read the lines in a witch-like voice. This made Shakespeare much more interesting and kept all of her students' attention. This, in turn, made it easier to grasp the concept of the play.

Huck and Jim

In English class we were reading the novel *The Adventures of Huckleberry Finn*. My teacher thought that we would get more out of the book if he read a few significant passages out of it in the dialect it was meant to be. Well, he was right. With him reading in two different animated voices, one for Huck and one for Jim, I got a better perspective about the novel and enjoyed it more than I had expected to.

Achtung!

Our German teacher uses quite a variety of vocal expressions. When he wants to emphasize a particular point or a pronunciation we're having trouble with, he will say it louder than usual. He sometimes even makes a siren sound whenever we read or say something particularly important.

The Changing Times

My eleventh-grade history teacher did something really creative with his voice that I thought helped me to learn about different time periods. When he was explaining a particular era in American history, he would use vocal expression that conveyed the sentiment most prevalent in that time—for instance, a happy, carefree expression for the 1920s and a sad voice for the 1930s.

Locker Room Follies

In high school gym class, we could get pretty rowdy in the locker room. Mr. W. would always tell us to be quiet, of course. But he didn't shout like most teachers do; he would say it real quietly. That really got our attention.

SEARCH FOR MORE ON ANIMATION IN VOICE

An Education Resources Information Center (http://www.eric.ed.gov/) search for the term "animation in voice" (or related term) and at least one other education-related term—an exercise that takes just seconds—reveals numerous citations. All of them, because they are announced in ERIC, have applications to education settings.

An ERIC search for the term "animation in voice" (or related term) with a variety of education-related terms reveals the following number of citations: "voice" and "teacher effectiveness": 49; "volume" and "teacher effectiveness": 230; "teacher voice": 40; "teacher's voice": 30; "effective teachers" and "voice": 4; "effective teaching" and "voice": 11; "voice qualities" and "teaching": 8; "voice quality" and "teachers": 15; "teacher volume": 95; "voice" and "enthusiasm": 27; and "voice" and "student engagement": 19.

In addition to exploring ERIC, you should consider searching other databases as well for books, articles, and programs related to the effective use of animation in voice in the classroom. You also are encouraged to search the Web using many of the ERIC descriptors presented in the previous paragraph.

THE MASTER'S VOICE

For further discussion of the concepts and skills presented in this chapter, read the following paragraphs in Appendix 2, Testimonials from Award-Winning K–12 Teachers and College Professors: Austin, Lefford and Yost, 2; Baleja, 3, 4; Borecky, 4; Clough, 1, 2; Light, 2, 4; Rogers (Martha), 3; Rotkin, 1, 2, 5; Steuernagel, 3.

CHAPTER

Classroom Space

People like to be close enough to obtain warmth and comradeship, but far enough away to avoid pricking one another.

—Robert Sommer

INTRODUCTION

Once upon a time, at the small Montgomery Bell Academy, boys entering their American literature class found the door closed and no sign of their teacher. When they knocked, however, they heard Mr. Pickering's voice inviting them in. Imagine their surprise when entering the classroom to not find him anywhere in sight. You may think you are reading the chapter about the tool of "suspense and surprise," but the meaningfulness of this classroom episode lies more in the fact that the next sound the boys heard was Mr. Pickering enthusiastically reading Thoreau—from under his desk! Their teacher's choice to read to them from such an unexpected spot made the students curious and unceasingly attentive (Pickering 2004). What a wonderful state of mind for students at the opening of a class period!

This episode provides us with one good reason to think about how we use the space of our classrooms. Are we doing so in a way that contributes specifically to the success of learning?

Another reason to give this issue some attention is that many times, a teacher, particularly a beginning teacher, may feel uncomfortable in the classroom. Perhaps forcing oneself to use the space of the classroom in a manner that *looks* comfortable not only would convey to students that the teacher *is* comfortable in that room but also would nurture an enhanced feeling of comfort within the teacher as well.

Thus, we now turn to consideration of constructive, purposeful use of the classroom space as a facet of the teacher-role that contributes to teacher confidence and to student learning. Imaginative use of classroom space is, therefore, a means, not an end in itself—a means of achieving positive learning outcomes. As one "acts" the role of teacher, just as with any acting, the space of the stage/classroom, with its scenery and finite limits, must be seen as a potentially beneficial tool.

PROXEMICS

The study of the communicative effect of the physical space between inter-acting people is known as proxemics. We learn from that field of study that people consciously or subconsciously choose to be in a particular spot in relationship to others depending on their interpersonal relationship, the context of the communication, and their particular goals (Hall 1966). Our interpersonal locations are interpreted as sending messages—of coldness, interest, intimacy, danger, love, and so on—whether we consciously intend them to or not.

It is on the basis of these principles of proxemics, then, that the actor or director plans the placement of actors for each scene. In real interactions with others, of course, we do not plan each and every placement of ourselves, but the prox-emic message is still present.

The teacher can apply proxemics in as deliberate a way as the actor does, by planning his or her placement during a class period. In addition, the teacher's awareness of the value of proxemic messages will allow relatively spontaneous decisions regarding where he or she should be in the classroom to convey a particular point.

There is a design firm in the state of Washington, Franklin Hill & Associates, that actually specializes in designing schools and classrooms to maximize their contribution to the quality of education. Their president, a former middle school and high school teacher, puts the issue into clear perspective: "School classrooms should have no bad seat. Poorly designed learning environments distort the information presented to our students hindering their ability to see, hear and participate. This hampers their ability to learn" (Hill, in Schibsted 2005, 29).

SPACE AND ITS LIMITATIONS

As oral communicators, both actors and teachers can benefit from being observant of the effect of space on the impact of their communication. Since nonverbal elements are part of the message communicated (be it dialogue or lessons), actors and teachers must, for instance, consider how well the listeners can see and hear them when they speak. The physical nature of the rooms within which we all must work will vary in terms of such things as acoustics and sight lines, and those elements will, in turn, impact the listeners' ability to attend to our messages.

The Responsive Classroom movement is particularly sensitive to the issues of classroom space. Their focus is the promotion of interactive learning in an atmosphere cognizant of variations in students' learning styles. Their research indicates that we serve our students' goals best when we create space that is an "organized, welcoming physical environment" (Clayton and Fortin 2001). No matter the particular room we happen to teach in, its space provides both opportunities and challenges.

As Lowman (1984) points out, some classes are held in rooms where the acoustics are awful. Students may hear an echo in some rooms, and in others the teacher may be inaudible to all students beyond the fifth row of seats. However, most classrooms, like most theaters, have been designed with good acoustics. It is, nonetheless, an issue of space to which the teacher may need to be sensitive. Some teachers, for instance, are reported to have roped off the rear rows of seats because of poor acoustics (Lowman 1984).

The issue of sight lines should also occur to teachers, just as it does to actors and directors. The question in this instance is, from what point in the classroom (or on the stage) can I be seen by listeners seated at various points around the room? Being seen by the listeners is, after all, a prerequisite to being heeded. A director will work from the set designer's drawings, which include sight lines to make decisions about where to place actors within the stage space. Such decision making is known as blocking.

Although such artificially predetermined decisions may seem far better suited to the theater than the classroom, the basic principles upon which blocking is based certainly carry over to the classroom. A review of these basic principles is in order here.

BLOCKING THE SCENE

A director or the actor involved must study the space available, the character's relationship to other characters on stage, and the character's specific motivation in order to determine the precise placement of the character within the stage space that would best convey that motivation and relationship to the audience. Placements must be compatible with established sight lines for the majority of the audience.

As the cast prepares for a performance, each piece of dialogue is thus blocked. During rehearsals, the blocking is reviewed and revised as needed to make sure its purpose is accomplished. Through rehearsing, the placement of the actors becomes firm and is ultimately perceived by the audience as integrated totally into the scene's creation of mood and idea.

The purpose of engaging in the tedious process of blocking is to place the actor in the precise spot on stage that will

- establish his or her relationship with the other characters on stage,
- emphasize the point of the lines delivered from that spot, and
- control and maintain the audience's attention.

Thus the actor's use of space is a nonverbal means of communicating.

Can a teacher do that same kind of purposeful planning of movement and placement within the classroom space? *Should* a teacher make such precise plans? Given the nature of the impact of space as a communicative message in any situation, the answer is a *qualified* yes.

BLOCKING THE CLASS PERIOD

Movement around the classroom will be most effective if planned in conjunction with a thorough review of the material to be presented on a given day. Some portions of a math lesson, for instance, are going to demand that the teacher be near the chalkboard, whereas other portions allow more options in using the classroom space.

Whatever the case may be—whether a teacher has many or few constraints on how the classroom space can be used—the goals of selecting the best use of space are the same for the teacher as they are for the actor. The teacher should place himself or herself in the classroom in such a way as to

- establish the desired relationship between teacher and students,
- provide emphasis for the most important ideas of the lesson, and
- maintain the students' attention.

If a teacher's material and style seem to result in a lecturing format in which many notes must be presented to the students, does that necessarily mean that the teacher must spend the whole class period by the chalkboard or the computer console? The answer is no.

A teacher's awareness of the proxemic effect of free use of space by a lecturer necessitates occasionally breaking away from the podium and chalkboard. Pedagogically, such movement is beneficial in that it allows the teacher to be more physically expressive, to establish meaningful proximity with the students, and to create a confident, professional image.

The podium is especially problematic in that it can be perceived as a barrier insulating the teacher from the students. Since most of us want our students to perceive us as *not* wanting to be distant, we need to get out from behind the desk or podium. Some consoles in technology classrooms are particularly challenging. Those that provide built-in units for all the computers and projectors that might ever be used in the classroom create a "Great Wall" of technology between the teacher and the students. Stepping out from behind that wall is no easy feat. We can conceive of several ways to break away from the chalkboard or podium during the lecturing mode, however. Such a planned break would allow the teacher to be in closer proximity to the students, thus conveying a greater interest in their responses and allowing for more control of classroom behavior, if needed (Geske 1992).

The break from the chalkboard can be accomplished when using a lecture format, for example, by planning and preparing overhead transparencies or flip charts of the desired notes. A student seated near the projector or chart can turn pages as needed, while the teacher is free to place himself or herself within the room where it makes the most sense for both holding the students' attention and emphasizing the key points of the material.

Another possibility would be to use poster boards placed strategically around the room in place of the chalkboard. The posters could be prepared in advance but revealed at the most appropriate moment or left with some blank spaces to be filled in as the teacher moved about the room.

Advance blocking of an *entire* class would, of course, be inappropriate because it would result in awkward movements and limit the spontaneity necessary for the learning process. But some consideration, in advance of the class meeting, of beneficial teacher and student placement during the lecture or discussion could be useful.

CLASSROOM SEATING

The classroom seating arrangement—a factor that both influences the students' attentiveness and constrains the teacher's use of space—deserves special attention as we consider the planned blocking of a class period. Teachers have long realized that students sitting in certain areas of the room tend to be more attentive and responsive than others. Although this is due in part to the tendency of more communicative students to select seats within the teacher's direct line of sight, the seat a student happens to be in is also a factor that can cause slight modification of his or her pattern of responsiveness (Hurt, Scott, and McCroskey 1978). It would follow that if we want to encourage students to be more responsive, we can move ourselves so that we will come within their direct line of sight, move the students, or both.

As we think about the possibilities of moving the teacher, the image of Professor Keating as played by Robin Williams in the film *Dead Poets' Society* (1989) comes to mind. Keating evidently was aware of the need to place himself in the most attention-getting position in the room, in spite of the constraints of the prep school's classroom. So we saw Keating in one memorable scene actually standing on the desk to deliver his lecture and, in another instance, kneeling down between rows of students so that they could huddle around him as he revealed an important insight about literature. Although these situations may seem extreme, they illustrate the range of options available that a teacher may want to "block" ahead of time in order to increase student attentiveness and learning.

Moving the students, on the other hand, is a somewhat more complicated undertaking, not as open to extremes. There are so many more people to move, and the possibilities are finitely constrained by the size of the classroom and number and type of desks involved. With a reasonable number of students in a fair-sized classroom, for instance, student desks can be arranged in a circle in order to promote multichannel communication (Billson and Tiberius 1991). Even the most inflexible of arrangements—chairs and desks bolted to the floor— can still allow some rearrangement of students, however. We should not be too quick to concede defeat.

One teacher dealing with this most inflexible of seating arrangements, for instance, developed a rotating seating chart. She had observed that certain seats in the room were "dead spots" because the students seated there had a poor view of the demonstration table at the front of the room. Certain other seats, however, were known to encourage the holders to be more attentive and responsive because of their bird's-eye view of the demonstration table. The teacher adjusted to this constraint by numbering the seats and establishing a regular rotation so that each student would move up one number each week of the course. Thus everyone had a turn at the "good seats."

Mentioning the table at the front of the room brings us to another important option for rearranging furniture to make best use of the classroom space. With the exception of lab rooms with demonstration tables needing certain gas and water hookups, most classrooms have a "front" only because that is where someone has arbitrarily placed the teacher's desk, wastebasket, flag, and so on. In other words, the "front" can be moved just by moving those accoutrements. By occasionally doing so, we change the students' visual focus during class and thus renew their attention.

In such typical straight-row classrooms, we would also have the option of simple rearrangement of students. Students can be moved in and out of the "prime seats" by a simple front-to-back periodic rotation. Another option would be to rearrange the student desks in some variation of small clusters (squares or parallel angles, for example). The advantage of doing so is greater student–student visibility (Walz 1986). Thus, students can hear each other better and be reinforced by their peers' responses.

Student seats should be placed so as to give the teacher a great deal of space to move and simultaneously put the teacher in close proximity to as many of the learners as possible. Thus, opportunities for creative use of space are enhanced, and it is easier to maintain attentiveness from *all* the students. In addition, as research has concluded, teachers are perceived more positively if they are occasionally within the student's personal space instead of maintaining a public distance.

The growing number of schools that encourage nontraditional student seating testifies to the credibility of these research conclusions. Classrooms using "learning centers" instead of traditional rows of desks are no longer so unusual. Science teacher Robert Wankmuller has found similar usefulness of nontraditional seating in the high school classrooms. He notes that in those rooms where he can establish two different seating areas, one for experiments and one for class discussion, students perform better. "Students need to know that different things are expected of them based upon where they are sitting. They have a different mindset for each area" (Wankmuller, in Schibsted 2005, 29).

To a certain extent then, teachers, like actors, can block their positions within the confines of the "scenery" (e.g., chalkboard, projectors, desks, walls) in order to enhance student attention, clarify focus, and establish intergroup relationships. Such blocking is done prior to the class by carefully considering the nature and substance of the material to be presented and both the limitations and creative possibilities afforded by the available classroom space.

SPONTANEOUS USE OF SPACE

Just as good actors can improvise on occasion, so can good teachers also make spontaneous decisions about where to place themselves, their students, or their materials within the classroom space. Such decisions grow out of the teacher's constant sensitivity to the students—their moods, levels of comprehension, and interests.

Recalling that the teacher's proximity to a student or students establishes the specific student–teacher relationship, we realize that there will be occasions when that relationship reflects a hierarchy of power, other times when a more caring relationship is indicated, and yet other times when the relationship is somewhere in between. Such variations cannot be blocked ahead of time.

Instead, as we are interacting with students—whether it be in a lecture, discussion, or practicum mode—we should be attentive to their feedback. One instructor who frequently has class in a large lecture hall reports, for instance, that students' postures and facial expressions often signal to him the need to come into their space to renew and refocus their attention on the material (Kurre 1993). Others, who more frequently use a class-discussion format for teaching, may note that students' nonverbal behavior indicates when the teacher needs to come to that group and when to keep his or her distance.

The point is that in order to use classroom space most productively as a teaching tool, one must be comfortable enough in the space to move about it spontaneously as dictated by the material and the student responses. The teacher has to be able and willing on a moment's notice to pick the spot that will indicate the relationship between him- or herself and the students and that will be most conducive to learning.

One could, for example, lean on the windowsill, sit in a student desk, stand in the doorway, or walk slowly among the student desks. Each of these actions represents a break from the typical or expected teacher behavior of standing by the desk or podium—a break that could change the students' perception of the teacher's meaning and/or attitude.

For instance, in conducting a student discussion of literature, a teacher may convey an attitude of respecting and encouraging student opinion by sitting in a spare student desk instead of standing at the front of the room. Standing at the front, after all, reinforces the perception of the teacher as the person "in charge" of the class. Thus, if the teacher notes that the students seem reluctant to share ideas, it may be that a change in space relationship is needed. By moving to sit at eye level with the students, a teacher can indicate or foster a different power relationship.

Similarly, at the college level, students have a different sense of who is responsible for leading the class when the instructor moves away from the front of the room. One of the authors has developed the habit of moving to the back of the room when students are talking about some group conclusions that members have written on the chalkboard. This seems to have freed the students to be more creative in their thinking instead of saying what they think must be the expected, or "right," answer.

This type of relatively spontaneous change in the planned use of the classroom space is enabled by teacher sensitivity to the dynamics of the learning environment. As with any communicative event, the teaching–learning event must be planned carefully, but with allowances for necessary adaptations to be made on the spot.

Spontaneity, though, can lead to some hair-raising experiences—literally. One of this book's authors, while speaking before a group of teachers at Darwin High

School in Darwin, Australia, decided to emphasize a point by leaping onto one of the classroom tables. Although he had assured himself that the table would hold his two hundred pounds, he neglected to take into account his six-foot, two-inch height *and* the classroom's slowly turning ceiling fans! His head just missed those swirling blades (Figure 6.1). It was almost an event everyone, *except* the author, would remember for a lifetime.

ACCOMMODATING SPECIAL NEEDS

One last reminder is necessary as we think about rearrangements of classroom space to enhance teacher confidence and student learning. That reminder is that whatever adjustments we envision should be made with the requirements for special-needs students in mind. Franklin Hill suggests that no student should be seated further than fifteen feet away from the focus of the classroom activity (Hill, in Schibsted 2005). For students with hearing loss or vision limitations, that maximum distance must be considerably reduced. Additionally, any "surprise" rearrangement of desks will pose a risk to those with certain vision impairments. Of course, whatever arrangement of chairs, desks, and tables used must always leave ample room for wheelchair-width aisles, as well.

SUMMARY

In the theater, actors and directors consciously apply principles of proxemics (the study of interpersonal space) to determine the best placement for each of the characters within a scene. This is done to help the audience understand the playwright's point in the scene. The blocking of positions is planned and practiced well in advance of a performance, with some allowance for improvisational movement under certain circumstances.

Similarly, an effective teacher will consider, prior to a class meeting, the best placement of the people involved in the class—teacher and students—to enhance the likelihood of meaningful learning. This planning may result in the preparation of certain teaching aids, in the rearrangement of furniture or seat assignments, or in rehearsed movements within the classroom space available. In addition, the teacher is always prepared to modify such plans and spontaneously make decisions about his or her placement in the room in order to achieve the goals of

- establishing the nature of the teacher-student relationship,
- emphasizing key points in the class material, and
- maintaining student attention.

These have always been among the goals of all teachers, but we are all creatures of habit and may feel uncomfortable moving around a classroom in new ways. Just as an actor learns a part gradually, so a teacher should attempt to learn new approaches to using classroom space gradually, developing new strategies to enhance achievement of old goals.

Figure 6.1
Teacher on Table Close to Ceiling Fan

Research conclusions unanimously confirm that teacher and student locations in a classroom affect their communication processes (Smith 1979). In teaching, as in acting, communication is, after all, the heart of the matter!

THROUGH THE STUDENTS' EYES

When surveyed regarding the use of space in the classroom, students offered real-life examples such as those that follow. Although each example refers to the use of space in a particular subject area, the application to other disciplines is evident.

Table Walking

One day, about five minutes after the students had filed into class, Mr. B. came running into the classroom and jumped onto the table. Talk about shock [surprise]! Our tables were in a circle, and he proceeded to walk around them, explaining the rules of the "math game." He would walk around reciting a math sequence of operations, and when and where he stopped (no one knew how long the math problem was [suspense]), that student would have to give the answer. The "game" definitely reinforced my math skills and yet entertained me at the same time.

Dealing with the Multitudes

My college Human Development class has four hundred students in it. Ordinarily, there is very little class participation under these circumstances. But this professor is different. He comes down from the stage area and walks around the lecture hall. This gets people to participate and makes learning more fun.

An Upending Discussion

Our German teacher in high school was explaining different customs and behaviors typical of the country. When we got to the part about driving on the autobahn, he had us turn our desks upside down and line them up around the room to "create" an autobahn. Then he explained the German rules of the road.

Cornering the Problem

In math class at my high school, a teacher used the corner or corners of the room as a focal point to show the x, y, and z axes of three-dimensional space.

New Flooring

Frequently in my college French class, the professor will ask us to arrange our chairs in a U shape, leaving wide-open floor space in the center. Then she spreads pictures around the floor pertinent to the day's lecture topic. That way, we can all see the pictures much more easily than if the same things were hung on a bulletin board.

SEARCH FOR MORE ON SPACE UTILIZATION

An Education Resources Information Center (http://www.eric.ed.gov/) search for the term "space utilization" (or related term) and at least one other education-related term—an exercise that takes just seconds—reveals numerous citations. All of them, because they are announced in ERIC, have applications to education settings.

An ERIC search for the term "space utilization" (or related term) with a variety of education-related terms reveals the following number of citations: "space utilization" and "teachers": 305; "space utilization" and "teaching": 200; "space utilization" and "students": 356; and "space utilization" and "effectiveness": 146; "space utilization" and "creativity": 9; "classroom seating": 45; "seating," "classrooms," and "interest": 14; and "creative classrooms" and "space" 2.

In addition to exploring ERIC, you should consider searching other databases as well for books, articles, and programs related to the effective application of space utilization in the classroom. You also are encouraged to search the Web using many of the ERIC descriptors presented in the previous paragraph.

THE MASTER'S VOICE

For further discussion of the concepts and skills presented in this chapter, read the following paragraphs in Appendix 2, Testimonials from Award-Winning K–12 Teachers and College Professors: Clough, 4; Grimnes, 1–3, 6; Mahoney, 3; McBrayer, 2; Steuernagel, 2–5.

CHAPTER 7

Humor

Humor helps to convert "Ha Ha" into "Aha!"

—Patrick J. Herbert

INTRODUCTION

As the story goes, Joe accompanied his friend to a joke-tellers meeting. At the well-attended gathering, members had such a large repertoire of jokes that they numbered each of them. Then, throughout the meeting, different members simply would stand and call out the number of a joke (e.g., number forty-two, number eighty-nine), and all in the audience would howl with laughter. Toward the end of the meeting, Joe asked if he could take a turn "telling a joke"—after all, it looked so easy. Joe stood, called out a number, and waited for an audience response. There was none. Joe's friend turned to him and said, "Well, some people can tell a joke, and some people can't."

Successful joke-teller or not, humor is everywhere. John F. Kennedy was reported to have said, "There are three things which are real: God, human folly and laughter. The first two are beyond our comprehension. So we must do what we can with the third" (Hunsaker 1988, 285). What can we do with humor?

On one hand, for both actors and teachers, humor should be the easiest skill area to address. Probably more has been written on the subject of humor than on any of the other acting/teaching skills highlighted in this book. On the other hand, humor is often seen as the most threatening of the skill areas. For teachers, humor may be even more threatening in that, for them, humor must serve a subject-related purpose, not simply entertain. Further, humor that "bombs" for an actor one night with one audience can be forgotten—a new audience will be in the theater tomorrow. For teachers, humor that "bombs" is remembered, not only by the students (audience) but also by the teacher.

According to Glasser, fun (what humor generates) is one of five basic needs that motivate human beings. It is no less important than the needs of survival, power, belonging, and freedom. Fun is nature's reward for learning. We agree.

"Students feel pain when a need is frustrated and pleasure when it is satisfied" (Glasser 1998, 26). Teachers are in a key position to help students experience the pleasure of having a need satisfied—including the need for fun. And, because needs typically are never met once and for all, teachers need to create the conditions for having fun—for learning—on a continual basis. Believe it or not, it is all right to laugh in school!

In spite of the anxiety, sometimes terror, that beginning users of humor might experience, it is worth the effort. "Humor, like sin, sun, and self-righteousness exists virtually everywhere people congregate" (Herbert 1991, 2). Humor holds great potential for positively impacting an audience, in the theater or in the classroom. Who can argue with the fact that learning is most effective when it's fun (Loomans and Kohlberg, 1993)? People who possess a real sense of humor can take it as well as hand it out. Don't be afraid to use humor (Enerson and Plank 1993). This, too, is true whether one is on the stage or in the classroom.

HUMOR: ITS IMPACT ON TEACHING

One of the most important qualities of a good teacher is humor.
—Gilbert Highet

Javidi, Downs, and Nussbaum (1988) report that award-winning high school and middle school teachers use humor significantly more than their non–award-winning counterparts. These award-winning teachers "played off" the self, the students, others not in class, and the course materials in order to clarify course content. Having a sense of humor is a positive teacher trait often listed by students when they are asked to rate effective teachers (Brown 2004). It has the proven potential to establish a positive learning environment (Sev'er and Ungar 1997) and is a critical component of effective learning in higher education (Hativa 2000) as well as in basic education.

The humor to which we refer here is *constructive* humor—nonhostile humor directly related to the educational message—not just a funny joke. "Humor is a valuable tool for establishing a classroom climate conducive to learning" (Kher, Molstad, and Donahue 1999, 400). Others, too, see humor as a teaching strategy to facilitate learning (Bergen 1992; Dinkmeyer 1993; and Torok, McMorris, and Lin 2004). If we allow such humor to be a vital part of the lecture or demonstration, we will add a strategy to our repertoire that is sure to stimulate student attention. The bottom line is that "students learn more when they're having fun" (Sullivan 1992, 36).

Specifically, humor is one of the best ways teachers can develop a solid relationship with students (Pollack and Freda 1997). Humor helps teachers and students establish a rapport with one another—the ability to see the frailties of human nature, to be able to laugh at oneself and not take oneself too seriously. Victor Borge is reported to have said that "laughter is the shortest distance between two people." Laughter is one of the most visceral expressions of being entertained. Laughter also increases the student's ability to absorb knowledge. Nonhostile humor, directly related to the educational message, can also help make taboo subjects, such as politics, more approachable. It is a powerful way to reinforce learning. Lundberg and Thurston's (2002) book title, *If They're Laughing, They Just Might Be Listening*, clearly connects humor to sound pedagogy.

Humor can take many forms, including that of playful exaggeration, an intentional expansion of emotional responses reinforced by gesture, posture, tone of voice, and role-playing. Such a form of acting, according to Starratt (1990, 19), "falls in between playing one's part with sincerity and playing an imposter or fraud." It recognizes that a play (or a class) "cannot tolerate relentless melodrama; neither can it sustain uninterrupted frivolity." This type of acting includes, among other exaggerated responses, "mock indignation ('How dare you, sir!'), mock surprise ('I never would have suspected!'), a playful moralizing ('That's what happens to little boys who disobey their mothers.') and stock rationalizations ('The devil made me do it!')." Observations about humor, no matter the form, reveal a concept that is multidimensional (Goor 1989).

Humor invites students to take risks in the classroom because it softens the blow of failure. In *Dead Poets' Society* (1989), Mr. Keating, played by Robin Williams, often uses humor to inspire his students to participate. One notable moment occurs when a student, Charlie, incorrectly answers a query about a certain poet. Williams makes the sound of a buzzer with his voice, giving the impression that the student is on a game show. The buzzing sound is followed with the line, "Incorrect, but thank you for trying." This creates immediate laughter from the other students, as well as from Charlie. The students were discovering for the first time that learning and participating in class, even if the incorrect answer is given, can be exciting, fun, and safe.

Civikly (1986) recommends that teachers who are considering the use of humor review, among other points, how humor has been used in class; identify comfortable humor styles; work on "planned spontaneity"; and evaluate (with student input) the humor used. Kher et al. (1999) point out the virtues of using humor in college classrooms to enhance teaching effectiveness even in so-called dread classes.

Whether surveying high school students or elementary school students, a "sense of humor" is regularly identified as a characteristic of best-liked teachers and identified as a characteristic lacking among least-liked teachers (Witty 1950). Similar views are held by college students with regard to their professors. Murray's *Teacher Behaviors Inventory* and Perry's *Instructor Expressiveness Construct*, found in Wlodkowski's book (1985), among other such communication-classification systems, cite "humor" as a key component of enthusiastic teachers. "Humor is also an excellent mnemonic device" (Larson 1982, 198). As a memory aid, humor can help students to visualize a concept, principle, or operation. Remember "Every Good Boy Does Fine" (the notes on the lines of the treble clef) or "My Very Extravagant Mother Just Sent Us Ninety Parakeets" (Mercury, Venus, Earth, Mars, Jupiter, Saturn, Uranus, Neptune, Pluto).

Theory, as well as empirical data, points out the close relationship between humor and creativity (Ziv 1989)—an added benefit to the increased use of humor in today's classrooms. Divergent thinking, as defined by Guilford (1959), is enhanced when fear of criticism from one's social environment (classroom) is reduced. "The tension release aspect of laughter and its contagious effects can influence group cohesiveness and thus reduce social anxiety" (Ziv 1989, 114).

Humor can be tendentious—it can help promote a point of view. Jay Leno's nightly monologue often combines domestic and international political events with humor to make pungent points. We laugh, but we also learn. According to Ziegler (1998), humor also can help teachers assess whether students grasp the concept that is the basis of the humor—if they laugh or smile, and do so at the right time, they probably have an understanding of the concept behind the humor. For instance, "a riddle or joke is funny only if both the expected and the unexpected meanings are understood" (Bergen 1992, 105).

We must remember, though, that humor is a tool that should never be used to lower the self-esteem of the student. One must be careful to note the difference between genuine humor, which allows us all to see our more vulnerable human side, and derision, which creates laughter at the expense of another person.

CATEGORIES OF HUMOR

The job of the teacher is to get students laughing, and when their mouths are open, to give them something on which to chew.
                                              —Elaine Lundberg and Cheryl Thurston

It soon becomes apparent when using humor that there are various kinds or categories of it. All have potential for livening up a classroom and contributing to student learning. When humor is used for pedagogical purposes, Neuliep (1991) places humor into the following categories:

- Joke (a relatively short prose build-up followed by a punch line): Did you hear the one about the young man who was hired by a supermarket? He arrived the first day, and the manager greeted him, gave him a broom, and said, "Your first job will be to sweep off the sidewalk in front of the store." The young man replied indignantly, "But, I'm a college graduate!" The manager responded, "I apologize. Here, let me show you how to do it!"
- Riddle (a puzzling question containing a problem to be solved): I am personally the number 79. They once tried to make me from 29. What am I? (McKay 2000). The answer is gold. Gold occupies the number 79 on the periodic table, and once upon a time, efforts were undertaken to make gold from copper, number 29 on the periodic table. For those of you who have a bit of extra time on your hands, how many ways are there to make change for one dollar? Try it. There are 293 ways.
- Pun (a play on words that sound the same but have different meanings): When his father, Claudius, asks Hamlet why he feels so moody, Hamlet responds by saying he is "too much in the sun." Remember that this response (Act 1, Scene 2, Line 69) would be delivered orally, so the audience could hear "sun," or it could hear "son"—just the pun Shakespeare intended. Here is one for the younger audience. What is black and white and read all over? Students hearing

this may well assume that the word "read" is actually "red," especially because the first two words in the sentence refer to colors. The answer to the riddle is "newspaper."

- Funny story (a series of connecting events or the activities of a single incident as a tale): "A funny thing happened on the way to the Forum . . . " We all have these kinds of stories, don't we? Just last month, one of the authors was in Australia, about to deliver a talk to roughly 200 education majors. As he exited his car in the university's parking lot and made his way to the auditorium, he opened a piece of taffy and popped it into his mouth. Big mistake. Seconds later he felt something solid mixed in with the taffy—a filling had been pulled out by the candy. The show had to go on! Needless to say, he did not drink any of the ice water that was offered.
- Humorous comment (brief humorous statement that does not fit in any other category): Shakespeare's *Romeo and Juliet* was "a tragedy that could have been averted if Verona had a decent postal system" (Boerman-Cornell 1999, 69).

We think that the categories of humor can be expanded. Here are a few others along with an example of each.

- Oxymoron (combination of seemingly exact opposite words): business ethics, military intelligence, genuine imitation, resident alien, working vacation, peace force, vegetarian meatloaf, pretty ugly, act naturally, rap music, soft rock, jumbo shrimp, and childproof (no second word is needed here, is it?).
- Murphy's Law (if it can go wrong, it will—and at the worst possible time): You have finished reading this book and have gathered up the courage to try some of these ideas for the first time in your first-period classroom. You are not feeling all that confident. As fate would have it, your principal has chosen this very period to sit in and observe you!
- Parody (a feeble, transparent, ridiculous imitation in voice or body): *Saturday Night Live* has been probably the king of parody on television. Think of the many U.S. Presidents, as well as entertainers and sports figures, who have been mimicked.
- Limerick (light or humorous verse form):

      There once was a principal named Harry,
      a wooden paddle he would carry.
      Through the halls he would swing it, up and down he would bring it,
      and not a lingering student would tarry!

- Deadpan (emotionless immobile face): You might remember Ben Stein, who has capitalized on his delivery of a deadpan look, whether as Mr. Cantwell, the biology teacher on *The Wonder Years*, or on his 1997–2002 television program, *Win Ben Stein's Money*.
- Knock-knock (call and answer form of a joke): Knock-knock. Who's there? (You finish it.)
- Irony (incongruity between actual results and expected results): It is ironic that although we say we value education, we often pay teachers so little that

many have to leave the profession. Note that this is "funny" only in the sense that incongruity exists between respect and salary. As coincidence would have it, a cartoon depicting just this very situation appears in *Phi Delta Kappan* (2005, 294). Check it out.

- Slapstick (exaggerated, unexpected movements and gestures): Think of the Three Stooges, or Chevy Chase and Steve Martin for more contemporary images, but tone it down a bit!

What is common to all of these categories? No matter the category, once people "get it," humor allows them to experience and appreciate a certain incongruity, absurdity, and ludicrousness about life (Sultanoff 2002). Humor also allows both the sender and the recipient to share the experience!

You may have noted that we have left sarcasm out as a category of humor. Although sarcasm can be funny, it also can be dangerous. *Webster's Seventh New Collegiate Dictionary* (1972) defines sarcasm as "to tear flesh, bite the lips in rage, sneer; a cutting, hostile, or contemptuous remark; the use of caustic or ironic language" (764). Shade (1996) adds to this brutal set of definitions the fact that sarcasm invariably wounds students' self-esteem. "Sarcasm humiliates, mocks, and makes fun of its victims . . . often leading to poor attitudes and deep resentments" (87). Avoid sarcasm at all cost.

By the way, if students don't bust out laughing at your attempts of humor, keep at it. You will get better. In turn, encourage your students to create and use humor. And be sure to respond positively to their attempts—laugh! And, if their effort at humor is not all that funny, *act* as if you find it funny; *act* as if you find the punch line surprising. With your support, they too will get better at creating and using humor.

Let students help you deliver humor in the classroom. Try David Letterman's approach. Share with them an example, such as where a principal announces his top ten reasons why it is "cool" to be a principal. Some of these reasons may include "lots of cool keys," "get to have an hour-and-a-half lunch with 350 friends," "gets to keep teachers after school," and "name sometimes appears prominently in print (graffiti)." We credit Principal Ron Wilson, of Abilene Middle School in Abilene, Kansas, for these reasons. Now, involve students. Ask them to help compose their own list of the "top ten reasons"—perhaps for scheduling chemistry (think flames, test tubes, and chemicals) or for volunteering to be in the upcoming Peter Pan play (think tights and swinging on wires suspended from the ceiling). Try asking them to brainstorm endings to sentences such as "You know that you are a bit anxious about your upcoming speech when you . . . ," "You know you are hooked on Shakespeare when you . . . ," and "You know you need to brush up on your Latin when you . . . "

GENDER AND GRADE-LEVEL DIFFERENCES

The early bird gets the worm, but the second mouse gets the cheese.

—Unknown

Are there gender differences in the use of humor by teachers and in student responses to it? Bryant and Zillmann (1988) conclude that, at every level, male teachers were found to use humor more often than female teachers. For instance, Bryant et al. (1980) found that college teachers used an average of 3.34 instances of humor during a fifty-minute class—3.73 instances for male instructors and 2.43 instances for female instructors. Gorham and Christophel (1990) report a much lower average of only 1.37 humorous attempts by instructors, but still confirm that females' frequency of humor was less (86 percent) than that of males.'

Humor favoring a particular point, though, is utilized by female professors (62 percent) to a substantially greater degree than by their male colleagues (43 percent). Males are more likely to use self-disparaging humor, whereas females are more likely to have a balance between humor directed at themselves and humor directed at their students. Self-disparaging humor works best when the speaker and audience are the same sex (Tamborini and Zillmann 1981). Male instructors who used humor generally received higher teaching evaluations, whereas females generally received lower evaluations.

Differences also exist within the audience viewing the humor. Bryant et al. (1980) found that for college students, sexual humor was more appealing to an audience of the opposite sex from that of the teacher. Gorham and Christophel (1990) report that male students are generally more positively affected—indications of learning, attitudes toward course content, and intent to take another course by the same instructor—than female students by teachers' use of humor.

The previous citations refer to college instructors who were teaching college-age students, not high school–age adolescents. Neuliep's (1991) study at the high school level reveals that high school teachers' humor differs from the humor of their college-level counterparts. High school and middle school teachers' self-reports reveal fewer uses of humor. No correlation was found between their years of experience and their frequency of humor use, and no differences were found between award-winning versus non–award-winning teachers. In high schools, "teachers also indicated that they use humor as a way of putting students at ease, getting students' attention, and for showing that the teacher is human . . . not as a pedagogical strategy for increasing student comprehension or learning" (Neuliep 1991, 354).

CARTOONS: A SAFE FIRST STEP

Humor is also a way of saying something serious.

—T. S. Eliot

One relatively safe way to begin using humor in the classroom is to incorporate into the curriculum cartoons that carry a message related to the subject being studied. A cartoon "can be useful in helping students to remember a concept or for reducing anxiety about difficult content" (Korobkin 1988, 157). Peterson (1980, 646) reports acquiring, in less than five years, several hundred cartoons with subjects related to his discipline of science. Students' recognition of the point of the cartoon involves a "spontaneous flash of insight that shows a familiar situation in a new light," not unlike the insight that accompanies scientific discoveries. This, he argues, leads to learning.

Neuliep (1991) refers to cartoons as "external source humor" or "third-party" humor. One of the authors, in beginning a discussion of alternatives to punishment, introduces the concept of in-school suspension, a version of the psychological principle of time-out, by the use of a cartoon. This cartoon, although outrageous and hilarious, uses a mental image and a play on words (e.g., in-school suspension versus students physically being suspended in a school) to make its point (Figure 7.1). The cartoon and the chuckles that follow help reduce student anxiety regarding the upcoming discussion of punishment.

The same author uses another punishment-oriented cartoon depicting two students, both of whom are dusting erasers. One student says to the other, "Hey, wait a minute! You're cleaning erasers as punishment? I'm cleaning erasers as a reward" (*Phi Delta Kappan* 1991, 501). The author's students, in attempting to explain the apparent discrepancy of the cartoon, begin to realize that whether something is a punishment or a reward depends on the perception of the child receiving it—not the perception of the teacher who is handing it out.

Still one more cartoon used by this author shows a father porcupine who is just about to paddle his son. The father says to his son, "This will hurt me more than it will hurt you." The cartoon highlights both the possible physical and emotional pain that administers of punishment can experience. This cartoon sparks comments from both teacher and parent audiences regarding appropriate and inappropriate discipline techniques.

Could these same messages or discussion starters have been delivered without the cartoons? Sure. But, like a picture, a cartoon is worth a thousand words. Further, cartoons add some welcome variety to a discussion. Lowe (1991) reports that cartoons are especially valuable in large classes, where they help maintain student interest, create a visual example of the topic at hand, and add some levity to the class.

Teachers, whether in training or in service, can start a collection of subject-related cartoons for possible inclusion in lectures via overhead transparencies. "It has been demonstrated that some cartoons of suitable type (e.g., visual 'puns') can be used with the intention of serving a direct teaching function such as facilitating the learning of definitions and symbols and promoting insights into difficult concepts" (Powell and Anderson 1985, 87).

Because of different subject areas, teachers will likely use different primary sources for amassing a cartoon collection, including professional journals within a specific subject area as well as journals relating to the teaching profession in general. Some wonderful cartoons are included each month in the scholarly journal *Phi Delta Kappan*, the sophisticated *The New Yorker*, and the witty *Atlantic Monthly*. At the same time, though, one should not overlook sources such as *Time*, *Newsweek*, and other magazines. Another great source would be the political cartoons on the editorial pages and the comic strips in newspapers. For a one-time use you might consider either showing them directly or, respecting copyright laws, displaying them on a data or overhead projector. Other sources would include books of

Figure 7.1
In-School Suspension

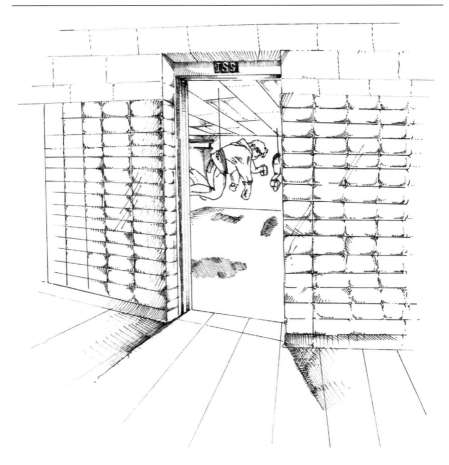

cartoons, such as Brooks' *Best Editorial Cartoons of the Year*, as well as the ever-growing wealth of Internet sources that are either free or available at a modest cost.

Finally, we may want to create our own cartoons. If a teacher does not have the "talent" to do so, he or she could always solicit students who do possess the talent and who, in fact, would be flattered to assist (Demetrulias 1982). One of the authors, on several occasions, has worked with commercial-arts students from local vocational-technical schools who have created original cartoons depicting his subject matter. On more than one occasion, the cartoons have been used not only in class lectures and workshop presentations, but also as pictorials to accompany journal articles and books published both nationally and internationally.

Newspaper comics seem to have something in them for everyone. Their appeal is shown in their longevity of publication. Comic books, an extension of comic strips, also have a widespread appeal to all age groups. Comic books are among the most widely read media in the world. In Japan, for instance, in 1994 almost 25 percent of the nation's entire publications were comic books (Kin 1995). What might comics, in any form, have to offer classroom teachers? Lots.

Before we leave the topic of cartoons, we would like to mention the use of stickers—yes, stickers! Stickers are sort of cartoon-like. Any parent or teacher knows the power over young children that stickers seem to have. Children love stickers, and they will do almost anything in the anticipation of receiving "award" stickers, "good job" stickers, or "thank you" stickers. One of the authors has saved some his daughter's elementary school worksheets. Many of these have scratch-and-sniff stickers on them. One, believe it or not, is a sticker that smelled like cucumber if you scratched it! We know there is a use for stickers with young children. We believe that there also is a use, in moderation, for stickers with older students—even adult students. Is it a little corny? Sure, but students of all ages seem to get a kick out of them.

Who doesn't like to be told, whether in words or in symbols (stickers) that they have done a "good job" or are deserving of a "thank you"? In fact, for conveying these messages to teenagers who, because of peer pressure, may be unreceptive to an oral message, stickers are just the trick. Be a little daring. Try peel-away stickers, hip word stickers, and, our favorite, scratch-and-sniff stickers. Don't overlook the time-honored rubber-stamp version of today's sticker craze. "Super," "Nice Work," and "Great Job" stamps or stickers on student work are always appreciated. Finally, consider motivational or message-laden buttons. They even work for adult audiences. One of the authors who teaches a graduate education course in Florida wears a button to class that says, "Spay the FCAT." For teachers who often are overwhelmed by having to dedicate much of their talent and time toward having students do well on the state's Comprehensive Assessment Test, the button is a small, but visible, humorous statement. It always generates both laughter and a discussion.

Where can you find stickers, motivational rubber stamps, and buttons? Ask any elementary school teacher. Look in the Yellow Pages for teacher-supply stores. By the way, consider this a "Thank You" sticker for reading our book.

BRINGING HUMOR INTO THE CLASSROOM—A GAGGLE OF IDEAS

Although not intended to be a definitive list of suggestions, the following list does represent a variety of ways in which humor can be brought into the classroom. Of course, humor *never* is used at a student's expense.

- Use a humorous cartoon to introduce a lesson. Encourage students to locate and then bring in their own subject-related cartoons, puns, and so on.
- Share a humorous event from your life in the form of "a funny thing happened to me on the way to the forum." Solicit such events from your students' lives.
- When a story or pun flops, try holding up your grade book and repeating the pun that has just flopped. Then there will be laughter.
- When citing a string of examples of a concept, end with a humorous or unexpected event. When teaching the classroom management concept of

"time-out," for instance, one could offer examples such as the child being made to sit in a corner, standing out in the hall, or spending a day with your accountant! When teaching the concept of "positive reinforcement," one could offer examples such as scratch-and-sniff stickers, consumables (e.g., candy), or a shiny, red Maserati!

- Include appropriate humor on tests. In a multiple-choice question, have one of the "a" though "e" choices be some outrageous distracter. Every once in a while, toss in Elvis, Kermit the Frog, or perhaps even your name.
- Encourage students to incorporate humor in answering test questions. Divergent thinking—creativity—will be enhanced.
- Bury, perhaps in a cigar box, humor that dies—and some of it will. Conduct a brief "grave-site" ceremony, and move on (Herbert 1991). If you are so inclined, you could slip into a short dance routine as Johnny Carson did when his monologue died.
- Start a humor board where everyone can put up their favorite cartoons, subject-related or not (your choice), with an award for the best one each week.
- Look for the humorous side of situations that probably are going to occur anyhow. Something that falls to the floor could elicit a "Gravity is proven once again" comment, or a truck backing up outside with a loud "beep, beep, beep" sound could evoke an "OK, whose wristwatch alarm is that?" remark from the instructor.
- Combine humor with other acting/teaching skills (e.g., use of props), such as donning a pair of "Wellees" (Wellington boots) while telling students, "We are going to do some 'deep' thinking today." Keep those boots handy for the times when students try to bluff their way through an answer. Bring out the boots, hold them up high, and say, "Boy, it's getting kind of 'deep' in here." In the future, simply holding up the boots will make your point and engender laughter.
- Have students write "humorous" lyrics to seasonal songs, perhaps Christmas carols, as does Patricia Thomas, a physics teacher from Northeast High School in Pinellas County, Florida. Join the students in traveling the halls singing the "carols." An example of such a "carol" would be "Gravity," sung to the tune of "Jingle Bells:

> A comet hits the earth.
> It's made of methane gas.
> It makes a giant force.
> Now isn't that so nice.
> Gravity, Gravity,
> keeps us on the ground.
> An apple fell on Newton,
> he said, what goes up comes down.
> Gravity, Gravity,
> mass times nine-point-eight.
> Remember, travel very fast,
> if earth you must escape.

Everyone finds the experience humorous, but like all of the acting skills high-lighted in this book, the humor has an academic purpose.

- Comment upon one's own hand-drawn overhead transparencies or chalkboard sketches with the statement, "It is pretty obvious why I didn't major in art."
- As a teacher of grammar—aren't all teachers?—show students Victor Borge's classic act in which he reads a piece of literature and, using sound effects, highlights the punctuation. Grammar will never again be seen as dull.
- Keep a skeleton (miniature will do) in the classroom closet—give it a name. Bring it out occasionally and "include" him or her in the class discussions. One could substitute a life-size picture of Albert Einstein or a full-size cardboard cutout of Joe Paterno (one of the authors did this) for the skeleton. Even a Chia Pet would do.
- When stumbling over one's words in a lecture (especially likely to happen early on a Monday morning), comment, "Gosh, I forgot to put my upper plate of dentures in this morning." You might keep a plastic set of "uppers or lowers" in your desk drawer for just such an occasion.

A POSSIBLE "HUMOROUS" BENEFIT OF HUMOR

A sense of humor is part of the art of leadership, of getting along with people, of getting things done.

—Dwight D. Eisenhower

A recent newspaper article by Oldenburg (2005), titled "Laugh Yourself Skinny," may have some application to today's classrooms. With obesity a serious problem in our country, perhaps humor, and the laughter that results from it, can serve two purposes. One, it can enhance student learning and heighten student and teacher satisfaction. Two, it can help people lose weight and, it is claimed, can lower stress levels and strengthen cardiovascular muscles. Wallinger (1997), too, supports this second claim relating to the therapeutic value of humor.

Buchowski, Director of Bionutrition at Vanderbilt University, has found that "ten to 15 minutes of laughter could increase energy expenditure by 10 to 40 calories per day, which could translate into about four pounds a year" (2005, 16). So can we eat calorie-laden foods with impunity? Unfortunately, the answer is no. "You'd have to laugh for 15 minutes just to burn off two Hershey's Kisses" (Buchowski 2005, 16). Fifteen years ago, Walter (1990) concluded much the same thing as Buchowski when he reported that "recent studies have shown that a good laugh provides a mini-workout for the body that actually burns us calories" (44).

Although physiology experts may say that laughing is not the most effective way to shed extra weight, it just may be an idea that is worth a laugh or two (Ross 2005). What do you have to lose? Get it? What do you have to lose? Just to prove that laughing can help you reduce weight, weigh yourself with a very, very accurate scale. Now, read the hypothetical dissertation title that follows (get ready to laugh): "Spikes vs. Platforms: The Relative Effectiveness of Two Height-Enhancement Techniques in the Reduction of Napoleonic Complex." If this hypothetical dissertation title didn't get you laughing, try the *Family Circus* (Keane 2005) cartoon where, just prior to the Christmas holiday, an elementary teacher asks, "Who can tell me what a subordinate clause is?" A student responds by saying, "One of Santa's helpers!" Surely this one got you laughing.

Now, after you have laughed, weigh yourself again on that very, very accurate scale and see if you have dropped a micro-ounce or two. Even if you did not "laugh yourself silly," the exercise of walking to and from the scale, twice, should result in burned calories. In either case, you come out a winner. [Note: The fictitious dissertation title noted previously comes from an article by Kher, Molstad, and Donahue 1999.]

SUMMARY

A merry heart doeth good like a medicine.

—Proverbs 17

According to Cornett (1986), humor can be a powerful instructional resource that helps teachers in a number of ways, including attracting attention, improving communication, soothing difficult moments, and reinforcing desired behaviors. The appropriate use of humor is a powerful tool that can help educators positively affect changes in a student's knowledge, attitudes, skills, and aspirations (Warnock 1989).

Having highlighted the power of using humor in the classroom, we consider it appropriate to offer some general cautions. While the intuitive benefits of humor may now seem obvious, there are recent research studies (MacAdam 1985, 329) that conclude that instructors who use humor may "contradict student expectations of just how a college teacher is 'supposed' to act." There appears to be less of a problem for K–12 teachers.

Sophisticated and subtle humor may be one of the hardest kinds of communication to understand and appreciate. It may demand a level of knowledge and intelligence that may not exist in some classrooms (Armour 1975). Not all students may catch the "point" in a pun. If it has to be explained, unintended embarrassment may replace the intended humor.

Another caution regarding humor applies to novice teachers. According to Wandersee (1982), beginning teachers may well decide to postpone using humor until they begin to feel confident in discipline, organization, and content mastery. Humor usage entails some risk on the part of the teacher. Too many risks too early in a teacher's career could backfire.

Recognizing the cautions just described, professionals still generally feel that humor holds the potential for helping teachers to teach more effectively. Humor can also help the teacher himself or herself. Humor and the laughter it precipitates may have medicinal value. Dr. Patch Adams's (1992, 1998) work backs up this claim. As a West Virginia physician, he used humor—complete with giant shoes and a red clown's nose—to help heal patients. According to Walter (1990), each time you chuckle or "crack up," your brain releases natural painkilling hormones, which, in turn, trigger the release of endorphins, natural opiates that can reduce pain, make eyes sparkle, and get the brain to work more effectively. He also claims that laughter can increase your feelings of self-esteem!

Humor, Humphreys (1990) argues, has positive effects on one's immune functions, pain, circulation and respiration, and physical illness. The medical and physiological impact of humor, often described as "gut" laughing or "stationary jogging," is well researched and well supported. Neilsen (1993), for instance, cites over one hundred references in support of humor's body- and mind-curing powers. In a stressful field such as teaching, curing powers can be helpful!

"One of the greatest sins in teaching is to be boring. It's a dull moment when there is no whetstone for the wit. Work mixed with fun goes better," says Baughman (1979, 28). Powers (2005), in his article "Engaging Students with Humor," agrees. Humor, according to Woods (1983, 112), "facilitates the task of teaching and learning and obviates strain." When students and teachers laugh together, for a time they stop being separated by individuality, authority, and age. They become a unit; they enjoy a shared experience. If that sense of community can be sustained and applied to the job of thinking, a more positive learning environment will have been created (Highet 1950; MacAdam 1985). We agree.

Properly used, humor clearly sends the message that you are confident, competent, comfortable, *and* in control. The fear of feeling foolish when attempting humor should be, in part, offset by the following aphorism: "Education should teach us to play the wise fool rather than the solemn ass" (Herbert 1991, 17). Although not all teachers can or should act like a Robin Williams or Jay Leno at the chalkboard, the thoughtful, spontaneous, or planned use of instructional humor can bring the wonder of play, wit, and wisdom (Korobkin 1988) into a classroom. Humor contributes positively to our perceived identity in the role of teacher—the "teacher-self." Clearly, humor is a skill that should be developed by all teachers.

One writer summarizes the teaching value of humor right in the title of her article: "She Who Laughs, Lasts" (Winter 2004). If you want to "last," then laugh; if you want to "last" longer, laugh more often!

THROUGH THE STUDENTS' EYES

One doesn't have a sense of humor. It has you.

—Larry Gelbart

When surveyed regarding the use of humor in the classroom, students offered real-life examples such as those that follow. Although each example refers to the use of humor in a particular subject area, the application to other disciplines is evident.

Like, Like . . .

Mr. C. will forever be my favorite teacher because he was entertaining. In order to break the monotony of learning geometry definitions, whenever any student tried to define a term and used the word "like," that student would have to stop immediately and walk a lap around the classroom. Once the student had completed this humorous act, he would sit down and then redefine the geometry term. This quickly led students to learn their definitions, and if they could not repeat them verbatim, they could at least describe them in plain and clear English. Trust me, not too many students in the class said "like" for any reason after the first two weeks.

Sick Herbie

My math teacher loaned his shiny metal chalk-holder, named "Herbie," to students when he asked them to do math problems on the front board. He told the students that Herbie rarely made a mistake. Any mistakes, if made, had to be due to a "sick Herbie." If he (Herbie) made a mistake, he would excuse himself to go to the trash can. Herbie then would return all cured—sporting a beautiful, long, white piece of chalk.

SEARCH FOR MORE ON HUMOR

Blessed is he who learns to laugh at himself, for he will never cease to be amused.

—John Boswell

We stated at the beginning of this chapter, "Probably more has been written on the subject of humor than on any of the other acting/teaching skills highlighted in this book." We would like to amend this statement by eliminating the word "probably." It is incredible how much has been written on the topic of humor given how little it appears to be addressed in either teacher-training or in-service programs.

An Education Resources Information Center (http://www.eric.ed.gov/) search for the term "humor" and at least one other education-related term—an exercise that takes just seconds—reveals numerous citations. The second set of searches listed in the following paragraphs links the term "cartoons" with at least one other education-related term. Again, a myriad of citations are identified. All of them, because they are announced in ERIC, have applications to education settings.

An ERIC search for the term "humor" with a variety of education-related terms reveals the following number of citations: "humor" plus "classroom": 819; plus "teaching methods": 299; plus "elementary education": 218; plus "secondary education": 10,100; plus "English": 2,057; plus "math": 10; plus "social studies": 56; plus "science": 202; plus "art": 148; plus "music": 90; plus "achievement": 87; plus "stress": 83; plus "physical education": 13; plus "teachers": 1,047; plus "teaching": 687; plus "learning": 657; plus "discipline": 78; plus "males": 109; plus "females": 138; plus "principals": 65; and plus "classroom techniques": 146.

Another ERIC search of the term "cartoons" with a variety of education-related terms reveals the following number of citations: "cartoons" plus "teachers": 179; plus "teaching": 525; plus "classroom techniques": 138; "learning": 543; plus "English": 1,072; plus "math": 16; plus "social studies": 239; plus "science": 215; and plus "art"; 135. We can only end this ERIC search on humor by exclaiming, "Wow!"

In addition to exploring ERIC, you should consider searching other databases as well for books, articles, and programs related to the effective use of humor in the classroom. You also are encouraged to search the Web using many of the ERIC descriptors presented in the previous paragraphs. Several humor-related Web sites follow:

Bibliography on humor and the education of adolescents and adults
http://www.teachtech.ilstu.edu/additional/tips/biblHumor.php
Using humor in the classroom
http://www.acteonline.org/members/techniques/mar04_featur3.cfm
Humor theory
http://www.redes.de/humor/theory.htm
Teaching with humor
http://www.etni.org.il/farside/humorme.htm

THE MASTER'S VOICE

For further discussion of the concepts and skills presented in this chapter, read the following paragraphs in Appendix 2, Testimonials from Award-Winning K–12 Teachers and College Professors: Austin, Lefford, and Yost, 2, 3; Clough, 5; Lisska, 1; Mahoney, 3; Rotkin, 1, 2; Smith, 3.

CHAPTER  8

Role-Playing

To be confident, act confident.

—James Eison

INTRODUCTION

Role-playing means temporarily transforming oneself into a different person by modifications of expression and appearance or by the use of props and language. To play a role successfully, one must become someone else and do so convincingly, at least for the moment. Obviously, it is a process that is totally synonymous with the profession of acting. In addition, it can be a very valuable tool for the classroom teacher.

Let us clarify at the start that our intention here is to address the means by which the teacher, *not the students*, can engage in role-playing. Considerable work has been done on the pedagogical value of student role-playing, and that is treated extensively in other texts. The rationale by which we decide to use student role-playing to intensify the learning experience, however, also applies to the use of *teacher* role-playing. Consequently, the teacher as actor is worthy of our consideration.

Actors, like teachers, are involved in role-playing at two different levels. The second, more obvious level is their involvement in the character of the play, but the first level is their involvement in the "role" of actor per se. The *person* James Earl Jones or Meryl Streep is slightly different from the *actor* James Earl Jones or Meryl Streep because the person must assume the role of a more confident and public self in order to succeed as an actor. Many actors are reported to have observed that they can feel a transformation of self occurring each time they don their makeup or costume or walk on stage. The transformation is not just into the character being portrayed but, more fundamentally, into the role of "actor." Because both levels of role-playing are appropriate for the teacher as well, both will be addressed in this chapter.

CREATION OF YOUR PROFESSIONAL PERSONA

Earlier in this book, we refer to Hanning's observations (1984) concerning the challenges of the beginning teacher. His comments are particularly apropos here: he suggests that the beginner can make himself or herself a better teacher by the process of "role mastery."

Teachers would benefit from that advice, regardless of career level. That is, consider the attributes, behaviors, and appearance that come to mind when you think of the role of "teacher." Each of us probably envisions some slightly different combination of features. Perhaps you see a straight-backed person walking with authority and pride; another may see a kindly, parental figure hovering about students with interest and concern. Whatever the visual image, it can serve as the basis for the creation of your own role—your "teacher-self."

The studies of Kress and Ehrlichs (1990), Butler et al. (1980), and Ostrand and Creaser (1978) all confirm that there are positive correlations between role-playing the part of a person one aspires to be and the development of one's self-esteem. Although these studies did not include the teaching profession, nonetheless their conclusions seem applicable. By *acting* like the professional you want to be, your self-confidence will likely improve, thus allowing you to *be* that professional. That hypothesis is confirmed in the experiences of many successful teachers who note that they are less shy and more dynamic when putting on their "teacher role" (Hanning 1984).

As with role-play in general, playing the teacher role may require some costuming in order to be most successful. In this case, of course, we are not speaking of theatrical costumes, but rather minor elements of attire that may make us *feel* more like that professional we aspire to represent. You may feel more like a teacher by carrying a briefcase, for instance, or wearing a lapel membership pin, high heels, or a particular necktie. There is no single "uniform" for the role of teacher. If a particular outfit or accessory makes you feel more confident in your teacher role, then wear it. It's that simple.

An example from a related professional area seems appropriate to include here because it is so telling of the value of costuming. The case in point was the experience of a member of the clergy queried about why she chose to wear the heavy ministerial robes on the hottest Sunday of the year. Her reply was that by wearing the "costume" of the clergy, she felt more confident in the role of pastor and thus was more likely to be received attentively and respectfully by persons unaccustomed to a woman minister. Her self-confidence, she felt, would have a positive impact on her communication success. Her experience is absolutely consistent with all that we know about self-confidence and communication and certainly testifies to the value of a little costuming for role-playing to create a persona.

Although some degree of a professional "costume" may be helpful in creating the role of teacher, it is not a prerequisite. The most important precondition for successful role creation is simply to have identified the characteristics of the teacher you aspire to possess. Then, using some combination of expression, posture, appearance, and language, act that role in your classroom. In doing so, remember that the goal of this teacher role-playing is the enhancement of self-confidence. One should not act the role to become manipulative.

CREATION OF A CHARACTER

In addition to playing the role of teacher, we can play an innumerable assortment of character roles in order to enliven our classroom instruction. Although acting the role of teacher will boost our self-confidence, acting the other roles may require a greater proportion of courage. Because role-playing is such a vivid and enriching instructional tool, however, it merits the effort. Many, many schools invite reenactors to visit their classes, portraying everyone from George Washington's soldiers to operators of the Underground Railroad to leaders of the Pullman strike. These are semiprofessional actors whose work has been proven to capture and hold student attention, making the actions and issues of that particular era come alive. Regular classroom teachers can get the same results with a little effort.

Interestingly, one veteran teacher/role-player was moved initially to attempt some role-playing as a remedy for his own shyness (Barto 1986). An English teacher and Thoreau scholar, Barto was struggling with the challenge of stimulating students when he remembered the advice of Thoreau himself: we should not be afraid to do things that others may consider "different" when our instinct tells us that "different" may be better. In this case, being different meant being Thoreau for a time. Let us take a closer look at the whys and wherefores of creating a character for our classes.

GOALS AND VALUES

One of the more memorable examples of educational role-playing occurred in a radio series some years ago called "Meeting of the Minds." The program, produced and moderated by Steve Allen, consisted of hypothetical conversations among great intellects of the past discussing contemporary issues. Allen, of course, played all the roles, from Aristotle to Zoroaster and everyone in between. The important point here is why Allen chose the role-playing vehicle for this program. His goal was an educational one: he wanted the contemporary public to appreciate the sage insights from the past and be stimulated to discuss the issues themselves. One could have attempted to accomplish that goal via a more conventional lecture-discussion approach. But, in Allen's view, that approach would not hold the listeners' attention or be very provocative; something more dramatic was needed. We would concur.

Role-playing enlivens material. By portraying a character pertinent to the specific subject matter, the teacher is able to make abstract concepts more concrete, to hold the students' attention, to clarify depths of meaning, and to stimulate student reflection on the material covered.

Numerous teachers who have tried playing a role confirm the success of the tool in motivating their students and provoking them to a more thorough understanding of the material. For instance, a political science professor in Idaho observed that his students answered test questions about characters he had portrayed in his occasional role-plays more accurately than questions about figures that had been discussed more traditionally in class (Duncombe and Heikkinen 1988). Others from disciplines as disparate as history, English, foreign language, and physical science all report that their goal was to motivate students (Carroll 1991; "Not so Rich" 1993; "Our Readers" 1982).

The current generation of high school and college students is definitely visually oriented. This has been attested to and decried in numerous arenas. Those teachers who engage in occasional role-playing are simply adjusting to that reality about their students instead of bewailing it. The students are more attentive and will learn better when presented with the material in a visually stimulating manner. Teacher role-plays accomplish this goal.

Not only is role-playing a motivating device for students; it is also a freeing device. By pretending to be someone else for a while, the teacher has created a situation in which students seem to feel freer to challenge and question ideas presented (Duncombe and Heikkinen 1988). After all, that person up front is not the grade-dispensing class mentor, but rather a member of Washington's army or a Puritan woman, for example. In one study in which the teachers role-played the part of their students, the observers noted that the students seemed to feel freer to discuss their problems than before the teachers acted out certain situations (Barcinas and Gozer 1986).

The goals, then, of teacher role-play are multifaceted. The strategy may be used to motivate students, to hold their attention, to clarify or intensify material, or to stimulate discussion. If any of these needs exist in our classrooms, the portrayal of a relevant character is a possible teaching tool to be considered.

Before we go on to describe the specific elements involved in doing role-play, it should be emphasized that this is a tool that can accomplish those pedagogical goals only if used in moderation. If the students become too accustomed to the teacher being someone else, the role-play has lost the element of surprise and has been diminished in interest value. To work, role-play should essentially be a tool kept in the "bottom of the tool box" to be used somewhat rarely for special emphasis and impact.

THE PROCESS

Everyone who has performed a classroom characterization agrees on one key point: it *must* be well prepared. Although we may use student role-plays on a somewhat spontaneous basis, teacher role-play will be only as valuable as the advance planning that has gone into it. That is where the process of role-playing begins.

Specifically, the teacher must begin by carefully choosing and researching an appropriate character to portray. It could be an obvious choice—the central figure in the material being studied—or it could be something more creative. The art teacher speaking *as* Andrew Wyeth is able to convey one perspective; speaking as Wyeth's model, on the other hand, would enable the development of a very different perspective. The character simply must be one that you, the teacher, are comfortable with (Barto 1986).

Research about the character should focus on biographical data as well as information about the times and setting in which this character lived. Sufficient information must be gathered to allow you to develop a sense not just of the person's actions, ideas, and achievements, but also of his or her feelings, values, and attitudes. One of the authors plays the role of legendary football coach Joe Paterno in teaching a lesson about being the subject of a media interview. For her to be able to answer questions that students will pose during this mock interview, she must learn the specific details of the current college football season and commit those details to memory for ready retrieval while she is "being Joe."

In doing such research, the teacher is ready for the second step in the process of character creation—deciding about costuming and props. By studying the character thoroughly, you will develop a sense of how this person would have dressed, stood, moved, and behaved. Knowing that, you must determine the degree to which you wish to recreate the person visually—a total costume may not always be necessary, appropriate, or comfortable. It is a matter of personal choice whether to *imitate* the character (full costume, props, and staging) or *suggest* the character (minimal costume and props, no staging). Some amount of props will generally make the role-player feel the part more fully and will assist in creating a more credible representation for the students.

Third, the dialogue must be constructed. In choosing what words to say, decisions should once again grow out of the research done on the character. Inasmuch as it is possible, using the person's exact words would be appropriate. That makes the characterization valid and conveys more clearly that the speaker is not Professor X, but a completely different character. When verbatim texts of the person's speech cannot be found or are not suitable, a script should be prepared using a manner of speech that seems consistent with the person's character and intellect. The more comfortable you feel with the character, the more you may want to build into the script some openings for spontaneous dialogue with the students. Be prepared to remain in character, no matter how the students respond.

Once the materials for the role-play are assembled and rehearsed, it is time for the final step in the process, the actual performance. There is no one right way to initiate the role-play in class. In some cases, it may be fitting to prepare the students in advance for the arrival of this character, having them do some research and prepare questions. In other cases, the teacher may simply appear in character unheralded and begin to speak. Both approaches have advantages and disadvantages that would need to be evaluated relevant to the particular class for which the role-play is intended.

No matter how the role-play is initiated, it is critical that it be brought effectively to a close. There should be an opportunity for "debriefing" either at the end of the class period or on the succeeding day to monitor the impressions the students actually had about the "guest." This is necessary because role-playing is such a dramatic device that it is possible some students may have gotten caught up in one of the characterization's special elements and missed the overall point. Naturally, a well-prepared and well-executed role-play will diminish the chances of such error. Check to be sure.

The teacher's creation of a character is a process moving from selection, research, planning, costuming, scripting, and rehearsing to presentation and review. If that sounds like the same process that an actor goes through in creating a character, it is not coincidental!

APPLICATIONS

The circumstances in which a character portrayal may be a suitable teaching vehicle are as numerous and far-ranging as the subject matter taught. A few specific examples may help you visualize the possibilities.

At the high school level, two noteworthy examples would be those provided by American history teacher Spencer Johnson ("Not so Rich" 1993) and English teacher David Barto (1986). Johnson portrays famous and "less than famous" citizens of eighteenth- and nineteenth-century America ranging from a Plains Indian to a member of Washington's army. His portrayals, done in authentic costumes, have earned him such a following that he is now a regular part of reenactment programs in the summer. Similarly, Barto's portrayals of Henry David Thoreau have earned him such acclaim that he has been asked to do various one-man shows at conventions and commemorative celebrations. He tends to use a little less elaborate costuming in the classroom than he does at conventions and commemorative celebrations, but he always tries to incorporate props appropriate to the character and times to help set the mood for his students.

It should be emphasized that neither Johnson nor Barto came into the teaching profession as actors. Rather, they "fell into" the role-playing technique out of the desperation of trying to find some way to motivate their students. In both cases, it worked so well that it is now a standard part of their teaching.

Similarly, a junior high science teacher in Pennsylvania, Dennis Murray, was looking for some vehicle by which he could excite his students at least a little about science (Carroll 1991). His reflections resulted in a decision to use the character of Tycho Brahe (sixteenth-century Danish astronomer) to "speak" to the students about the principles of physical science (Photo 8.1). This has turned out to be a very wise decision. His full-costumed Brahe, speaking with the arrogance for which he was known, has stimulated students in a way no standard lecture could have done. In his case, the dramatization even includes background music and staging, in addition to the custom-made costume.

A less elaborate, but equally successful, example of teacher role-play is the "two-hat" technique used by political science professor Stanley Duncombe (Duncombe and Heikkinen 1988). The gist of the technique is a staged debate

Photo 8.1
Tycho Brahe

between real or hypothetical persons representing opposing political viewpoints. Duncombe plays both characters and distinguishes the speakers simply by putting on a hat appropriate to the different characters and positions. While the costuming is minimal, the characterizations are no less valid, given that they grow out of considerable research.

One of the authors has used a version of this "two-hat" technique in the form of a t-shirt that he dons when staging a hypothetical debate between B. F. Skinner, a behaviorist, and Carl Rogers, a humanist, and the opposing philosophies they represent. The t-shirt, prepared at one of those shopping-mall kiosks that place pictures on almost anything (calendars, coffee mugs, hats, t-shirts), has pictures of Skinner and Rogers facing each other as if in heated debate. This same author also uses Duncombe's "two-hat" technique in the form of a collection of baseball-type caps, each of which is adorned with pictures of famous men and women representing his subject area.

Although the stagecraft of these examples varies considerably, the quality of preparation is the same. After much work, the teachers have chosen to recreate a character whose presence in the classroom has been a riveting presentation enhancing the impact and meaningfulness of the subject matter.

STORYTELLING

A variation on role-play involving significantly less staging but having similar effects is storytelling. A much simpler and briefer technique than the role-playing we have described, it is still a form of role-play in that the teacher takes on a different persona, the role of narrator. The art of the storyteller is a time-honored tradition in many cultures and has carried over very effectively to the classroom. No matter the age of the students, there is still a noticeably captivating effect when one says "once upon a time" or something equivalent.

One of the most legendary of classroom storytellers points out the educational power of a story to hold students' attention, teach values, and nurture the imagination (Shedlock 1951). That perspective was confirmed by more recent research on the value of narratives. This research concluded that the opening of a story signals to students that literal meaning is being highlighted or emphasized (Nussbaum, Comadena, and Holladay 1987). Thus, the storytelling episode stimulates and refocuses their attention.

Whether the story told be truth or fiction, it is told best if told simply. The teacher should play the part of narrator as well as any and all other characters in the story using slight modifications of posture or expression or masks to suggest the identity of the character speaking. As with the more extensive role-plays, storytelling may incorporate some dialogue with the students. However, because storytelling should usually consume no more that ten or fifteen minutes, inviting student dialogue may result in an inappropriate and misleading digression that detracts from the story's point.

MIME

A particularly unique role creation available for the teacher is the role of a mime. By removing dialogue from the role portrayal, a teacher is challenged to convey a message or concept to the students with facial expression and movement alone. There is some evidence that mime's lack of words challenges students to think more analytically and sparks their creativity (Arterberry and Sawatzky 2006). An elementary teacher might, for instance, teach a lesson on table manners via mime. Doing so would force the students to pay very careful attention to the actions that are typical for a mannerly person without being distracted by "table talk." At the secondary level, a history teacher might portray the experience of being in a war or an English teacher the creative process used by poets and novelists.

Mime is a more challenging form of acting than that used in the other examples we have described here. It might be considered as an "advanced" level of

Photo 8.2
Elementary Role Playing

role-play suited to teachers who have already developed some comfort with the basic form of character portrayal.

SUMMARY

Teacher role-playing is the pedagogical tool probably most resembling the tools of the actor. Consequently, it may be the most difficult for many teachers. If a teacher's self-confidence is still "under construction," the one role-play that is ideal is the role of teacher itself. We benefit by acting in the way that we think confident, successful teachers act because we actually grow into the role, *becoming* confident master teachers ourselves. Once that self-esteem begins to develop, we may want to try the creation of character roles to further enhance our teaching. All role-playing should be carefully planned, rehearsed, and presented in a well-organized manner. By doing so, you will have added another enlivening tool to your repertoire.

THROUGH THE STUDENTS' EYES

When surveyed regarding the use of role-playing in the classroom, students offered real-life examples such as those that follow. Although each example refers to the use of role-playing in a particular subject area, the application to other disciplines is evident.

Storytelling

My sociology teacher is very effective because he makes an effort to show that he truly cares about his students and their grasp of the subject matter, which is difficult in a class of eight hundred students. He does this, in part, by telling stories that we can relate to in an entertaining manner that holds our attention. It's much easier to learn in this positive, friendly environment.

My Friend George

My eleventh-grade history teacher was very enthusiastic about his subject. When explaining something, he would act as if he knew George Washington or whomever it was he was talking about. He would laugh about something that person had said or done just as if he were there while it was happening. He didn't just teach history as if it were a collection of facts; he taught it as if it were a story about someone he knew.

High Official

My teacher stood up on his desk [space utilization] and, with a silly smirk on his face, looked around the classroom as if he were superior to us. On his shirt he wore a paper sign that said, "F for fluorine." Then he exclaimed, "I am the highest official on this planet called electronegativity!" On the desks were copies of the periodic chart. Then it hit me—we, the students, were elements on the periodic chart—all with lower electronegativities than fluorine.

The Russians Are Coming

My tenth-grade teacher showed up for class dressed in a long, red Russian robe that prominently displayed a hammer and sickle and a small star above them. He told us that the robe stood for revolution, the hammer and sickle represented united workers, and the star stood for the Communist Party. He began the history lesson by speaking a little bit of Russian. He then played the Russian anthem for the class, while at the same time demonstrating a short Russian dance by folding his arms in front of him and moving his legs about. I don't know about the rest of the class, but the costume and dance left a visual impression with me and helped bring the lesson into focus.

Please Excuse My Dear Aunt Sally

My algebra teacher, Mrs. U, dressed up as a wretched old woman named Aunt Sally. She then began her lesson on the correct order of mathematical functions: parentheses (Please), exponents (Excuse), multiply (My), divide (Dear), add (Aunt), and subtract (Sally). All I had to do was think of Aunt Sally and her gnarled cane in order to remember the order of mathematical operations.

SEARCH FOR MORE ON ROLE-PLAYING

An Education Resources Information Center (http://www.eric.ed.gov/) search for the term "role-playing" (or related term) and at least one other education-related term—an exercise that takes just seconds—reveals numerous citations. All of them, because they are announced in ERIC, have applications to education settings.

An ERIC search for the term "role-playing" (or related term) with a variety of education-related terms reveals the following number of citations: "role-playing" plus "teaching": 124,000; plus "student interest": 1,450; plus "student achievement": 2,530; plus "elementary teaching": 194; plus "secondary education": 275; plus "science teaching": 1,030; plus "English teaching": 806; plus "social studies teaching": 146; and plus "math teaching": 130.

In addition to exploring ERIC, you should consider searching other databases as well for books, articles, and programs related to the effective use of role-playing in the classroom. You also are encouraged to search the Web using many of the ERIC descriptors presented in the previous paragraph.

THE MASTER'S VOICE

For further discussion of the concepts and skills presented in this chapter, read the following paragraphs in Appendix 2, Testimonials from Award-Winning K–12 Teachers and College Professors: Harrison, 3, 4, 10; Kurre, 1–7; Light, 3; Mahoney, 4, 5; McBrayer, 1, 3; Richardson, 2, 3; Smith, 1, 4–9.

CHAPTER

Props

Give me a lever long enough and a prop strong enough,
I can single-handedly move the world.

—Archimedes

INTRODUCTION

Perhaps Archimedes placed a bit too much confidence in his "prop." This prop, though, is central to the success of his goal of moving the world. Classroom teachers may not be asked to move the world, but they are asked to motivate students—at times, a task of seemingly equal difficulty. It has been argued that many school programs err on the side of too much book work and too little hands-on work (Sukow 1990)—and the latter often relies on the use of props.

Although actor Hal Holbrook may be able to stand on a propless stage and command the attention of an audience as he portrays Mark Twain, most stage and film productions rely heavily on the use of props. In fact, awards are given for such props—for example, costumes. Holbrook, in fact, does depend heavily on the costumes he wears to give credibility to his Twain.

If a picture (a two-dimensional image) is worth a thousand words, then a prop (three-dimensional) must be worth much more. For the actor, props help set the stage, conveying information that is crucial to the film or play's message.

CLASSROOM-APPROPRIATE PROPS

I love to come in and play with a wig or glasses or clothes. I love using props.
I'm from the Peter Pan Sellers school of trying to prepare for a character.

—Dan Aykroyd

Although the actors' props are essentially limited to artifacts and costumes in the theater, the options are considerably more extensive in the classroom. Actual artifacts can be used, provided that they are portable and house-trained!

Other low-tech or no-tech props include the chalkboard, flip charts, posters, Velcro board, and photographs. We should emphasize that the chalkboard's lack of dimension, color, and creativity makes it the least desirable prop, by the way. In addition, we currently have access to a growing variety of high-tech props that are the subject of another chapter (Chapter 10).

Whatever the form, classroom props, like those in the theater, set the stage. (See Photo 9.1.) They provide context and character. Additional purposes, however, are served in the classroom. For the students, props may clarify information; props may capture and hold their attention; and props may make the classroom material more memorable. In some cases, of course, a single prop may accomplish all three purposes. Such seems the case in Professor Ron Berk's classroom when he teaches statistics with the aid of a human "T-score" whose scarf is blowing in the wind as music from *Titanic* plays in the background (Bartlett 2003).

At the elementary school level, some students especially benefit from the tactile nature of props. Manipulatives provide an additional sensory channel for learning which complements some students' unique learning styles. One elementary building in our area has a wall in each primary classroom that is covered in a rough fabric that allows the easy attachment of small placards. This is known as the "Word Wall," and the placards used are each a single word—new vocabulary for the week. The fabric allows children not just to place new vocabulary words in a prominent spot, but also to move them around as they experiment with using the new words in sentences.

One purpose of using props in the classroom renders a special benefit to the teacher and, thus, indirectly to the students. That purpose is that using the prop gives the anxious teacher something to do with his or her hands. By keeping physically busy, the teacher is less likely to be perceived as nervous. In this circumstance, the props also serve the function of "notes," reminding the teacher of the sequence of points to be made in the lesson.

PROPS GENERIC TO ALL CLASSROOMS

I trained as a theater actor and you had a bare stage and you had to pretend, one prop and you were in the middle of 8th Avenue and traffic is just going by.

— Benicio Del Toro

Most of the props we listed earlier can be used in just about any classroom, no matter the subject area or grade level. In fact, virtually all classrooms come equipped with the all-purpose chalkboard or white board, flip chart, overhead projector, and computer. Other props can be considered universal in that, with a little imagination, the same prop can serve very different purposes in a variety of classrooms.

Take, for example, an apple. In an art class, the apple may be used as a still-life prop to be painted. In a chemistry class, the apple (in both its peeled and unpeeled state) may be used to test the reaction of oxygen. The significance of

Photo 9.1
Props, Props, and More Props

taking a bite out of the forbidden apple may be explored in a religion class. The historical accuracy of Newton's having been hit on the head with a falling apple could be investigated. As shown in the film *Stand and Deliver*, Jaime Escalante, a Bolivian-born Los Angeles calculus teacher, used an apple to teach fractions. Each of these lessons could have been taught by the teacher's use of words alone. But the apple makes those words much more captivating and memorable!

What about using a piece of taffy as a prop? One college professor we know takes several pieces of saltwater taffy with him to class. After covering a particularly challenging concept, he stops talking and slowly chews the taffy—"digests" it—a function that he would like his students to emulate mentally regarding the subject matter just presented. The time used to chew the taffy provides the pedagogically sound equivalent of "wait time." After the "food for thought" has been digested, he entertains questions or comments.

How about using a beret as a prop? One instructor creates a Marcel Marceau costume by simply donning a beret. The beret "signals" to the students that she is going to begin using mime—acting without words—to review the assigned lesson. Students try to guess what specific event or behavior is being mimed. Only students who have read the lesson are able to guess correctly. Students of all ages look forward to this creative diversion from the traditional worksheet lesson review.

Lowman (1984) suggests that even an everywhere-present, taken-for-granted book can be an effective prop. He cites the positive effect of a teacher reading a quote directly from a book rather than from his or her notes. The words may be the same, but the dramatic impact is different. Reading from a book adds a dimension of reality. Lowman points out that the prop does not have to communicate anything directly; it is not even critical that students can see it closely. Props, books or otherwise, in this instance, are used to add credibility and enhance interest.

PROPS UNIQUE TO SPECIFIC SUBJECT MATTER

When I used to do musical theatre, my dad refused to come backstage. He never wanted to see the props up close or the sets up close. He didn't want to see the magic.

—Nia Vardalos

Naturally, there are some props, artifacts in particular, that have narrower applicability in the classroom. Each of the sciences certainly has an array of props unique to the field. Biologists use animals—both alive and dead! Chemists use beakers, test tubes, Bunsen burners, and so on, and the physicist relies upon generators and scopes. Or does he?

We know of one physics professor, Jonathan Hall, who demonstrates the concepts of force and pressure by having an eager undergraduate student nail two pieces of wood together—on a bed of nails placed on the teacher' chest (Photo 9.2). In an experiment not all that different from the Indian guru who astonishes followers by "sleeping" on a bed of nails, Professor Hall dramatically makes his point about the dispersal of force!

Even a subject such as accounting, which doesn't seem to lend itself to creative use of props—not much beyond the sample ledger sheets—can be considerably enlivened by diverse props. A professor friend of ours describes how such household basics as a picnic basket, kitchen measuring devices, linens, and a wastebasket can be used to teach the accounting concepts of a "T" account, the liability/capital equation, inventory pricing, and the closing entry, respectively.

USING STUDENTS AS PROPS

One special set of props is the students themselves. Everyone, though not necessarily volunteering to do so, loves to be "on stage." Several examples capitalizing on that ham in all of us follow.

Photo 9.2
"Nailing" a Teacher

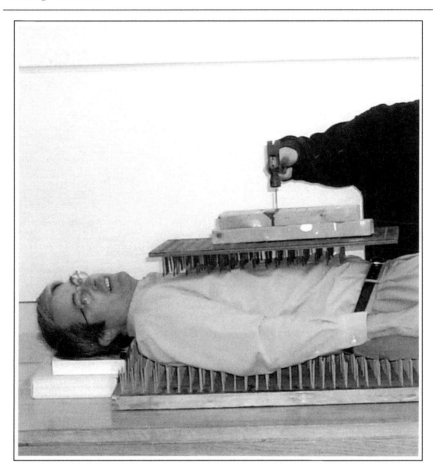

Displacement Theory

One instructor we know teaches the "displacement theory" in chemistry by assigning three students to play the role of elements. While one girl is assigned the role of chlorine (Cl), two boys are assigned, respectively, the roles of sodium (Na) and potassium (K).

Na and Cl are instructed to hold hands, forming NaCl (sodium chloride), and walk slowly across the room. K has eyes for Cl. Because K is the more active element, he wrestles with and displaces Na. The net result is KCl holding hands, and Na, the less active element, left all alone—displaced. A memorable lesson!

Why Does Ice Float?

Another professor in physics tackles the mystery of "Why does ice float?" by using student props. Until students realize that water is the only liquid whose solid form is not heavier than its liquid form, students take the floating ability of ice for granted. In order to demonstrate the phenomenon, nine students are asked to stand together in three rows of three, playing the role of molecules. The teacher pretends to lower the thermostat and asks them to show what would happen. Naturally, they move closer together—they become more dense (i.e., heavier) and, thus, sink to the bottom just like the cold water does in a swimming pool.

Then the teacher surprises them by explaining that between 4 and 0 degrees centigrade, water molecules actually move farther apart, not closer together. The result makes the frozen form (ice) lighter, thus causing it to float.

Discrimination

Who doesn't recognize Jane Elliott's "blue eyes versus brown eyes" impression-forming activity used in so many psychology and sociology classes to teach elementary school children about the effects of prejudice and discrimination? In this case, the entire class of students is used as props, participating in an elaborate charade where the teacher divides them into two groups—those with brown eyes and those with blue eyes. Alternately, the teacher makes one group superior and the other inferior, and then they switch. Students report learning lessons about stereotyping and discrimination in such a deeply emotional way that the lessons are never to be forgotten.

Holding Your Breath

A psychology professor demonstrates the concept of stereotype threat—the theory that people try to live up to or down to a stereotype held of them. Sadly, this works against minorities when they are stereotyped as being less capable. The professor does this by asking which students own or have owned a dog. Then she says that research shows that dog owners are better able to hold their breath than non-dog owners. Next, she asks the dog owners to stand. Finally, she asks everyone to raise one of their arms high in the air and, on the count of three, begin holding their breath. When students are no longer able to hold their breath, they are to lower their hand. Sure enough, the "dog owners" are able to hold their breath longer. Was the research verified? In actuality, two things accounted for the difference in breath holding. One, standing makes it easier to hold one's breath. Two, being told (i.e., establishing a stereotype) that dog owners are *supposed* to be able to better hold their breath then established a stereotype threat.

A Shakespeare Festival

A high school English teacher makes Shakespeare come alive by hosting a festival. The students and the teacher attend the event in costume—from either *Macbeth* or *Hamlet*, two of the plays they have studied. In addition to performing scenes from the plays, the students and teacher prepare and consume period foods and drink. Students not only make their costumes and prepare the food (both props), but also must create props for their scenes.

A Normal Curve: On a Grand Scale

A math teacher enlisted the entire ninth grade of his three-story high school building to help demonstrate what a normal curve looks like when a human characteristic such as height is "graphed." Rather than simply graphing data on a piece of paper, he had all of the ninth graders go out on to the parking lot (emptied of cars) and line up according to their height. Earlier, he had placed chalk marks along a straight line marking heights in intervals of one inch. Once all of the students had lined up according to their height, the teacher went to the third floor overlooking the parking lot and took a digital picture of the "normal curve." Pictures of the almost perfect normal curve were displayed not only in the instructor's classroom, but also in prominent places around the school. The students labeled themselves in plus or minus standard deviations from the mean. Every year the ninth grade looked forward to being "props" for this grand scale event!

PROP BOX

Acting is all about big hair and funny props. All the great actors knew it. Olivier knew it, Brando knew it!

—Harold Ramis

A prop box is more or less a "hope chest" of prop and costume items the teachers think may be useful for some future lessons as well as those that they need immediately. What does one use for a prop? The answer is anything and everything. Where does one get his or her props? The answer is anywhere and everywhere. Put together a prop box and have it ready for your use and the students' use. Keep adding to it. Ask colleagues what props they have successfully used and put those in the box. Ask students for suggestions of what to include.

If the teacher has decided to use props, costumes, special lighting, or any other kind of "staging," help should be sought in locating suitable free materials for the prop locker before deciding to invest any money in purchasing the items. For instance, the college or school custodial staff may be your best source of knowledge about what materials are lying around the buildings that could be used. Naturally, the theater department would be another good resource. It is this alertness to the possibilities of props that has led to one author having a file drawer filled with Slinky toys, whistles, fat rubber bands, and an assortment of cardboard tubes!

If teachers must go shopping, they should start with yard sales. One professor's two-hat technique depends upon the hats salvaged from yard sales and junk stores. Either he has purchased them himself, or others, knowing of his teaching style, have picked up some unique hat for him that they happened to run across (Duncombe and Heikkinen 1988). Such a network of friends is the teacher's costume or prop crew. It's not Agnes de Mille, but it is still a very fruitful resource "behind the scenes."

As previously noted, the teacher seeking to use certain acting devices will benefit from storing all creative ideas that come to mind. So the "prop box" may have many things other than props, such as a collection of humorous cartoons, striking anecdotes, creative ideas for rearrangement of classroom space, great opening lines, and more. Journaling of personal stories is an effective and easy way to build such a resource. Every event that happens to you or that you read about that leads you to say "that's really interesting" ought to be written down in your journal. You never know when one of those stories will be just what you need! Building one's acting/teaching repertoire should be an ongoing process.

Any time teachers feel themselves going a little stale, they should check their repertoire for innovative ideas they may have stored away for just such an occasion and have forgotten about. Most teachers can attest that creative ideas come at the most inopportune times. So a teacher's file may include notes jotted on napkins, concert programs, airline ticket folders, or grocery lists. Teachers should make notes whenever ideas come to mind, file them, and check back on them periodically.

As has been stressed by numerous pedagogical scholars, good teaching results from good planning: setting goals and objectives and selecting strategies for accomplishing them (Eison 1990). But, as is learned from the field of acting, those strategies won't simply become apparent, nor are there any resource manuals listing all available strategies so that a strategy may just be selected. Instead, an active repertoire of personally suitable strategies must be developed. A huge list of possible strategies to choose from may be generated by jotting down instructional techniques that are heard or read or that suddenly pop into a teacher's head.

GUIDELINES FOR USING THE PROPS

This is external preparation that requires no significant time or a support crew; it just takes thinking ahead.

—Alexander Graham Bell

Whatever the nature or purpose of a prop, they all come with risks. Murphy's Law is certainly applicable when it comes to props. Nearly every teacher has stories of props that flopped because a light bulb was burned out, or the fish died, or the supplies didn't arrive in time, or it rained on the poster, or the dog ate it! Like any good actor who double-checks all the props before the curtain goes up, a teacher should rehearse with the prop prior to class and make sure it is working.

The best prop is that which is large, clear, and visible to all of the students at the same time. So check the movie, the poster, or the artifact and make sure it can be seen well. Are all the necessary pieces there? Do you have the proper equipment for displaying the prop—an easel, a projection screen, a display table? Do a "dry run" of all experiments to make sure that the procedure will result in the desired conclusion—every time!

Generally speaking, props should be displayed, not passed around the room. Passing just increases the odds of Murphy's Law kicking in! If every third grader has to hold and pass on the beautiful crystal, it is going to get dropped somewhere along the line. In addition, passing an object is a distraction to all the students in the class, who are watching it go around the room instead of focusing on what the teacher is saying about it. Also, it is quite likely that the object will still be in some student's hands *after* the teacher is already done explaining it, diminishing its usefulness as a clarifier.

Keep props simple enough to be clear. "Remember that a visual aid should be exactly that—an aid, not the complete source of information" (Bradley 1981, 267). This means displaying just the main gear in a linkage assembly, not the entire contraption.

Display the prop *only* when you are actually speaking about what it depicts. Until that moment and after than moment, it is a distraction, so keep it out of sight. The only exception to this rule is when you want to use the presence of the prop to heighten the students' suspense about the topic for which it will be used.

Finally, there is one more risk in using a prop. It does draw attention—both the students' and the teacher's. It is very tempting to look at the prop while speaking about it, even if that means looking down or back—and thus, away from the students. Considering what we emphasized earlier about the value of maintaining eye contact with the students, looking at the prop is a temptation that is too dangerous to succumb to. Practice with it sufficiently so that you know exactly where the various parts are that you will be pointing to, and then you should not need to look much more than a quick glance when actually teaching with it.

SUMMARY

Do you remember "show and tell" days of kindergarten years? The prop, the "show," was used to promote the real reason for the exercise, the "tell." And it worked! The teller's word was more informative through the use of the prop.

From the talking letters of Sesame Street to the fascinating forensic tools of CSI, from the Royal Shakespearean production of *Richard III* to the second-grade holiday pageant, from the smelly, slimy creatures of the biology lab to the glamorous posters of the English or foreign language classrooms, props are a key ingredient in helping to set the stage and convey the intended message.

In addition to the "pizzazz potential," a good prop also can provide a sense of security for the teacher. Whether used as a part of a demonstration or held up as an example, a good prop can clarify an idea and enliven an otherwise less-than-stimulating concept.

THROUGH THE STUDENTS' EYES

When surveyed regarding the use of props in the classroom, students offered real examples, including those that follow. Although each example refers to the use of props in a particular subject area, the application to other disciplines is evident.

38th Parallel

Mr. B, my high school history teacher, made the study of World War II and the Korean Conflict more interesting because he had experienced both first-hand. While talking about his personal experiences, he showed us some of the weapons, clothing, and equipment used during those conflicts. I learned more in this class than in any other dealing with American wars.

Roy G. Biv

Mrs. T brought in a very large doll that, literally, was dressed in every color of the rainbow. This prop, introduced as Mr. Roy G. Biv, represented the color spectrum as displayed in a rainbow. To this day, I can recall that doll and the colors of the rainbow in their proper order.

Here, Catch!

When learning the names of objects in French class, the teacher would toss the item (such as a banana) to a student and call out its French name. The student would then toss it back while, at the same time, saying the item's name. What could have been a boring vocabulary drill was made much more interesting.

Wear It with Pride

When we were learning about classroom discipline models, my instructor all of a sudden ripped off his shirt, only to reveal a t-shirt with the faces of six different discipline authors on the front. On the back, he had pictures of B. F. Skinner (behaviorist) and Carl R. Rogers (humanist), representing a dichotomy of discipline philosophies. For the rest of the class hour, these folks were constantly on display for us.

Let George Do It

My high school biology teacher used a skeleton, named "George," as his laboratory assistant and, of course, to show things about human anatomy. George was so popular that someone even tried to run him as a candidate for student government.

Off with His Head

My high school English teacher brought in a mini-guillotine and cut pieces of carrots and other vegetables when we studied A Tale of Two Cities. We cheered on the "executions," just like the citizens of Paris had done. The vegetable slices were distributed to students, who continued to talk about the book well after class.

Pavlov's Dogs

Our psychology professor used a real lemon to demonstrate classical conditioning. You see the lemon, and you begin to salivate, even though you try to resist. On a different occasion, she announced that we were going to have a pop quiz. Faces flushed, heartbeats increased, palms sweated—all at the mere mention of "pop quiz."

Treasure Chest

I haven't thought about it for years, but my third grade teacher had a treasure chest full of things such as scratch-and-sniff stickers, decoder rings, and buttons. She announced that it was not her job to decide when students were deserving of rewards; it was theirs. Hence, the contents of the treasure box were there for our taking. During the first week, students took handfuls of "rewards." By the second week, most of us were weaned from dependency on external rewards—just what the teacher had planned in the first place.

Slinky

In science class, the teacher used a Slinky to demonstrate how seismic waves move through different materials. For some reason, "seeing" the motion of the wave just made more sense than viewing the diagrams in the textbook. This same teacher used chemical Tinker Toys to teach us how to construct molecules. Having used these toys to demonstrate concepts in class, he bragged that he now could write the cost of them off of his income tax [another acting/teaching tool—humor].

SEARCH FOR MORE ON PROPS

An Education Resources Information Center (http://www.eric.ed.gov/) search for the term "props" and at least one other education-related term—an exercise that takes just seconds—reveals numerous citations. All of them, because they are announced in ERIC, have applications to education settings.

An ERIC search for the term "props" with a variety of education-related terms reveals the following number of citations: "props" plus "teaching": 157,000; plus "elementary education": 1,460; plus "secondary education": 2,480; plus "student interest": 1,020; plus "student achievement": 1,520; plus "science teaching": 666; plus "English teaching": 649; plus "social studies teaching": 98; and plus "math teaching": 135.

In addition to exploring ERIC, you should consider searching other databases as well for books, articles, and programs related to the effective use of props in the classroom. You also are encouraged to search the Web using many of the ERIC descriptors presented in the previous paragraph.

THE MASTER'S VOICE

For further discussion of the concepts and skills presented in this chapter, read the following paragraphs in Appendix 2, Testimonials from Award-Winning K–12 Teachers and College Professors: Austin, Lefford, and Yost, 2, 3; Grimnes, 4; Hall, 2; Harrison, 3–7; Richardson, 3; Rogers (Betsy), 1, 4.

CHAPTER  10

Technology Props

The upcoming generation is going to amaze us in ways we're just beginning to understand—if we can just keep up!

—James Daley

INTRODUCTION

The age of technology has arrived and brought changes everywhere. Now that's an understatement! We all have had to learn digital technology for simple things like using the telephone or watching television and are observers of the technology used for much more complicated operations in manufacturing, global communications, medicine, and transportation.

Those transformations have certainly not been lost in the worlds of theater and education. The technology has created a vast new world of "props" available to the performer and the teacher alike. Like the traditional props discussed in the previous chapter, there are many similarities between the two worlds and how they can capitalize on technological innovations. In movies, they are called "special effects" and include everything from the creation of believable flying creatures to enhanced views of microscopic realities. Even in live theater, technology has created new prop possibilities via projected images, creative sounds production, and sophisticated artifacts.

The classroom has seen an absolute explosion of possibilities as technology has given the teacher new tools for clarifying and enhancing lessons. A list of a school's technology purchases just since 1990 would likely include televisions, DVD players, overhead projectors, interactive whiteboards, 3-D data projectors, iPods, laptop and podium-mounted computers and software to support streaming video, presentation software, Webcasts, course-management software, and electronic chat. With more options, of course, come more challenges.

PURPOSES AND OPPORTUNITIES

Just as with any prop, the instructional technology we use in the classroom is meant to serve the purposes of clarifying information, capturing and holding student attention, and making ideas memorable. It is critical to keep those purposes in mind as we discuss the options newly available to us, lest we fall for the notion of using the technology simply because we can. That caution aside, it is also important to note that the technology does create opportunities to accomplish the props' goals more extensively and in more detail than what we could possibly do with chalk and slate.

A mere twenty years ago, a cell biology lecture would be enhanced with simple handouts and transparencies representing the microscopic structures of the cell's interior. Today's biology teacher, instead, is using projections of an actual living cell displayed through the computer or a linked microscope and 3-D data projector. Down the hall, a classroom discussion of opportunities for research in outer space can now be enlivened by enrolling the class in a live conversation with astronauts working on the space station. In the art room, a class that used to sit through the interminable "slide show" is now engaged in a Web tour of the works in the Louvre and can zoom in to study the fine details of any one of the paintings. Even in the elementary school, students whose parents wrote "country reports" based on encyclopedia articles are now creating their reports by chatting electronically with their peers in elementary schools around the globe and presenting those reports with PowerPoint. The opportunities are endless!

Technology has given us the means in the theater to help audiences listen more closely and, in the classroom, to help students learn more and remember it longer. No one in the entertainment industry is more aware of technology's possibilities than George Lucas of *Star Wars* fame. His landmark work in the creation of special effects has revolutionized the movie industry. More importantly for those of us who teach, he has recognized the potential for similar technology-driven transformation in education and has put his considerable wealth toward that goal. The George Lucas Educational Foundation is now a major player in funding research and implementation of instructional technology, giving us all opportunities to learn more about this valuable "prop."

A great actor may use just his voice and a few simple props to create a character and hold us spellbound. That is one choice. Technology tells us there are many other choices that we ought to at least consider. That is exactly the case in the classroom. A recent article in *Edutopia*, the publication of the George Lucas Educational Foundation, reported the results of a teacher survey in which the teachers were asked, "What technology is most effective in the classroom?" Although several teachers identified particular software that has helped their classrooms, some chose to nominate the lowly piece of chalk in the hands of a skilled teacher. As one answered, "A well-prepared teacher. She or he has the capacity to inform, challenge and open minds. Using a variety of media—chalkboard, computer, presentation tools—and enthusiasm, a teacher can open a window in any subject" ("Sage Advice" 2005, 42).

Using technology, like using other props, is a choice we make. We should be aware of the range of options available and their relative value. Then decide whether any one of those options will help our students learn.

LIMITATIONS AND RISKS

Any casual conversation around the office coffeepot will reveal that instructional technology has its advocates and its doubters. The latter would likely endorse the observation of then-presidential candidate Adlai Stevenson who, in a speech at Columbia University, said "Technology, while adding to our physical ease, throws daily another loop of fine wire around our souls." That may be a little extreme. However, the research on the deleterious effects of relying on e-mail and voice mail instead of waiting to speak to an individual in person certainly indicate there are some serious downsides to technology-assisted communication.

A noted scholar and teacher, Edward Tufte, has become somewhat famous of late for his scathing attacks on the classroom reliance on PowerPoint. His research indicates that presenting a lecture accompanied by a series of bullet-pointed slides causes students' analytical abilities to deteriorate (Tufte 2003). As we all know, high school and college students are inclined to write down whatever we put on the board or project on the screen. From Tufte's research, it seems that students are functioning as mere information recorders, not as thinkers, when the class period is dominated by this use (or misuse) of the technology.

Because the wide-ranging use of instructional technology is relatively new (PowerPoint was created in 1984 and took ten years to become widely used), no research on long-term benefits or risks of technologically delivered information is yet available. Research on the short-term effects is not conclusive and includes many articles indicating that Tufte may be right. One librarian conducted a comparative study of three different ways of presenting his standard library orientation. One version relied completely on the ubiquitous bullet points on PowerPoint slides; a second used occasional slides to offer examples of points orally explained; a third used no technology at all. Students were tested on their recall of information covered. The best scores were earned by those in the second group, and the worst were earned by those in the PowerPoint-reliant group (Kapoun 2003).

This work speaks to the risk of "underusing" the technology; that is, using it for very simple tasks for which it provides no educational benefit and not exploring the more complicated but educationally valuable occasional uses available. The teacher who simply puts his or her notes on a series of PowerPoint slides to accompany a lecture is a little like the cook who uses the microwave only to reheat leftovers. The machine *can* do that, but that is not its *best* use.

So many teachers have made this mistake that students frequently complain that they have become bored by PowerPoint. The technology has actually caused them to become disengaged.

In addition to these concerns about pedagogical effects of technology props, there are some pragmatic concerns as well. Above all is the cost! Converting a classroom to a "smart room" equipped with a variety of projection devices and wireless technology can cost $10,000 per room. That figure puts the equipment in the room—but maintaining it is another expense that will add to the school district or university's ongoing budget needs. We suppose that proponents of "smart rooms" picked that name because they want you to believe that what existed prior must have been "dumb rooms." Of course, no one wants that.

A school's computing capacity may also create some limitations given that older buildings may require rewiring in order to handle the load from multiple computers and projectors in every room. Although grants are often available for initial equipment purchases and installations, maintaining them is usually the financial responsibility of the school. Every time a program fails to work or a light bulb burns out, technology creates another doubter.

Another pragmatic limitation is the ability of the teachers to keep up with the constantly changing technology. When the authors took college classes in instructional technology, the things we learned to use were mimeograph machines and overhead projectors—and that was not that long ago! Each year, a new technology aid is invented and marketed; software is constantly upgraded; and our "old" systems are rendered obsolete by the manufacturers. Even if initial teacher training includes the latest technology, the teacher will have to discard that skill and learn several new ones with each passing year (Norris and O'Bannon 2001).

The limitations and risks of instructional technology may cause some teachers to avoid it altogether. It's just too frustrating, some say. In one of the author's teacher-training classes, students were required to teach a "mini-lesson" using PowerPoint. Of the eight students who were to present on one particular day, six of them were unable to do so because their programs didn't work. On another recent day, the power went out on campus. When it didn't come back on after about fifteen minutes, several teachers canceled their classes because they felt they were unable to present the material without technology. These are the kinds of stories that get around quickly and cause many to despair about the actual benefit versus risk of technology.

One computer science professor spoke to that concern from his own experience and came to the wise conclusion that the seriousness of the risks depends on the teacher's motivation in using the technology in the first place. "Digital technology can enhance our students' learning, but only if our goals for our students learning drive its use" (Creed 1997). If all we want to do is "play" with the newest instructional devices, we are misusing them. A search of articles about the rationale for using instructional technology yielded many reasons like its "ease," "availability," "colorfulness," and "compatibility." The same can be said of crayons! That doesn't justify using crayons all the time anymore than it justifies using PowerPoint or transparencies in every class. The actor does not use fireworks in the theater, even though he could. Instead, he or she chooses the most appropriate technology for the setting and for the goals in that setting. That is the lesson for us as teachers.

BEST PRACTICES

The experience of the most successful teachers who have embraced technology yields several important suggestions that should guide the selection and use of these advanced props. We focus here on eight recommendations that are most useful in most classrooms.

Choose a Particular Technology Prop Specifically to Enhance Learning

If the teaching goal is to stimulate student reflection on and analysis of some new material, the best tool may likely be an interactive whiteboard. This technology allows computer-generated images to be projected on a board on which the students can write, adding their own questions or suggesting relationships among the details presented. This allows students to see the basic information in a clear, colorful, and memorable format, but also feel empowered to generate their own insights about the information.

By contrast, if the teaching goal is to have students understand a specific block of unarguable information, a PowerPoint-assisted lecture may be the best thing. Use occasional slides that incorporate strong, clarifying graphics with the basic terms you must explain in the lecture.

If the teaching goal is to stimulate students' personal reflection, course-management software provides the best opportunity to draw out even the most reserved students, allowing them to comment via electronic chat rather than face-to-face. There are numerous programs available, including ANGEL, Moodle, DyKnow, and others, that seem to have the effect of creating online learning communities (McHugh 2005).

For consideration of complicated statistical tables, on the other hand, the best tool is probably a detailed handout—no technology at all. In that format, the students can better see all the data that has to be analyzed in the relationship rather than being presented with only segments of the data that can fit onto a single slide, thus distorting the material's impact.

Prepare Backups in Case the Planned Technology Fails

As noted previously in our discussion of risks, technology, in all its beauty, can fail to perform. It seems that the more complex the technology, the more things that can go wrong. Being prepared to deliver material with technology aids and being foiled in the execution should not cause a teacher credibility–destroying frustration.

If you have planned a set of PowerPoint slides, make a copy of the slides into transparencies—a strategy made very easy within the program itself. If a computer glitch interferes with accessing or showing your slides, you can still present the material via the overhead projector. The same can be done for the interactive whiteboard. Just print (a color printer is an asset here) the image you intend to use and make it into a write-on transparency. If the class size is small, you could simply hold up the printout while walking around the classroom—working the crowd. The result may not be as effective, but it's far better than canceling class!

When preparing for a class in which you want to use any form of technology, ask yourself what you will do if it fails. Can you rent a video or DVD in case the streaming video doesn't work? Can you read the inspiring words of a great speech yourself if the video doesn't work? Can you prepare individual handouts in case the projected images don't come through clearly or the power fails?

Select Uncomplicated Images

Web images include many that are easily viewed and whose meaning is easily discerned. But there are also images as complicated as those in *Where's Waldo*. Remember that anything that you decide should be seen by the students is intended to clarify, not confuse. So select the photo of a sea anemone that is taken from an angle omitting all the other sea creatures around it; select a cut-away diagram of the internal combustion engine, not the outer view; select a graph made with sharply contrasting colors, not shades of a single color, and so on.

Unless your classroom has been equipped with the latest innovation in projection screens, whatever image you project on the screen will be slightly distorted by the effect known as "keystoneing," making the lower part of the image appear narrower than the upper part. Look at the image you want to show and ask yourself how it will look if keystoned—will its meaning still be clear?

Simplicity of images also relates to the backgrounds and fonts selected for created slides. The backgrounds available are numerous; choose the least complicated ones so that students' eyes will be drawn to the words or images in the foreground.

Minimize the Content of a Single Slide

Whether using transparencies, PowerPoint, or interactive whiteboard, any single slide should be uncluttered. The industry's "rule of thumb" is that single slides should be constructed in observance of the "6 × 6 Rule" (Brooks and Bylo 2004). This means that a slide should not have wording (or its equivalent) that exceeds six words across and six words down.

Students are going to glance up at the slide. If they can't make sense of the material in that first glance, they will either give up or quit listening to the teacher in order to concentrate on figuring out the material on the slide. Either way, they are no longer engaged in the teaching–learning dynamic.

This directive should be especially remembered when selecting or creating graphs and tables. Margin-to-margin numbers are just too hard to see, focus on, and comprehend. This challenge suggests that, as tip number one suggested, complicated statistical material should be presented on paper, not on screen.

Keep the Room Relatively Lit

Many people believe that projected images are visually most appealing if viewed in a room darkened like a movie theater. Although that situation may make the image especially striking in the theater, it invites naps in the classroom!

Any DVD, video, webcast, PowerPoint, or transparency is visible with most of the lights on in the room. It is not necessary to turn them off. Succumbing to that temptation prevents the students from making notes while watching the projected film or image and emphasizes an expectation of student passivity. Both of these results are disastrous to the learning process and may increase classroom-management problems with younger students.

Instead, if the particular graphics are low contrast, just turn off or lower the lights that are right in front of the screen. Leave every other light in the room on.

If students complain that they can't see what's on the screen (some will), invite them to come sit in the front row or move the chairs to increase the number that are close to the screen.

Use Optional Features to Enhance, Not Detract from, the Lesson

Presentation software and course-management software both come with a wide array of options. When first becoming familiar with the technology on your own, explore all the options, deciding which will be useful to you and when.

Some selections can be made when the hardware and software is initially installed in your classrooms. For instance, those using rooms equipped with computers for each student have learned to request the optional feature that ties the podium computer to each student computer, allowing the teacher both to make sure students are on task and to check their actual progress on classwork.

Options you may select just for a particular lesson include colors, fonts, backgrounds, sounds, imbedded pointers, reveals, and transitions. As mentioned before regarding the issue of selecting simple images, fancy fonts, cluttered backgrounds, and decorative noises all run the risk of drawing the students' attention away from the material you actually want them to focus on. They should be avoided.

The software allows you also to choose various ways of revealing the words and images on a single slide. This is another way to provide that concentrated focus on just part of the slide at a time without having to use any pointer at all. Keeping the value of simplicity in mind, choose a reveal that is silent. The imbedded pointer, on the other hand, is a very useful device. Typically, we want to call the students' attention to a specific part of the image projected. Some teachers can be found standing in front of the screen and pointing at it with their hand or pencil—really bad idea! If you do that, the image is now partly projected on your shirt! Some like to be able to walk around the room as they speak and therefore, choose a laser pointer. This can fill the bill nicely, although one has to be careful of inadvertently pointing it at a student's eyes. The imbedded pointer solves all of these problems because it can be triggered and moved from anywhere in the room via the remote mouse and keeps the screen free of distracting images.

Speak to the Students, Not to the Screen

It is tempting to ask every reader to recite that tip aloud three times! It is a simple suggestion with major benefits, but is frequently disregarded.

You are the person who prepared the slides or transparencies or who selected the video clip—you know what is on the screen! Other than a quick glance to make sure the program didn't misfire, your eyes should be on the students when using any instructional technology.

Direct eye contact, as addressed elsewhere in this book, contributes to a trusting relationship between teacher and students and helps to sustain student attention and good behavior. Do not break that bond by falling for the temptation to look at the colorful image on the screen behind you.

SUMMARY

In the area of technology props, perhaps more than any other lessons we take from the theater, careful selection of one's tools is vital to the enthusiastic teacher's success. The best teachers are not the ones who incorporate all the latest "bells and whistles," but rather the ones who choose the best bell or whistle for the moment. The hardware and software available can be daunting. However, because making these materials available is big business, there are many resources available to help us all sort through the options and wisely decide what to ask our districts to fund.

THROUGH THE STUDENTS' EYES

When surveyed regarding the use of technology props in the classroom, students offered real examples, including those that follow. Although each example refers to the use of technology props in a particular subject area, the application to other disciplines is evident.

Magic!

In my statistics class, the professor uses a projector to display the screen of the graphing calculator. He then enters changes in some figures, and we are able to see the graphs and curves change as a result. It makes the point very memorable.

Football

Our high school physics teacher used televised sports programs to illustrate principles of physics. For instance, clips from football games that were available from ESPN were specifically illustrative of different principles of force and motion.

Fill in the Blanks

In chemistry class, our professor uses PowerPoint slides to accompany his lecture. Then he puts the notes on the classroom-management software, but leaves some key terms and concepts out. That way, when we go online to check the class notes, we have to fill in the blanks based on what we noted during class. That makes us pay attention better in class.

Private Drives

I went to a tech school that provided "non-swappable" hard drives for each student. So, each of us could save all of our information and personal work on our own drive.

Plain and Fancy

We had interactive PowerPoint lectures every day in chemistry, which is common in many classes. But in this one, pictures, visuals, examples, and movie excerpts were included. It was evident that a great deal of time had gone into the PowerPoint, and that made it more interesting. When teachers throw together plain, boring PowerPoint presentations [also very common], they are not effective learning tools.

Wall-to-Wall

We were learning how to use graphing calculators in twelfth-grade math. The teacher used a projection device to show the calculator screen on the wall. Without this device, the lesson would have been near to impossible.

Twofer

In my college biology class, the professor uses PowerPoint slides that are displayed on an interactive whiteboard so that he can add drawings to the slide to emphasize a point.

SEARCH FOR MORE ON TECHNOLOGY PROPS

An Education Resources Information Center (http://www.eric.ed.gov/) search for the term "technology props" (or similar concept) and at least one other education-related term—an exercise that takes just seconds—reveals numerous citations. All of them, because they are announced in ERIC, have applications to education settings.

An ERIC search for the term "technology props" (or related term) with a variety of education-related terms reveals the following number of citations: "PowerPoint" and "teaching": 106; "PowerPoint" and "lectures": 31; "technology" and "teaching": 19,322; and "technology" and "student interest": 133.

In addition to exploring ERIC, you should consider searching other databases as well for books, articles, and programs related to the effective use of technology props in the classroom. You also are encouraged to search the Web using many of the ERIC descriptors presented in the previous paragraph. Among several technology props–related Web sites are the following:

George Lucas Educational Foundation (GLEF)
  http://www.glef.org
Internet4Classrooms
  http://www.internet4classrooms.com
SMARTer kids
  http://smarterkids.org

THE MASTER'S VOICE

For further discussion of the concepts and skills presented in this chapter, read the following paragraphs in Appendix 2, Testimonials from Award-Winning K–12 Teachers and College Professors: Austin, Lefford, and Yost, 2, 5; Baleja, 5, 6.

CHAPTER

Suspense and Surprise

It is by surprises that experience teaches all she designs to teach us.
—Collected Papers of Charles Sanders Pierce, Vol. V

INTRODUCTION

What common complaint do many students have about schools and classrooms today? "They are boring." When asked "What is boring?" students respond, "The teachers, the curriculum." What common complaint do many teachers—after the first several years' idealism has tarnished—have about teaching? "It is boring." Actually, teachers mask the word "boring" in such responses as, "The kids just don't respond; they don't show much of an interest," or "I get so tired of having to teach the same thing period after period, day after day." It is clear that teachers, too, are bored.

That all students and teachers at some time become bored is axiomatic. The introduction of suspense and surprise into teaching can help resolve this common complaint. According to Ramsell (1978, 22), "When we are reacting physically and emotionally to surprise, boredom cannot be part of that response." Most, if not all, children love suspense and surprise (The Teacher Institute 2005). All human beings come into this world with what is known as epistemic curiosity—curiosity about knowledge. This serves as the basis of their love for suspense and surprise as they set about acquiring their knowledge of the world. Both teachers and students have something to gain through the use of suspense and surprise.

CREATING THE TWO ELEMENTS

Surprise is the greatest gift which life can grant us.

—Boris Pasternak

Although both suspense and surprise are included in this same chapter, there are differences between the two. Suspense is something that is developed over a period of time as the story or event unfolds. Intrigue, especially dramatic intrigue—whether on stage, in film, or in the classroom—helps develop this suspense. Creating intrigue, and hence suspense, is possible in physics (Why does the earth stay in an orbit around the sun?), in mathematics (What is the probability of at least two students in the same room of thirty having the same birthday?), or chemistry (What is "heavy" about heavy water?). Suspense is equally possible, and useful, in history (Why did Napoleon hold his hand inside his coat?) and literature (What would have happened had Tom Sawyer not been crafty enough to get his friends to help with the work of painting the fence?). With a little imagination, no subject matter is alien to suspense.

Surprise, on the other hand, is said to depend on unexpected events or special effects (Comisky and Bryant 1982). "Surprise takes place when a student is presented with a phenomenon that violates expectations derived from existing beliefs" (Vidler and Levine 1981, 274). An established expectation is challenged by a contradictory, unexpected event. Cognitive dissonance (the theory that people experience tension when a belief is challenged by an inconsistent behavior; Festinger 1957) is created. Such a dissonance, when one gets what is not expected, is understood even by four-year-olds (MacLaren and Olson 1993).

An example of a surprising cognitive dissonance was when one of the authors led a discussion with his graduate education students surrounding the controversy about keeping the words "under God" in the Pledge of Allegiance. This was a particularly relevant topic because many school districts require that the pledge be said in classrooms. When people are asked why the words should not be removed, the most common justification offered is "It's traditional; it has always been in the pledge. Why take it out now?" Almost the entire class is surprised when they find out that the words "under God" were added to the Pledge of Allegiance only about fifty years ago under the Eisenhower administration. Seemingly, the motivation to add the words was an effort to clearly juxtapose a God-fearing America with the "Godless" Communists in the Soviet Union. Are you surprised?

Should an event, effect, or outcome be totally unexpected? Murray (1984) argues that with surprise the "cart should come before the horse." We are much more likely to perceive surprise if we have reason to expect it. This sense of a shared surprise creates a shared experience helping to bond the audience and the actor—the students and the teacher.

The unexpected interjection of suspense and surprise helps teachers to be more spontaneous (Friedman 1995). Suspense creates tension; surprise generates tension. This tension prompts us to attempt to resolve the dissonance, to explore further for answers, to ask "why?" questions, and to search for cause-and-effect explanations. We are, in fact, motivated! Order is sought for unexplained events. It's the chase, not necessarily the achievement, of order that is so stimulating.

Both elements, suspense and surprise, are accompanied by physiological changes (e.g., rapid breathing, gasping air, flushed face), behavioral patterns (including distinct facial expressions, for example), and subjective experiences (Meyer et al. 1991). Suspense and surprise create an emotional impact on students' senses, and "the more you involve your students' senses, the more you sharpen their ability to learn" (Wells 1979, 53). Suspense and surprise are critical elements for effective learning in higher education (Hativa 2000) as well as in basic education.

THE UNPREDICTABLE REAL WORLD

No surprise for the writer, no surprise for the reader.
—Robert Frost

Too often teachers teach as if the world were predictable. It isn't—or at least most of it isn't. The black-and-white world of clearly right and wrong answers is a fallacy. Poetry and literature are not predictable. Psychology and sociology are not predictable. Even mathematics and chemistry are not predictable. Ask any scholar in his or her field. They will tell you this is so. We don't know whether it is part of some grand plan, but the world, not just schools and classrooms, would be boring if total predictability prevailed.

How can suspense and surprise be used in schools? Lowman (1984) suggests that teachers use the elements of suspense and surprise when they enter the classroom. After all, actors pay attention to this all-important, stage-setting entrance. What successful entertainer would simply, without fanfare, walk onto a stage? Rock stars have their accompanying fireworks and smoke, live theater has its dimming of the house lights and the raising of the stage curtain, and television has its "and now, live from New York, it's *Saturday Night!*"

Although it is usually preferable for teachers to get to class well before its official starting time, a variance from this format can be "surprising" and "suspense-building"—"Where could the teacher be? It is almost time to start class." A teacher might also work on varying how he or she actually enters the room. Whereas predictability breeds contentment, the unexpected breeds attentiveness. One could burst into the room and, while rapidly walking to the front of the room, begin lecturing. Consider varying exits, too. Perhaps a colleague could step in at the end of the class and announce in that classic entertainer-exiting style, "(your name) has left the auditorium!" See Chapter 12 for more detailed treatment of entrances and exits.

Students would be better served if they were taught that the world is full of the unexpected—suspense and surprise. Not only would teachers' use of the unexpected, then, be a sound pedagogical tool its use would reflect the reality of the world. Without the feelings of uncertainty and insecurity that accompany suspense and surprise, learners quickly fall into a state of complacency and overconfidence where unthinking approaches to problem solving are mechanically applied. Unfortunately, such an approach to problem solving dominates many of today's classrooms.

Step-by-step "recipe solutions" regularly are applied (and reinforced) to get results without thought occurring about either the process or the result. What high school chemistry lab exists today where students do much more than don a white coat and safety goggles, play scientist, and "discover" exactly what the instructor had intended to be discovered? Where is the "discovery"? Why not assign experiments that give students unexpected—surprising—results? A fellow chemist, Chirpich (1977, 378), agrees that "it is good to include some experiments that are more dramatic and that arouse student curiosity." This is good advice for all subject areas.

STORYTELLING

Eureka!

—Archimedes

One hears the water running. The camera pans toward the Bates Hotel bathroom where, silhouetted behind the curtain, the unsuspecting woman is taking a shower. One hand of the mystery intruder is shown raised, holding a long butcher knife. The other hand is about to grasp the shower curtain and rip it aside. Twenty-five years later, this scene from Alfred Hitchcock's thriller *Psycho* continues to create viewer suspense and surprise.

Then there is the campfire story of the young couple parked on lovers' lane. Steamed windows accompany some adolescent necking. The music on the radio is interrupted by an announcement: "An escaped murderer, nicknamed 'The Hook' due to his having one artificial arm, is rumored to have been seen in the area. Beware." The frightened young couple quickly put the car in gear and speed away. Upon arriving at the young lady's home, the boy gets out and walks around the car, planning gallantly to open the door for his girlfriend—only to find a bloody "hook" hanging on the passenger-side door handle! Do you have goose bumps?

Effective storytellers have long known the power and persuasion of using suspense and surprise. Storytellers are part and parcel of human existence. Whether gathered around a primitive campfire or a formal dining-room table, storytelling was, and in many societies continues to be, an important medium for the transfer of knowledge and skills. Then and now, storytellers teach.

Whether in film or on stage, a story is told. The audience, often purposefully deceived by the movie's or play's plot, waits with anticipation to see "whodunit." Suspense and surprise are often used to grab, as well as hold, the attention of the audience. Did the butler really do it? Will the damsel in distress be saved? Will the roadrunner ever be caught by the coyote? What is the big secret in the movie *The Crying Game*? In *Dallas*, who really shot J.R.? Would Robert Barron ever find the girl of his dreams? Tune in next season.

In the classroom, teachers can infuse their presentations with that kind of suspense. They can create a sense of dramatic tension and excitement that comes from expecting something important or unusual (Lowman 1984). Lectures can be delivered as if a story were being told. The excitement of discovering an unfolding plot, using only "clues" that have been dropped along the way, can heighten student suspense. Teachers can act as if they, too, are just now discovering the plot. They can share in the students' suspense.

According to Lowman (1984, 92), "Superb lecturers share many qualities with storytellers. They, too, save the conclusions or most crucial points until the end, having teased the students along the way with preliminary findings or interpretations. . . . Almost any instructor can learn to be a good storyteller if he or she relaxes inhibitions and reacts to the suspense inherent in most content."

Watch the eyes of a child sparkle with anticipation at the parent's or teacher's opening line during story hour, "Once upon a time . . ." No matter how many times the line is used, the effect is the same. The child is excited about the unexpected. The child is spellbound. Watch a high school or college student's face as she wonders what the author means in the opening lines of the novel A *Tale of Two Cities*: "It was the best of times; it was the worst of times." How can it be the "best" and "worst" of times at the same time? The apparent discrepancy builds suspense.

RELATIONSHIP TO OTHER ACTING SKILLS

Mystery is at the heart of creativity. That, and surprise.
                                                                                —Julia Cameron

Almost anything teachers do that is seen by students to be out of the ordinary will be viewed with curiosity. Therefore, each of the other acting/teaching skills highlighted in this book, if not part of a teacher's usual repertoire of behaviors, has the potential for creating suspense and surprise.

Unexpected animation in voice—perhaps a shout (surprise), perhaps a whisper (suspense)—can do the trick. Animation in body, possibly conveyed through sudden demonstrative body movements, can create both surprise and suspense. Greeting students on a Monday morning after having unexpectedly moved their desks into a new seating pattern might do it. Students wonder, "Gee, what's up?" A teacher playing a role, complete with supportive props (e.g., costumes), can be surprising and can heighten suspense. Content-related humor, delivered at just the right moment, can be surprising. Teachers should keep their eyes open for opportunities to evoke suspense and surprise when using other acting/teaching skills.

BRINGING SUSPENSE AND SURPRISE INTO THE CLASSROOM

When I was born I was so surprised I didn't talk for a year and a half.
                                                                                —Gracie Allen

Although not intended to be a definitive list of suggestions, the following ideas do represent a variety of ways in which suspense and surprise can be brought into the classroom. In those circumstances where the suggestions appear content-specific, use your imagination to envision how the basis of the suggestion could be used in other subject areas.

- Do not always announce to students what activities will take place during the class period. Let each activity, revealed one at a time like the layers of an onion, help create suspense and surprise.

- Use self-disparaging comments in moderation. Before doing so, one should have a healthy rapport with students. Mild self-disparaging comments, not the Rodney Dangerfield "I get no respect" variety, are unexpected in the students' experience. Students find it surprising to hear teachers "pick" on themselves for a change. Skillful teachers exploit their own fallibility (Rubin 1985).

- Feign mistakes in a form of teacher role-playing. Rubin (1985, 135) argues that students "are delighted when a normally accurate teacher makes a mistake." They are surprised. The use of a feigned reaction is "neither deceptive nor dishonest in spirit when the purpose is altruistic." Aware of this, enterprising practitioners occasionally engage in a bit of "planned error." The teacher could accompany this error with an exaggerated display of consternation or despair. The more the teacher "hams it up," the more surprising it is. Students then can be asked to help correct the error—a useful, but surprising, pedagogical tool.

- Feign laryngitis. A professor whom we know feigned laryngitis on the day that a wrap-up discussion was scheduled for an earlier off-campus, field experience. In an uncharacteristic fashion, the discussion was dominated by students. All the teacher could do was gesture and, perhaps, scribble boldly on the chalkboard, "Tell us more." "Why is that?" "What about such and such?" Imagine the students' surprise when, while leaving the classroom at the end of an exciting class, the instructor said, in a clear voice, "I will see each of you on Wednesday."

- Feign "giving in" to a view that you don't really support. For instance, one of this book's authors contrasts the classroom-discipline views of behaviorism and humanism. While the teacher identifies characteristics for both philosophies, it becomes clear to students that personally he supports the often less-popular humanist position that shuns the providing of punishment and rewards. As the period continues and students make their compelling arguments in favor of behaviorism, the author finally appears to "give in" and says—with all the sincerity possible—"I give up; it's too hard trying to defend humanism. I think that just maybe you are right; behaviorism is the preferred position." Students are so surprised at his change of heart—perhaps they just feel sorry for him—that they immediately set about trying to convince him that humanism is the better view!

- Use "what-if" exercises. A what-if exercise asks students to extrapolate information, to go beyond what is known for sure and venture into the suspense of the unknown. What if the Germans had won World War II? What if ice did not float? What if we reduce by half the size of the House of Representatives? What if people were regularly to live to over one hundred years old? Today's computer spreadsheets (e.g., Lotus 1-2-3) allow us to play what-if games with numbers, such as the return expected for different proposed interest rates. Every discipline has a past and a future. Both are ripe for surprising what-if exercises.

- A professor the authors know starts out asking her students, "What are the three most important words in real estate?" If you have not heard this question before, you might be surprised to find out that the answer is the same word, three times—*location, location, location*! Another professor uses a version of this question with his education majors, "What are the three most important words in education?" The students are a bit surprised to learn that the three words are *expectations, expectations, expectations*. This same professor sometimes places the word *expectations* on three separate cards and then, just before class, "hides" them somewhere in the room. When he asks students, "What are the three most important words in education?" he walks around the room and "pretends" to find the cards he has hidden. To add some additional drama, the professor looks surprised each time he finds one of the cards.
- A music teacher the authors know has a partial outfit for the Lone Ranger— white hat and mask. While wearing the hat and mask, the teacher plays the theme song from *The Lone Ranger* television program. The students are surprised to find out that the theme song for a children's cowboy program is actually the *William Tell Overture*! It is claimed that, among the middle-aged, only a true intellectual can listen to the *William Tell Overture* and not think of the Lone Ranger. The authors, then, must not be true intellectuals!
- A psychology professor teaching the principles of operant conditioning asks, "What is it called when a teacher *supplies* a reward to a child?" Her students reply, "Positive reinforcement." The teacher responds, "Correct!" Then she asks, "What is it called when a teacher *removes* a reward from a student?" The majority of students reply, "Punishment." The students are more than a bit surprised when the instructor responds, "Wrong!" Why is it wrong? The definition of negative reinforcement is removing an aversive stimulus (i.e., pain or discomfort), not removing a reward. Removing a reward is called "time-out." What, then, is punishment? Punishment is the supplying of an aversive stimulus. To be sure that students have a grasp of these operant conditioning terms, the instructor asks, "Do children look forward to receiving positive reinforcement?" The students' response should be "yes." She then asks, "Do children look forward to receiving negative reinforcement?" For those who understand the definition of negative reinforcement, there is no surprise. The answer is "yes." For those who are still confused about the definition, they find the "yes" answer very surprising.
- Watch the faces of kids in their middle-school science class when the volcano that they just built "explodes" and spews out steam. Even though they were told it was going to explode, even though they knew it was going to explode, and even though they knew *why* it was going to explode, the suspense is still there until it does explode.
- Bait students. Ask students to do something that, although it appears possible, can't be done. For instance, using a bull's-eye target, teach students the concepts of "validity" and "reliability." Tell the students that you are testing a rifle's validity and reliability. Pretend that you have five shots to fire at a bull's-eye target (Figure 11.1). Show the students what a "reliable" and "valid" pattern

Figure 11.1
Bull's-Eye Target

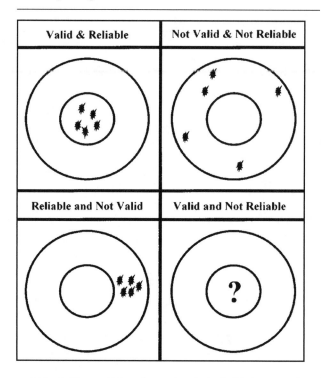

of shots would look like—all five shots closely (reliably) grouped in the bull's eye (valid). Ask them to create shot patterns for the three remaining combinations: valid and not reliable, not valid and reliable, not valid and not reliable. It looks easy, but it is impossible to do. There is no way to have a pattern of shots that is "valid" and "not reliable." By definition, all things that are valid are reliable! Surprising? Yes! Remembered? Yes!

- Still another version of baiting is telling enough of a story, or revealing enough of an event, to pique their curiosity. "Once baited, the audience wants to find out who wins, who loses, whether the villain receives his just desserts" (Rubin 1985, 113). One of the authors teaches the "Roadblocks to Communication" from Thomas Gordon's *T.E.T.: Teacher Effectiveness Training*. When introduced to these twelve roadblocks, students realize that they unknowingly use them all the time. Just when the students are begging to know what alternative behaviors they could use, the instructor announces, "Sorry, but we are out of time. We will have to wait until tomorrow to find out about Gordon's alternatives." Healthy suspense is created. This is precisely the format of every good television program or movie for which each show is one episode in a series. Think of the suspenseful "cliffhangers" of the Friday episodes of daytime soap operas or the conclusions of each installment in the *Lord of the Rings* trilogy. The viewer *wants* to return to learn more.

- Go back and reread the authors' example about "Why does ice float?" in the chapter on props. In this example, students are surprised when they are first told that ice should not float. It is just inconceivable to any audience that something so common in their lives can seemingly violate nature's laws. We call upon readers to come up with their own discipline-related examples.

- Change the rules once in awhile. One teacher we heard about has a variation on the popular game of musical chairs. Instead of pitting students against each other so that one child has to lose each round, she designs the game so that the children act cooperatively with everyone a winner. How does she do this? In her version of the game, when the music stops and a chair is taken away, if a child can't find an empty chair, he or she simply sits on another person who is on a chair. The objective of the game is to see how few chairs are eventually needed to accommodate all the children. An extra benefit to this version of the game is that children do not need to run around or fight for a seat.

- Provide students with the opportunity for meaningful guessing—call it forming hypotheses if you like—before solving or presenting solutions (Johnson 1973). The anticipation associated with guessing "whodunit" or "what color the powder will turn the solution" heightens the suspense. As an example, try using a form of overhead transparency burlesque. Take a picture related to the day's lesson. Prepare an overhead of it, and then cover portions of it with a bunch of Post-Its. During class, show the picture on the overhead and slowly reveal more and more of it by removing Post-Its. Periodically, stop and ask students to predict what the picture is all about or what might still be hidden under the remaining Post-Its. This exercise is guaranteed to create suspense and surprise.

- Buy a musical jack-in-the-box at a toy store and "equip" it with the ability to grasp a 3" x 5" card or some other way of holding a message. When it comes time to deliver the day's message—homework assignment, who will be the designated lab assistant for tomorrow, what is the answer to an earlier posed question—crank the crank and watch the students stare at the box in anticipation of Jack popping out with the message. It never fails to surprise them. Those with a few years under their belt may remember Groucho Marx's quiz show where he announced that if any of the players said the "secret word," a plucked duck (yes, a duck!) held by a wire would drop from the ceiling, and the contestant would win $25. The contestants and audience never ceased to be surprised. (And no, it was not a real duck.)

- The announcement of a "pop quiz" is always an attention-getter, of course! But, you might surprise the students even more if the "quiz" only has one question. One of the authors does this in beginning a discussion of semantics by asking the class just to identify a simple item (simple, but foreign to them). As they struggle to come up with an answer amid concern about their "quiz" grade, the answer is revealed and serves as a good starting point to discuss the arbitrariness of linguistic labels.

- Use an accomplice. In an administration of justice course, one instructor had a primed student burst into the classroom, "shoot" him with a water pistol, and then quickly exit—not the usual classroom experience. Students were then asked to describe the perpetrator. Few could do so accurately. The lecture on the reliability and validity of eyewitness testimony followed.
- Display a prop that is destined for later use and let students wonder about its use until later in the class period. Who would not experience a feeling of suspense if a teacher walked into class, placed a paper bag (obviously full of something) in a prominent place, and then proceeded to "ignore" it? It would have our curiosity piqued. Suspense, and possibly surprise, is created. Students would be paying attention.
- Play music from *Jaws*. It doesn't get much more suspenseful than this. Enough said!

SUMMARY

This suspense is terrible. I hope it will last.

—Oscar Wilde

In a list of a handful of components for teachers' success, House (1988, 640) highlights one letter "s" in the word *success* as surprise. She describes the personal feelings of "renewed awe and wonder and surprise" that she experiences when studying her disciplines of science and mathematics. These same feelings, we believe, are shared by most successful teachers in any subject area. The trick is for teachers to convey this sense of suspense and surprise to students.

"People seem to enjoy being placed in suspense" (Zillmann and Hay 1975, 308). This fact is evident from the earliest measures psychologists made of kindergarten children, when the children expressed a clear preference for stories with a suspense theme (Jose and Brewer 1990). Whether it is Hitchcock's classic *Rear Window* or Spielberg's thriller *Raiders of the Lost Ark*, it is clear that theater and film directors know and exploit this fact. Although teachers cannot be expected, especially on a daily basis, to present such attractive themes of good and evil forces (e.g., man-versus-man, man-versus-nature), teachers can capitalize on those opportunities that do exist.

Do kids like suspense and surprise? The authors need only to remind the readers of the interest—no, the passionate interest—that children show in reading *Harry Potter* books. The books are thick, there are lots and lots of words, and pictures are kept to a minimum, yet children (and many adults) cannot put them down. What is the attraction? Suspense and surprise!

THROUGH THE STUDENTS' EYES

When surveyed regarding the use of suspense and surprise in the classroom, students offered real-life examples such as those that follow. Although each example refers to the use of suspense and surprise in a particular subject area, the application to other disciplines is evident.

Paper Drive

For two weeks, Mrs. A., my high school English teacher, asked us to bring in all of our old newspapers from home. We didn't have the slightest idea why we were doing this. Finally, she broke the suspense and told us to divide into groups of three, use our creativity, and "make" something from *Beowulf*, a topic we had been studying for the past week. Our group made a huge model of Grendel. I think the activity was a good stress-breaker for the class.

Blindfolded

For composition class, we would do a composition describing something with one of our senses. Then that sense would be blocked. For instance, we would be blindfolded and asked to describe what was put into our hands, on our tongues, and under our noses.

Duck!

When lecturing about making observations in science, Mr. M. proved that you can't always rely on seeing-is-believing. To prove this point, he showed us a good-sized rock, which he then threw at a student. The student ducked to escape the rock, which turned out to be simply a hunk of Styrofoam.

Is the Principal Coming?

To help us learn the metric system, Mr. A. brought in his electric jigsaw and actually cut a wooden meter stick into important lengths (e.g., centimeter, decimeter). To say the least, we were surprised. He even "posted a guard" in the hall to watch out for the principal (suspense). Because it looked as if we were getting away with something, everyone paid attention. Each student was given a length of the meter stick (a prop) and was required to have it with him at all times and be prepared to produce it upon demand.

ESP

My psychology teacher fooled the class (a little bit of role-playing) by claiming to be able to communicate with a colleague through extrasensory perception (ESP). He did it so convincingly that, upon revealing the purpose of the activity, we were surprised at how easily all of us were fooled.

Soap Bubbles

Our engineering teacher gave us the problem of connecting the cities of Boston, Chicago, New Orleans, Atlanta, Spokane, and San Diego with the least amount of concrete (shortest path) possible. Is this a complicated problem? Not really. The surprisingly easy solution was to place pegs (representing the cities) between two pieces of Plexiglas, and when this was dipped in a soap solution, the resulting soap film connected the pegs with minimum surface area—hence distance—possible. "Amazed" is a better word than "surprised."

SEARCH FOR MORE ON SUSPENSE AND SURPRISE

An Education Resources Information Center (http://www.eric.ed.gov/) search for the term "suspense" or "surprise" and at least one other acting-lessons term reveals numerous citations. All of them, because they are announced in ERIC, have applications to education settings.

An ERIC search for the term "suspense" with a variety of education-related terms reveals the following number of citations: "suspense" plus "student learning": 973; plus "student achievement": 668; plus "student creativity": 30; plus "elementary education": 780; plus "secondary education": 1,349; plus "teaching": 93,300; plus "teaching English": 1,190; plus "teaching math": 177; plus "teaching social studies": 41; plus "teaching science": 297; plus "teaching boys": 48; and plus "teaching girls": 33. Although we did not conduct a search of the term "surprise" with a variety of education-related terms, we have every reason to believe that it, too, would generate lots of citations.

In addition to exploring ERIC, you should consider searching other databases as well for books, articles, and programs related to the effective use of suspense and surprise in the classroom. You also are encouraged to search the Web using many of the ERIC descriptors presented in the previous paragraph.

THE MASTER'S VOICE

For further discussion of the concepts and skills presented in this chapter, read the following paragraphs in Appendix 2, Testimonials from Award-Winning K–12 Teachers and College Professors: Carroll, 2–5; Hall, 6; Light, 3; Lisska, 3–7; Mahoney, 2; McBrayer, 4, 5.

CHAPTER

Making a Dramatic Entrance and Exit

Well begun is half done.

—Anonymous

INTRODUCTION

This introduction, like all the chapter introductions in this text, serves as an entrance. If it is not crafted correctly—that is, if we don't create something that catches your attention and motivates you to read further—you might tune out what we have to say next. If we don't create an attractive entrance, you may not want to enter the world that follows, and our message will be lost. A lot is at stake.

BEGINNING AND ENDING: THE COMMUNICATION PRINCIPLE

As everyone knows from having taken an English or speech class, the opening and closing of any message are critical to the message's overall impact. This general principle is especially true in oral communication because listeners are most alert at the beginning and ending of the message. Thus, any and every message ought to begin in a way that captures the listeners' interest and attention and ought to end in a way that makes the message memorable. We see the incorporation of this principle in advertising, public speaking, and private conversations and, of course, in theater and films.

MEMORABLE ENTRANCES

Many actors and actresses have created memorable, almost signature, entrances. There was Fonzie on *Happy Days*, Lenny and Squiggy on *Laverne and Shirley*, Johnny Carson on *The Tonight Show*, and even Dr. Phil. For more years than most viewers can remember, Johnny Carson's entrance would be announced by Ed McMahon saying, "Here's Johnny!" Sometimes Johnny would "fight" with the curtain while trying to emerge from backstage. Was this unplanned, or was it really sort of comedic entrance, setting the audience up for Johnny's monologue that followed?

Speaking of memorable entrances, all one has to do is mention the television program *Seinfeld*, and an entrance comes to mind—Kramer! Cosmo Kramer may well be the king of memorable entrances. As a point of trivia, Kramer *entered* Seinfeld's apartment 284 separate times, and each time, he did it with pizzazz.

Not all actors' entrances have to be exaggerated to be noticed. Recently, one of the authors and his wife went to an autograph-signing by Gary Burghoff, better known as Cpl. Walter "Radar" O'Reilly, from *M*A*S*H*. Radar spends his winters living in a motor-home park nearby. About one hundred people were lined up at an outdoor picnic pavilion, eagerly waiting his appearance. Without any fanfare, Radar walked up and stood at the end of line just as if he, too, were a fan. Imagine the impact on his "audience" when folks at the end of the line turned around and saw him standing there. Low-key or high-key, entrances are important.

PAGEANTRY AND ENTRANCES

Every exit is an entrance somewhere else.

—Tom Stoppard

Recall the grand beginnings so carefully crafted for every Olympic Games of the modern era. The pageantry, the torch lighting, and the parades of athletes all are coordinated to draw in the viewer and heighten his or her expectations of the events to come. The same effect is created by the dramatic arrival of the stars at a movie premiere, the sweeping searchlight openings of every Chicago Bulls home game, and the trumpet blasts announcing the play's beginning at the Stratford Festival in Canada. The audience members are virtually on the edge of their seats, ready to receive an exciting message!

The raising of a curtain in the theater is an attention-getter; it is a signal that one's focus should be directed toward the stage. It signals something is about to happen; something is about to be revealed! It may not be practical, or desirable, for teachers to hide behind curtains prior to the start of class, however. After all, unlike actors, teachers have a responsibility to monitor their charges at all times

Yet educators could duplicate the positive effects of raising a curtain. One math teacher who the authors know brings to school her daughter's toy plastic stage (about 18" by 18")—complete with a curtain that can be opened and closed. With the curtain closed, she places the stage on the edge of her desk. When it is time to start class, with a bit of exaggerated fanfare, she raises the curtain to reveal the day's assignment or the answer to a previously assigned

Photo 12.1
Dramatic Entrances

problem. Sometimes she invites students to help create the accompanying fanfare to the curtain raising. With this unusual beginning, the teacher conveys that exciting learning is about to take place.

Another faculty member the authors know starts her fifth-grade class by standing in the doorway with a clearly visible stopwatch hanging around her neck. She says nothing—there is no nagging or cajoling students whatsoever. She just stands there like a statue—like one of those people found on the street who amaze their audience (and collect a few coins) by remaining motionless. The stopwatch does all the work. It controls the students' entrance. The watch is a critical part of executing Jones's (2000) Preferred Activity Time (PAT). PATs include activities, usually content related, that the teacher knows her students really enjoy. Students can increase their time for PATs, done on Friday afternoons, by beating the clock. The teacher announces at the start of the year how much time he or she allows for transitional activities, such as getting into class, getting seated, and getting ready to work. If students complete the transition faster than the allotted time, the saved time goes toward PATs. If they take more than the allotted time, then that time is deducted from PATs. This form of an entrance works because students love to waste a teacher's time but hate to waste their own time!

ENTRANCES (AND OPENING LINES)

The teacher's entrance into the classroom is no less important than the actor's entrance onto the stage (Greenberg and Miller 1991). Both signal, or at least should signal, that it is time for something to happen. Performances are to begin, classes are to commence, or meetings are to start. When starting a meeting, our dean would walk to the front of the room, remove his watch, and place it on the lectern in front of him. Given that every room on campus had a large wall clock, why did he need to place his watch in front of him? He used it to signal to faculty that it was time to start the meeting. We got the message.

What ritualistic entrances or opening lines do you use? One educator we know rings a musical triangle (see the chapters on vocal animation and classroom management) to signal the starting of class. Its tinkling sound travels to all corners of the room. Another teacher we know walks to the center of the room (i.e., the stage), stands erect, and simply announces, "Let's begin." It signals to everyone that class (on time, of course) is to begin. If results are not forthcoming, the same statement in the same tone of voice is repeated. It takes two times at most. Greenberg and Miller say that "if the entrance does not get the audience's attention, it should be reassessed" (1991, 435).

Teachers could pass out "tickets"—really just jazzed-up worksheets or other assignments—to the class the day before. The tickets could then be collected at the door just like at the theater or cinema. Students with tickets are invited in for the day's "performance." Everybody knows that the "ticket" in question is simply a ruse.

For teachers, who, unlike actors, have to meet with the same group of students over and over, a consistent entrance (opening line) is recommended. Procedural routines also offer predictability, something many students need and value.

ENDING ON A HIGH NOTE: EXITS (AND CLOSING LINES)

The classroom should be an entrance into the world, not an escape from it.
                                                                    —John Ciardi

When it comes to ending a television show for the season, the episode "Who Shot J. R.?" on *Dallas* probably still leads the pack. When it comes to ending a television show for good, *Seinfeld*, *M.A.S.H.*, and *Cheers* will always be noted for leaving the viewing audience with memorable images of the show and its themes. When it comes to ending a concert, who can forget the way that Elvis did it? After his last song and in spite of raucous applause demanding still more, over the loudspeaker it was announced, "Elvis has left the building!"

We, like Eggleston and Smith (2002), argue that creative and purposeful classroom endings or exits are just as important as their entrance counterparts. Yet, according to Maier and Panitz (1996), in their article "End on a High

Note," when it comes to teaching, the pedagogical literature is surprisingly sparse on the topic of class endings. Fortunately, creative teachers, equipped with the acting lessons highlighted in this text, can strike out on their own to fill this ending/exit void.

Teachers may want to avoid the commonly delivered closing statement "Now, in conclusion . . ." This signals to some students that at that very moment class is over. Notebooks begin to close, one after another, filling the last moments of class with a shuffling sound. One teacher we know anticipates this student behavior and instructs them, in unison, to "slam their books closed." Once the books have closed—taking just a second or two—the remainder of the class time is available for the teacher's concluding remarks.

A MARQUEE: THE PHYSICAL SIDE OF AN ENTRANCE

Most clubs, theaters, and cinemas like to boldly advertise. The advertisement is meant to capture the attention of passersby and act as an invitation to enter. Their most visible form of advertisement often is their marquee.

Why shouldn't teachers use a marquee—advertising to students a bit of what is in store for them? Why should the entrances to classrooms all be alike, all having at most a room number and a teacher's name and—well, that's about it. How boring! A marquee can whet the appetite of both students who are walking by and students lucky enough to enter the teacher's classroom.

A teacher could place a marquee (homemade or perhaps constructed by the school shop), made out of poster board, cardboard, or plywood, over the classroom door. It could be painted, it could have a "slot" to insert teacher-prepared and regularly changed messages, and who knows—it could have lights powered by batteries! We understand, of course, that many teachers move from room to room, and thus a permanent marquee may be out of the question. But, just because the idea will not work for every teacher does not mean that it can't work for many of them.

For those marquees designed to permit the words to be regularly changed, students can experience a sense of anticipation and wonder each time they see the marquee and the messages displayed on it. What does Mrs. Knouse's marquee mean by the words "Shakespeare on rye served today?" What does Mr. Bennett mean when he advertises, "Roaches: Man's best friend!" What does Ms. Carroll mean by her marquee that says, "Lincoln: What did he really keep under his stove top hat?" We don't know for sure what these marquee messages mean, but we would like to find out.

What messages would you place on your marquee? Let your imagination run wild. One first-grade teacher known to the author recently converted her classroom doorway to look like a cave opening—and not just any cave, but the cave of a dinosaur. This "marquee" loudly conveyed to the entering students that their class day was going to be an adventure! Thus, the children started the day with high attention and anticipation.

WHAT IS ON THE MARQUEE?

The more obvious aspect to the marquee is the one just described—the physical entrance complete with bright colors and flashing lights. But there is another part to the marquee—the message placed on it! Surely, playwrights and movie producers spend time, effort, and money trying to come up with play and movie titles that they believe will capture the attention of theater- and moviegoers. Teachers should do the same thing. Consider the title (a form of a marquee) of George Plitnik's three-credit university honors seminar. This professor of physics labels his course, "The Science of Harry Potter." He could have named it "Physics 101." Which marquee (i.e., course title) do you believe will best capture and hold the interest of students? Plitnik's demanding course is always full—and not just with engineering and science students!

What's in a name or marquee? When Japanese sports cars first came into the United States, Datsun (now called Nissan) named its contender Fair Lady. This was a bad choice. It had to compete with European cars that had racy-sounding names such as MG, TR-6, and JAG. And at the time, the United States was offering muscle cars with marquees such as GTO, Barracuda, and BOSS Mustang. What's in a name? What is in a marquee? Everything! Nissan now calls its sports car a 350Z! Which is more likely to bring young folks into the showroom, ready to buy?

Think of the impact 007 would have had if his entrance, his opening line, was "My name is Waxman, Horace Waxman!" Somehow, saying "Bond, James Bond" has more impact.

SUMMARY

Ambady and Rosenthal's (1993) research shows that an audience's evaluation of a teacher is formed in the first thirty seconds of the first class! And these evaluations were found to be similar to the evaluations students gave teachers after the entire semester. These first minutes, in fact, these first seconds, count! Clearly, first impressions are lasting impressions. Knowing this, teachers should consider carefully their first encounter with classes—their dramatic entrances. And in anticipation of future classes, they should give equal consideration to their dramatic exits.

SEARCH FOR MORE ON DRAMATIC ENTRANCES AND EXITS

An Education Resources Information Center (http://www.eric.ed.gov/) search for the term "entrances" or "exits" and at least one other education-related term—an exercise that takes just seconds—reveals numerous citations. All of them, because they are announced in ERIC, have applications to education settings.

An ERIC search for the term "entrances" or "exits" (or related terms) with a variety of education-related terms reveals the following number of citations:

"dramatic entrances" and "classrooms": 53; "dramatic entrances" and "teaching": 236; "dramatic entrances" and "teachers": 222; "dramatic entrances" and "motivation": 62; "dramatic exits" and "classrooms": 18; "dramatic exits" and "teachers": 73; "dramatic exits" and "teaching": 71; and "dramatic exits" and "motivation": 12.

In addition to exploring ERIC, you should consider searching other databases as well for books, articles, and programs related to the effective use of entrances and exits in the classroom. You also are encouraged to search the Web using many of the ERIC descriptors presented in the previous paragraph.

PART 3

Epilogue

CHAPTER

Behind the Scenes, Loosening Up, and Preparing for That Step across the Classroom Threshold

Take the first step in faith. You don't have to see the whole staircase, just take the first step.

—Martin Luther King Jr.

INTRODUCTION

An actor is vividly aware that the performance seen by the audience is a mere fraction of the work involved in staging a play. It is an *important* fraction, but still a fraction. The bulk of the work happens "behind the scenes" out of sight—just like the bulk of an iceberg is out of sight underwater. That is the reminder for teachers: most of the work that makes the classroom come alive happens behind the scenes. Some of this behind-the-scenes work is physical, and some of it is mental. Both are necessary to take that all-important step of crossing the classroom threshold—day after day.

For an actor, the behind-the-scenes category includes endless hours of personal preparation as well as the coordinated contributions of a large support crew who attend to the staging issues of lights, sound, props, and so on. Without that background preparation by all parties, the performance itself could be of very poor quality, no matter how great the actor's presentational skills.

Likewise for the teacher, "behind the scenes" refers both to personal preparation and to preparing the accoutrements of the performance with the help of some support staff. When one thinks of preparation in regard to teaching, content mastery is probably what comes to mind. Content mastery certainly is vital, but it has been amply treated earlier. In this instance, preparation refers to preparing for the *act* of teaching, not preparing the subject matter per se. Such preparation requires attention to the teacher's "spirit," if you will, and to the "things" of the stage called a classroom.

Although teachers may feel they are "in it alone," at least when they close the classroom door, they have to perform as if they have an entire entourage to help them. Unfortunately, they don't have these human resources—they have to do most all of it on their own. Teachers must be their own director, playwright, editor, script supervisor, announcer, costume designer, prop manager, set designer, sound and light technician, ticket taker, rigger, and grip. We would add the theater jobs of stand-in and understudy, but these are luxury human resources that definitely are not available to teachers.

How important are all of these roles to the stage and cinema? They are very important. For instance, imagine a movie where no one has kept track of the flow from scene to scene. Just last week, one of the authors went to a popular movie where it looked as if sections of film from all of the individual scenes had dropped on the floor, been retrieved in no particular order, and then spliced together to make the final version of the film.

In any performance, whether in the classroom or in the actors' world, someone has to keep track of the details. Imagine the chaos in classrooms if teachers could not keep track of their "scenes"—what was taught today and what needs to be taught tomorrow.

INTERNAL PREPARATION

Although we discussed the importance of teacher passion in Chapter 1, we return to it here. It is that important! Richard Weaver, a noted communication scholar, asserts that the problem with college teaching is that so few faculty have a "passion" for teaching (Weaver 1981). His position is shared by many others, including students. If the faculty member sees the teaching task as simply a job, it will be impossible to generate the enthusiasm necessary to perform it well. All that has been suggested in this book regarding the tools of teaching is valueless if used by a mere technician. The user must be an artist—one for whom the teaching–learning process is anticipated joyfully and executed with dedication.

Another scholar reminds us that the etymology of the word "professor" is the reference to a person able to make a profession of faith in the midst of a dangerous world (Palmer 1990). Seen from this angle, then, to be a professor requires some courage of conviction. One must be willing to present the issues, the ideas, and the challenges whether students are motivated to listen or not. It is the professor's task to create that motivation by allowing his or her *passion* for the subject matter and for the teaching–learning process to be evident.

Recapturing that passion is what internal preparation is all about. Like actors, teachers must feel a commitment to express themselves before going on stage. That commitment is what gives teachers self-confidence. In the midst of the pressures of outcomes-based assessments, performance reviews, troubled students, and funding shortages (and the list goes on and on), teachers must remind themselves why they got into the business of teaching. It is the magic of learning, the challenge to make a difference, the wonder of knowledge. Do these ideas sound familiar? Every teacher who can recapture that passion within is prepared to handle the tools and techniques of the classroom.

LOOSENING UP

Confidence is preparation. Everything else is beyond your control.
—Richard Kline

When one of the authors plays tennis with his daughter, she first stretches this and stretches that and takes a brief run around the perimeter of the court. She warms up—just what one is supposed to do prior to setting foot on the tennis court (i.e., the stage for the afternoon). Her dad does none of this. After playing several sets of tennis, it is clear that the daughter made the right decision. Someday, maybe he will learn to warm up. Don't follow his example. Warm up now.

One should prepare ahead of time for any task, whether it is tennis, acting, or teaching. By reading this book, you are preparing ahead of time to be a more enthusiastic and engaging teacher. Although we have introduced a series of specific acting/performance skills to help you do your teaching job better, we recognize that sometimes teachers—new and seasoned—can be so nervous or anxious about stepping over that classroom threshold that they are unable to capitalize fully on their newfound acting knowledge and skills.

According to Sandler (2006), "when a threshold is crossed, the actor transcends into the character's life and body, leaving behind all aspects of the actor's personal life and body." He cites Michael Chekhov's (1991) position that actors (teachers, too) need to envision an imaginary line, and when that line is crossed, their personal baggage and negative energy are left behind. Their entire focus, then, can be on the role they have to play—actor or teacher. Sandler even suggests that a teacher draw an actual line across the entrance to his or her classroom. Even a subtle line, known and seen only by the teacher, may be sufficient.

This stress is not unique to teachers. Actors and actresses regularly report feeling stressed, nervous, tense, anxious, and apprehensive about setting foot on stage—their version of a classroom. In fact, the acting world has a name for these debilitating feelings—"stage fright." It is interesting that there is no such term, other than "performance anxiety," for teachers who may be experiencing these same feelings. Even this alternative term, "performance anxiety," is not unique to the teaching profession—it is shared with the acting, sports, entertainment, and business worlds.

Some educators find walking into the classroom anxiety-laden. One professor reports that quickened and shallow breathing and a headache often accompanied him through the classroom door. Another teacher reported having nightmares that the clock hands were moving backward while he lectured and he was running out of material (Showalter 2003).

Still another professor—actually, one of the authors—recalls having bad dreams in which he arrived at class completely unprepared. A first-grade teacher in a private school dreams that she is in front of the class in her underwear. She realizes that something is not right, but she doesn't know what it is. A high school math teacher reports having a recurring dream that he's late and can't find the class he's supposed to teach. These anxiety-laden bad dreams regarding irresponsibility, lack of preparation, and downright terror are common-enough teacher dreams that they have been investigated by one of our Penn State colleagues, Michael Berube (Showalter 2003).

It does little good to tell such anxious people, "relax," "calm down," "don't worry," or "take it easy." What is needed, and what we do in this chapter, is to offer readers specific strategies that can help them reduce these debilitating feelings and make it easier for them to enter the classroom with confidence.

The anxiety that is normally felt by all humans before having to speak in front of an audience is not foreign to teachers. Just because we want to teach does not necessarily mean that we are fully comfortable with that first moment of standing alone in front of a room full of new faces. The reaction to even the slightest degree of anxiety is a physiological reaction (heart racing, shortness of breath, and so on), and therefore, the best ways to address the anxiety are physiological as well. We suggest in this chapter a number of exercises both to limit the development of anxiety and to minimize it after the fact.

WELL BEFORE CLASS: PRACTICING ALONE

- Reread this book.
- Realize that you have something to offer the audience.
- You do not need to eliminate all fear, nervousness, and anxiety. According to Danson, "Fear is actually a terrific desire to do well . . . teachers need to learn to manage that desire and make that nervous energy an ally rather than an enemy" (Danson, cited in Showalter 2003).
- Good preparation is one of the best antidotes to feelings of anxiety—do not leave the preparation until the last minute. Get your presentation down pat.
- Practice Glasser's Choice Theory (1998). Glasser asks us to visualize an automobile, with each of the four wheels representing a component of our behavior—left front (*action*), right front (*thinking*), left rear (*physiology*), and right rear (*feelings*). His argument is that although the rear wheels propel the car, the front wheels determine the direction the car will go. He also argues that we can control our *actions*, and we can control our *thoughts*. If you are *feeling* anxious and if *physiologically* you are stressed (i.e., sweaty palms, increased heartbeat) about going into the classroom, you can redirect these debilitating conditions by using positive *thinking* and *actions* to redirect your life! Think positive *thoughts* and engage in productive *actions* that are likely to contribute to your success as a teacher. The positive *feelings* and settled *physiology* will follow.
- Also, practice Glasser's Learning Pictures (1998). He argues that people are motivated to engage in activities that they believe lead them closer and closer to their picture of an "ideal world." For those who perceive teaching as a career, their picture of an "ideal world" would include opportunities to prepare

and deliver exciting lessons—over and over. All the time and energy that is required to design and deliver these lessons is well spent; it results in movement toward that "ideal world."

- Check out the room where you are scheduled to teach. Are the needed materials there—chalk, overhead, screen, and room-darkening blinds? Is it important to have tables and chairs versus just student desks? What is your "plan B" if the resources you expected to be present are not there? Now is the time to get everything straightened out!

- Form an argument to defend the use of acting/performance skills in the classroom. Throughout this text, we have tried to help you make this case. By forming your own argument, not only will you better convince yourself, but you also will be in a better position to respond to others who might try to dismiss the value of using these skills in the classroom.

- Get your prop box out, the one you were asked to prepare in an earlier chapter. Now think of a topic that you are planning to teach in the near future. Close your eyes, reach into the box, and grab a prop at random. Now imagine how you would use this prop to teach the topic under consideration. Repeat this exercise.

- Seriously consider taking an Acting 101 course at your own school or at a nearby college or university. Working with a community theater also may be helpful. Use the buddy system—enroll with a friend!

- Develop a series of stretching and relaxing exercises that you will be able to do routinely and inconspicuously on a regular basis. You might have a set of first-thing-in-the-morning exercises that include stretching the jaw and neck muscles to prepare your articulators for fluent, extended speech. Add to your repertoire some quick arm, shoulder, and leg stretches to recharge your oxygen supply later in the school day.

- Use vocal exercises routinely to keep your vocal range broad and flexible. An easy one to do is "scaling from ah." To do this, just say "ah" in your normal tone, and then go up the scale from that point about eight or ten tones; go back to the initial "ah" and go down the scale about five or six tones. Most humans have a speaking range of twelve to sixteen tones, yet only use about half of that. By stretching your range via this kind of exercise, you will find that your voice is capable of much more expressiveness, making it easier to show your enthusiasm for your subject matter.

WELL BEFORE CLASS: PRACTICING WITH OTHERS

- Practice, practice, practice—it is supposed to make perfect. Practice some of your early lessons with an audience such as your family, friends, or colleagues. No actor would go on stage without having first rehearsed his or her lines and delivery—usually with an audience (albeit a small one—the director and fellow actors). Why should you? This is your career, so launch it successfully. Do all that you can do to succeed the first few times because nothing breeds success like success!

- Practice using emotion—body and voice—in your delivery. Do this with a party-type game that will be fun for everyone. Ham it way, way up; you can always dial it back! Place the following Shakespeare quotes on 3" × 5" cards and distribute them among the game players. Take a moment and learn your assigned lines so that you can maintain eye contact while delivering them. Crank up your emotion. *Hurl* these lines at each other! *Project* these lines. A few of these lines follow.

  > "Out dog! Out cur! Thou drivest me past the bounds of maidens' patience!" (*A Midsummer Night's Dream*, Act 3, Scene 2)

  > "Hence horrible villain! Or I'll spurn thine eyes like balls before me; I'll unhair thy head: Thou shalt be whipped with wire and stewed in brine, smarting in lingering pickle." (*The Tempest*, Act 1, Scene 2)

  > "Thou art a hodge-pudding, a bag of flax, a puffed man. Thou are old, cold, withered and of intolerable entrails." (*The Merry Wives of Windsor*, Act 4, Scene 5)

  > "Why you baldpated lying rascal. Show your knave's visage with a pox to you! Show your sheet biting fact and be hanged in the hour!" (*The Taming of the Shrew*, Act 4, Scene 1)

- Play a time-honored game of charades. In fact, play it lots of times. Select book or movie titles that contain opportunities to use gestures. This form of mime—acting without words—is great preparation for classroom deliveries.
- Play a game called Gibberish. In this game two players take turns giving a speech on a subject of the audience's choosing. One player orates in gibberish just like Andy Kaufman did playing Latka on *Taxi*. The other interprets in English. Exaggerate the gibberish and accompanying gestures. Have fun with this one. For instance, after the first player delivers gibberish for about a full minute, have the second player interpret it by saying just "Hello." The audience will be in stitches.
- Try Fortunately and Unfortunately. This is a game that makes you think on your feet and improvise—just like actors and teachers have to do every day. You and your friends sit in a circle and, moving clockwise, deliver one sentence at a time, each beginning with "Fortunately," or alternating between "Fortunately" and "Unfortunately." Don't just create each sentence; *deliver* it! Spice it up a bit by having the person delivering his or her sentence point to the next candidate. Keep the story going, often taking a humorous path, until a satisfactory conclusion occurs.
- Review in your own mind those annoying habits that your own previous teachers had. Get others in your group to do the same thing. Because everyone has a history of having had teachers, all in the group—teacher-bound or not—have something to contribute. Consider how these distracting teacher habits interfered with the message they were trying to deliver. After the group exercise, take an honest look at your own delivery—perhaps seeking input from others.

- Play the prop box game. Either use your own prop box or ask everyone in the group to bring a prop. Think of topics that you could teach in your class. Take turns at closing your eyes, reaching into the box, and grabbing a prop at random. Take sixty seconds to think how you will use the prop as the basis for teaching your topic. Teach the topic using the prop. Variations include having the audience select the prop that will be used or selecting the topic that will be taught.
- Get together with a few colleagues and take turns teaching a brief lecture to each other on a topic representing your subject area. Five-minute-or-so presentations should be enough. Critique each other's presentation—not for what the presenters did, but for how they could have used one or more of the acting lessons in this text. Brainstorm possibilities. Start off your critique with, "Have you considered using . . ." or "I wonder how effective it would have been if you had . . ."
- With colleagues discuss the often-delivered advice to new teachers, "Be yourself." Now that you have read this text, do you find this advice useful? If so, why? If not, why not?
- Gather a small collection of children's books—especially those with pictures. The pictures suggest (and only that—suggest) the feelings that the characters in the book are experiencing. With a group of friends or colleagues, take turns reading the same passages out of these books. Each person should try to deliver the reading with his or her own interpretation of these feelings. Pay attention to the variety of interpretations. You might get some ideas—new, clever, innovative, and maybe even daring.
- Take turns being a puppeteer. Use a finger puppet, hand puppet, or puppet on strings as your "special friend." This friend could pretend to be a recognized expert on such and such topic. Practice carrying on a conversation with your friend about a topic you might teach that typically has more than one point of view. Issues such as invasion of privacy, individual rights, and academic freedom all guarantee that the interaction could get heated! Carry on the conversation so that your audience of friends, family, and colleagues (later to be your students) can overhear you. Try being a ventriloquist if you want. Take turns being the puppeteer.

Have you noticed that most, if not all, of these learning exercises that are designed to loosen you up are fun to do? After all, learning is fun(damental)! They are especially fun to do when you can do them with others. When practicing these fun exercises, you do them with family, friends, and colleagues. When you actually use what you have practiced in the classroom, the benefit of these exercises, once again, can be fun—fun for you and fun for your students. These experiences will help make your teaching more enjoyable for you and for your students.

JUST BEFORE CLASS BEGINS

- Pause for a moment to prepare emotionally for entering the classroom (Lowman 1984). In that moment, clear your mind of extraneous issues, review the plan for this day's lesson, and recommit yourself to the challenge of the teaching–learning process. That sort of mental preparation is exactly what most great actors do just before taking the stage. It is a habit that transfers well to the theater of the classroom.

- Develop a number of routine relaxation techniques that can be used before a lecture (e.g., stand up in your office, close your eyes, focus on your toes, and work though your entire body, slowly tensing, releasing, and wiggling each part of your body).
- Practice deep breathing. When people are nervous, they tend to take shallow breaths. The result, decreased oxygen, makes you light headed, jittery, and clammy. Breathing deeply tells your body—and those in the audience—that everything is OK.
- Stand with your feet about six inches apart, arms hanging by your sides and fingers unclenched. Gently shake each part of your body, starting with your hand and then moving to your arms, shoulders, torso, and legs. Concentrate on shaking out the tension.
- Rotate your shoulders forward and then backward. Rotate your head slowly clockwise and then counterclockwise.
- Mentally rehearse the successful delivery of your lecture—imagine yourself at the front of the classroom, speaking fluently and effectively and responding to students' questions.
- Once you feel relaxed, think positive thoughts about yourself as a teacher—"I am an effective teacher," "I am a confident speaker," "I am a confident teacher," "I know the subject matter well." This is a form of positive imaging—athletes, stand-up comics, and motivational speakers all do it.

ONCE CLASS BEGINS

- Arrive at class early and prepare your materials on the desk or podium. Check the equipment, lights, and any other resources vital to the presentation. Remove any distractions that might work against you.
- If all seems in order, chitchat with those who arrive early. It will help relax them and you.
- Don't attempt to speak or lecture for the entire class.
- Know that your feelings of anxiety and tension are not as noticeable to the audience as they are to you.
- Allow yourself the time to pause—locate needed material, glance at notes, and get your thoughts together. This is the equivalent of providing yourself that pedagogically sound concept of "wait time."
- Remember, even the best presenters make mistakes. The world will not stop spinning—we guarantee it. If you pick up and continue, so will the students.
- Avoid repeated throat clearing. Not only is it often perceived as a sign of nervousness, but it also is both distracting and ineffective. When one clears the throat, the two vocal folds are brought together with very high impact.

This can harm the vocal folds if continued repeatedly. Instead, try swallowing or sipping water to help remove the excess mucus in your throat.

- If your throat feels dry during class, sip the water again. Do *not* sip coffee. The caffeine in the coffee actually dries out the vocal folds, making you less able to speak expressively. Water, on the other hand, is the tonic that restores a healthy voice.
- Move out from behind the desk or podium. Work the crowd.

SUMMARY

Teaching is harder than it looks! Don't let anyone tell you otherwise. Stepping across that classroom threshold takes courage. And to take this action as a professional, it also requires knowledge, preparation, and practice. Perhaps the Boy Scouts say it best when they tell their members to "be prepared." This is good advice for all of us to follow.

CHAPTER

Classroom Management

Discipline is not a nasty word.

—Pat Riley

INTRODUCTION

How do acting skills and classroom management fit together? It would not be surprising if, while you were reading previous chapters, you had already given some thought to how acting skills might contribute to more effective classroom management. With teaching being such a demanding profession, and discipline being part of that demand, it is comforting to know that effective use of acting skills can benefit *both* instruction and classroom management. In this chapter we offer several specific applications of how acting skills can contribute to more effective classroom discipline.

Acting skills can be used to engage students and, hence, decrease the likelihood that discipline problems will occur in the first place. And acting skills can be used to handle discipline problems when and if they occur.

PUTTING ON AN ACT

One of the joys of teaching children is watching them do what they naturally do. Parents know this, too. Sometimes what they do is seen by teachers as hindering their teaching. Students can be so exuberant that they seem annoying and frustrating, moving teachers to question, "Why am I here?" But what students do also can be seen as cute, funny, and, at times, downright hysterical. Their hormones are running their lives. They are forming, breaking, and reforming alliances. They are trying to "save face," and when academic challenges are overwhelming, they are thinking up and trying to deliver effective excuses. When they find themselves caught with their "hand in the cookie jar," and being inexperienced at being especially clever, their efforts are often transparent to teachers.

Photo 14.1
Teaching Classroom Management with "Friends"!

For instance, in a preschool class observed by one of the authors, a four-year-old boy punched the little girl sitting next to him during their drawing time. It was only a four-year-old punch, so no real harm was done. But the teacher, wanting to keep order, spoke sternly to him, saying, "Little boys don't punch little girls." With a completely dumbfounded and confused look, the boy responded, "But I just did." On one level, his comment was a funny revelation of his naïve sense that what the teacher said had to be wrong because his own actions had contradicted her words. Tempting as it would have been to smile at this confusion in a youngster still learning word usage, smiling would have, unfortunately, suggested a tolerance for "talking back" that could have damaged classroom decorum in the long run.

Teachers should respond to discipline infractions as if they have "seen it all." This is relatively easy for seasoned teachers because they have, in fact, seen it all—or at least most of it. For new teachers, the task might be a bit more difficult. At any rate, sometimes teachers need to *act* in a stern manner, *act* in a disapproving manner, *act* in a disappointed manner, and, for some, even *act* in a mean manner when inside themselves they are resisting all temptation to break out in raucous laughter. Experienced teachers know that giving in to this temptation actually may reinforce the undesired student behavior. So as effective disciplinarians, teachers hold in their laughter, control their temptation to smile, and resist sending even the hint of a message that says, "I really thought what you did was cute."

In Jones's *Tools of Teaching* (2000) discipline model, teachers are encouraged to practice their *act*—practice their act of looking bored when confronting a misbehaving student. Teachers are taught to avoid even having the corners of their mouths curl up at the last moment, which signals that, in reality, "I found what you were doing funny." When some students' misbehaviors are just so cute that it is almost impossible to resist smiling at them, Jones instructs teachers to look not directly in the students' eyes but at a point on the forehead just above the students' eyes.

This advice is not all that different from that given to actors who when delivering their lines in a comedic situation must resist the temptation to laugh. Harvey Korman and Tim Conway had such trouble keeping a straight face when working with one another on the *Carol Burnett Show* that their hysterical outtakes have been made into a television special. Take after take was required to complete the scene. Teachers do not have time for take after take.

ANIMATION IN VOICE

Animation in voice includes, among other characteristics, pitch, volume, and rate. When it comes to classroom management, if calmness signals strength (and it does!), then a teacher's high pitch, combined with loud volume (i.e., screaming) and rapid rate, becomes a scream and signals weakness. Although more purposefully varied use of pitch, rate, and volume conveys teacher enthusiasm, misuse can convey a teacher out of control, a teacher "losing it," or a teacher who has let students get under his or her skin.

A higher-than-necessary volume in voice when disciplining a student ignores the sound pedagogical truism, "praise in public, chastise in private." A teacher's voice being too loud also is likely to result in distracting an entire class away from its productive work to become, instead, a "peanut gallery" of observers watching the teacher's discipline efforts. On the other hand, a quieter volume (along with a conversational rate and pitch), combined with proximity control, is likely to keep discipline efforts focused on the one misbehaving student—where it should be.

Another successful classroom-management tool, especially one that can be used to get the attention of students whose attention might be wandering, is to lower one's volume. It is amazing how a reduction in a speaker's volume can cause listeners to lean forward and listen more carefully.

Sometimes order and discipline are enhanced by using no voice at all. As the saying suggests, "It takes two to tango," so if only one person is talking (i.e., the student), there can be no "tangoing!" Refusing to verbally "tango" with a student often can diffuse a discipline problem. The Jones discipline model (described a bit later) has teachers doing 80 percent of their disciplining with their mouths closed.

Another example of not using one's voice to establish classroom management is the use of signals that convey a pre-explained message. One faculty member we know purchased a musical triangle and uses it to convey, among other things, that it is time to get ready for lunch, time to return to seats following group work, or time to move on to the next portion of the exam. How much more pleasant it is for students to hear a chime from a musical triangle than to hear a teacher's voice trying to scream above the din of the classroom. Many teachers use the blinking of classroom lights as a less intrusive signal for indicating a change in activity or a request to quiet down. In the theater, the audience is called back to the performance by dimmed lights or chimes and not by someone screaming, "Let's get back to our seats!"

ANIMATION IN BODY

Another acting-related skill that is effective in establishing and maintaining classroom management is animation in body, or actually, *lack* of animation in body. Jones, in his books *Positive Classroom Discipline* (1987) and *Tools for Teaching* (2000), stresses the value of remaining totally inanimate. He recommends that teachers practice, and then deliver, their best "boy, am I absolutely bored" look in response to students who are misbehaving. It takes the wind right out of their sails.

He recommends that teachers think of their dirty laundry or some other boring chore, make slow (but deliberate) turns in the direction of the perpetrator, take two deep breaths before saying anything (thus not appearing startled), and hang their hands and arms limp at their sides (not crossed in front of their chests or provocatively set on their hips). The nonverbal message to the student is clear, "Your antics are unimpressive. Ho, hum. Are you through yet?"

Jones (1987, 2000) describes a hierarchical series of limit-setting teacher behaviors for students who range from what he calls "penny-ante gamblers" to "high-rollers." All involve little or no animation on the part of the teacher. A minimum of talking, too, is suggested. Jones's limit-setting behaviors, in order of seriousness, all involve teachers swinging into *inaction*.

Whether lecturing or moving about the room helping students, when a teacher spots a misbehaving student, immediate action (or inaction) is warranted. Jones (1987) suggests using, among other tactics, implementing "The Look," "Moving in," and "Palms and Prompt."

The Look

Turn around fully, in a regal fashion, and face the disruptive student.

Make good eye contact.

Relax (two relaxing breaths).

Say the student's first name loud enough to be heard.

Relax (two relaxing breaths).

Wait (look unimpressed, even bored). (See Photo 14.2, "Expressions for Classroom Management." This provides time for the student to decide to behave.)

Moving In (if required)

Same as the look, but now walk (slowly and deliberately) to the edge of the student's desk, with your legs just touching the desk.

Relax (two relaxing breaths).

Wait, and maintain eye contact (look bored—really bored).

When student returns to the designated task for at least fifteen seconds, lean over and offer a sincere "Thank you."

Move out—return to where you were originally in the room.

Turn and watch the student (two relaxing breaths).

Palms and Prompt (if required)

Same as for the look and the moving in, but now place palms flat on the student's desk. In doing so, the teacher now has even closer eye contact with the student.

Relax (two relaxing breaths).

Prompt the student by telling him or her exactly what you want to be done.

Wait, and maintain eye contact (look bored—really, really bored).

When the student returns to the designated task for at least fifteen seconds, lean over and offer a sincere "Thank you."

Move out—return to where you were originally in the room.

Turn and watch the student (two relaxing breaths).

Although some of these behaviors may seem, at first, to be unnatural, the more a teacher practices these actions (e.g., looking bored, turning in a regal fashion), the more genuine they will appear to students. After all, isn't this exactly what an actor or actress must do when asked to play a challenging role—practice until his or her actions become believable to an audience?

The teacher's calm and business-like manner (at least it should appear that way on the outside) denies students the attention they are craving through such misbehavior (Dinkmeyer, McKay, and Dinkmeyer Jr. 1980). Calmness displays confidence; willingness to take the time to deal with the problem reveals commitment; proximity reinforces intensity. These three ingredients, heightened through successful acting, almost guarantee results.

The power of using nonverbal messages needs to be stressed. These behaviors can be a nonoffensive (safe) means of reminding others who it is that possesses greater power and higher status. Nonverbal behaviors "associated with dominance include eye contact (even staring), relaxed but not slumped posture, expressive and expansive gestures, touch initiation, classic clothing and personal artifacts,

Photo 14.2
Expressions for Classroom Management

expansive use of space, and poised, straightforward posture" (Andersen 1986, 48). See Photo 14.2, "Expressions for Classroom Management." More experienced teachers use these dominance-expressive behaviors; less experienced teachers tend to behave in nonverbally submissive ways. These two sets of behaviors convey two distinct images. It takes just a moment or so for students to note the difference. By the way, even a smile goes a long way toward maintaining classroom management. Teachers need to become skilled in *performing* these several looks.

Although the emphasis in the previous paragraph is on stopping inappropriate behavior, nonverbal behaviors can also be used to start or encourage appropriate behavior. Smiling, eye contact, nodding, and supportive gesturing—at the right moment—are among the nonverbal responses teachers can offer that are likely to heighten desired student interaction. These behaviors signal that the teacher is interested in what the student is saying. Stimulating student interaction can be further encouraged by another example of teacher inaction—using a pause. Ten to fifteen seconds of a well-placed pause can do wonders to stimulate participation.

CLASSROOM SPACE

One of the authors had a teacher named Brother Shad—at least that is what everyone called him. He was a very old English teacher who never got up from his desk. Students thought, because of his movement limitations about the room, that they, especially those in the back of the room, would be able to get away with murder. Wrong! Brother Shad had lined the sides and back of his room with photographs of past classes, allowing students' movements and antics to be clearly reflected in the mirror-like glass covering the photographs. He could see all. He, like any good actor or teacher, had planned his use of space carefully! He had done his work "behind the scenes."

A recognized ingredient of successful classroom management is possessing "with-itness," as Kounin (1970) calls it. Being "with-it" means knowing what is going on at all times, knowing who is doing what, when, and where. Effective use of classroom space, one of our acting/teaching skills, can help teachers be "with-it."

Proxemics, a topic discussed in the chapter on classroom space, has its classroom-management equivalent—proximity control. It is easy to understand that students are less likely to misbehave when a teacher is standing close to them. It should be of no surprise to anyone that mischief-makers try to keep as much distance as possible between themselves and their teachers. Effective use of classroom space can thwart such students

A teacher's presence can be made known to students who are seated farthest away even when it is inconvenient, or even impossible, to be physically next to them. This can be done by carrying on some sort of running "joke" or good-hearted bantering with students seated in the back rows. Best done before class or just as class starts, such behaviors demonstrate that the teacher is tuned in ("with-it") to the far reaches of the classroom. In a raised lecture hall, the professor might ask, "Just checking, is the oxygen too thin that high up?" While announcing the assignment for tomorrow, the teacher might stop partway through and, as if on a soundstage, ask for sound check: "Am I coming through loud and clear back there?"

Creative use of classroom space in the form of rearranging student desks to reduce the distance between a teacher and students or to create more accessible paths or aisles can contribute to more effective classroom management. But effective use of classroom space is not the only acting/teaching skill relevant to classroom management.

HUMOR

"Attentive students will engage in fewer discipline problems." To that end, classroom management is enhanced by teachers making regular and effective use of the various acting skills (including humor) presented in this text to keep students engaged. On an even more practical note, consider the title of Lundberg and Thurston's (2002) *If They're Laughing, They Just Might Be Listening*. Getting students to listen, alone, supports the use of teacher humor.

When humor is used as a supplement to, and not a substitute for, teaching, its most positive benefits to classroom management come forth. Effective use of humor reinforces the teacher's superior position in the classroom. Psychologists recognize that it is "the superior that most often uses humor in communication with the inferior" (Vizmuller 1980, 266). In this context, the words "superior" and "inferior" are not derogatory terms; they simply specify status or position.

A recognition by the students of a teacher's higher status enables that teacher to use French and Raven's (1960) legitimate power (authority granted someone because of their position) more effectively. Students, too, recognize the confidence that accompanies a teacher's successful use of humor. The belief is that only a confident, in-control teacher would risk using humor. Effective use of humor also enhances the teacher's use of French and Raven's (1960) expert power (authority granted someone because of their knowledge or skill level) more effectively. The perception is that only competent people are brave enough to use humor.

In addition to these general principles of humor, there are endless examples of specific applications of humor that can affect classroom discipline. A subject-matter–related riddle, funny story, or pun seems to have the power to capture a learner's attention regardless of age, gender, grade level, or subject. By being attentive, the student is behaving.

For instance, a riddle can initiate some healthy competition to be the first (individual or group) to figure it out. Directed competition is healthy; it is productive. It can channel, in a constructive way, students' need to compete. The funny story or pun can create a shared experience. People sharing a common experience are more likely to feel part of a group and, as a result, less likely to do something to damage it, that is, misbehave.

Almost all research on classroom management recommends that rules be established. After all, it is unreasonable to expect students to follow the rules if they do not know the rules. Normally, presenting the classroom rules should occur at the beginning of the school year. Yet imagine the possible demoralizing effect on students when their first introduction to a new teacher and subject matter is "Here are the rules that you are expected to follow!"

More creative teachers can use humor to introduce both "teacher pet peeves" and "classroom rules." A teacher could introduce his or her "Top 10 Peeves" in the same way that David Letterman announces his trademark top-ten lists. One could insert a few humorous peeves in the list such as "My number 8 pet peeve is when a student parks his Ferrari in my parking spot." Note that this would be even funnier if the teacher had a classroom full of fourth graders. A teacher might want to ask students to create a list of their "Top 10 Peeves," too.

Classroom rules themselves can be introduced with a bit of humor. For instance, "Students will raise their hand and be acknowledged before speaking, or they will receive three swats with a wet noodle." Or the warning "Students should walk to and from lunch" could have an ending such as "or they will have to . . ." (Add your own funny ending!) The result of these introductions to "peeves" and "rules" will be laughter. Gee, what a great first experience to have in school!

HUMOR WITH "DOWN-UNDER" SLANT

Humor can be an excellent tool for diffusing tense situations. This works best at the onset of a possible discipline problem. This is why teachers need to be ever alert in order to handle "little fires" before they have a chance to grow into "raging infernos."

A suggestion of how humor could be used to diffuse a problem comes from Bill Rogers, a discipline guru from down under in Australia. Say you are teaching, and students are working at a task in their seats or at their lab tables. Out of the blue, Sam hollers, "Oh, sh--!" Obviously, something happened that upset Sam. There are many ways a teacher could respond. Some ways are likely to result in the problem escalating, whereas other ways are likely to diffuse the problem.

A favorite thing of one of the authors to blurt out in times of frustration is "Oh, ka gee gee beads!" "Ka gee gee beads" is a term that the author created many years ago, delivered in the context of telling his son and daughter (and occasionally students), "You are full of Ka gee gee beads!" No one, including the author, ever knew exactly what "Ka gee gee beads" were, but everyone did seem to know what was meant when a "Ka gee gee beads" message was sent. Readers are welcome to use this relatively meaningless expletive. Assuming that the teacher knows Sam and knows that this unacceptable word just "slipped out," Rogers suggests responding by saying (while hamming it up with exaggerated body motions), "Where? Where? Oh my! Where?" while, at the same time, looking around the floor area and lifting one's feet as if to avoid stepping in it. This might be followed by the teacher *acting* as if he or she just realized that there really was no doodoo on the floor. The teacher then might say, "Thank goodness there is no smelly mess on the floor to clean up; it was just Sam upset enough to spout forth scatological expletives." At this point everyone is attentive. At this point the teacher has a "teaching moment" on the word *scatological* as well as a chance to teach the students to handle the temptation to utter an unacceptable expletive. The teacher might end by saying, "Thank you, Sam. We have all learned a new vocabulary word. In the future, if you are really upset and feel the need to blurt out something, try 'Oh scatology!'"

SUSPENSE AND SURPRISE

Suspense and surprise are acting skills that can contribute directly to improved classroom management. Go out of your way to learn good things about your students: their work in other classes, family, part-time jobs, efforts and accomplishments in sports, and participation in extracurricular activities, for instance. Actually, this is not very difficult to do and is not time-consuming either. Just keep your eyes and ears open. Try talking with fellow faculty; try reading the school newspaper.

Armed with a knowledge of these "good" things, set about to surprise students by "dropping" the news when they least expect it. At the beginning of your class, you could say, "Joe, looks like you really had quite a soccer game on Saturday"; "Wendy, that was a creative way in which you helped organize the food drive for the homeless shelter"; or "Bill, how does it feel to be the only one to get a perfect paper in Mr. Sands' class?" Don't dwell on any one item. That's not the point. Don't give students the time to think how you know what you know. Just "drop" the bit of surprise information, and go on with the scheduled lesson.

The effect of delivering this unexpected (surprising) information is twofold (Tauber 1999). First, it conveys to your students that you are tuned into their lives beyond merely what they are doing in your class. This helps teachers develop what French and Raven (1960) call referent power—a sense of common purpose, one person identifying with another. Two, it keeps students "on their toes" as they wonder *how* you seem to know so much about them. They start to think that if you know this information, maybe you are also in a position to know when they might be trying to get away with something. You come off as being someone who must have eyes and ears everywhere.

USING ACTIONS TO CONVEY EXPECTATIONS

As noted earlier, the three most important words in education are expectations, expectations, expectations! When teachers convey positive expectations *and* when students perceive these positive expectations, discipline problems are lessened. On the contrary, when students perceive negative expectations being sent their way, they are likely to fulfill those expectations and trouble often arises.

The expectations, or self-fulfilling prophecy, process goes like this:

- Teachers form expectations.
- Teachers act on those expectations conveying what level of *achievement* and *behavior* is expected from each child.
- Teachers keep treating students in a differential manner over a period of time.
- Eventually students fulfill the teachers' high or low expectations.

The bottom line is that teachers tend to get what they expect! Like it or not, some children are naturally the recipients of more positive teacher expectations.

When classroom teachers are asked, "How many think that you are relatively good judges of character?" most hands are raised. And when they are asked, "How many of you like to be wrong?" no hands are raised. The impact of this is that teachers often make judgments (i.e., form expectations) about students' behavior and achievement based on factors such as race, gender, family affluence, given name, eye color, height, attractiveness, and so on and then seek evidence to justify those expectations. Therefore, because first impressions often are lasting impressions, expectations—positive or negative—tend to stick!

How do acting skills impact expectations? Acting skills impact expectations because teachers must *act* in a way to convey those expectations. Teachers who are knowledgeable of how the expectations process works can control how they *act* toward children. They can *act* in a way that conveys positive expectations to a student even if in their hearts they may not hold high expectations for that student. Plus, if they *act* convincingly, they can get the student (and perhaps themselves) to believe these positive expectations.

As a case in point, a student for whom one of the authors held low expectations asked for help. By acting as if holding high expectations of her (turning to face her while responding, looking directly in her eyes, and verbally focusing on her strengths), the teacher conveyed positive expectations that definitely enhanced the student's self-esteem. How do we know that these teacher actions convey positive expectations? We know because these are exactly the teacher actions that we engage in with students for whom we do hold high expectations!

"THANKS, I'D APPRECIATE THAT"

One special classroom-discipline technique involves the teacher *acting* as if she believes her request will be honored. It goes something like this: A journalism teacher wants Lisa to help return all of the newspapers and magazines strewn about the room to their rightful place on the shelves. Or an elementary teacher wants David to empty the overflowing pencil sharpener. How does the teacher get the students to carry out her requests? She simply *acts* as if the students will do what she has asked them to do. Her *actions* include both words and body language. She says, "Lisa, would you help me by returning the newspapers and magazines to their rightful place on the shelves?" The teacher then immediately says, "Thanks, I'd appreciate that. It would be a big help." She continues her *act* by turning and walking away, showing she trusts that Lisa will respond positively. For the other child, the teacher says, "David, would you empty the overflowing pencil sharpener? That would save me a lot of time." Once again, she follows her request by saying, "Thanks, I'd appreciate it," and then she turns and walks away. It is hard for students to resist doing what they have been asked to do, especially when the teacher has already thanked them for doing it!

MUSIC TO SOOTHE THE SAVAGE BREAST

Sometimes music—certainly a performing art—should be in the forefront as in a musical, rock band, or military marching band. Sometimes, however, music works best in the background; it's there, but not the major focus. In this situation we often find music playing softly in the background. We hear it (though most of the time, we don't really hear it consciously) in a department store, in a grocery store, or in a mall. It is there for a purpose. "Music has charms to soothe the savage breast, to soften rocks, or bend a knotted oak" (W. Congreve, *The Mourning Bride*, Act 1, Scene 1) in all of us. Music has a calming effect. It can lower our stress and anxiety levels.

Schools can use music to accomplish the same goal with *both* students and teachers. Soothing background music (but not capable of putting people to sleep) can be played in the cafeteria, in the library, and in the hallways during class changes. It also can be played in classrooms during seatwork, lab exercises, and transitions between activities and as signals for starting and ending tasks. If music can help calm harried shoppers in a mall during a holiday, it has a good chance of calming students and, hence, improving classroom management.

Consider compiling your own CD of songs—perhaps with input from students. After all, both you and the students will be doing the listening. With today's inexpensive technology, this task has never been easier. Although it may date the authors, some of our personal favorites include "Be True to Your School" (The Beach Boys), "We Are Family" (Sister Sledge), "Yakety Yak" (The Coasters), "Don't Worry Be Happy" (Bobby McFerrin), and—just once in awhile to keep the kids on their toes—"Happy Trails" (Dale Evans). Other types of music can work just as well. Consider playing some classical music selections, songs from *Mister Rogers' Neighborhood* (i.e., "Won't You Be My Neighbor?" "You Are Special," and "I'm Proud of You"), and—well, the list is endless!

SUMMARY

The common ingredient in all acting skills that can contribute to classroom management is the skills' impact on perceived teacher enthusiasm, which, in turn, secures students' attention and holds their interest. A paper bag (*use of props*)—containing something—that the teacher has placed in a prominent location and the *suspense* it elicits can grab students' attention that might otherwise be directed elsewhere. Finding the mathematics teacher dressed in a short-order cook's outfit (*role-playing*), as Jamie Escalante did in *Stand and Deliver*, would hold most students' interest that might otherwise have been misdirected.

A teacher's *animation in voice* (e.g., even just a whisper) can have significant attention-getting power, possibly diverting students' temptation to chitchat with a neighbor and thus cause a disturbance. Moving the front of the room to the back, through the simple operation of writing on the "back" (now front) chalkboard, makes surprising use of *classroom space*. Students hiding in the back are now right there in the front. Displaying an editorial cartoon (i.e., *humor*) that relates to the day's lecture can silently engage an entire class that just moments before had its attention diverted in a million other directions. And so go the many examples that can be offered.

Teachers who incorporate acting skills into their teaching will be better able to secure students' attention and maintain their interest. Plain and simple— attentive, interested, and engaged students are less likely to misbehave.

SEARCH FOR MORE ON CLASSROOM MANAGEMENT

An Education Resources Information Center (http://www.eric.ed.gov/) search for the term "classroom management" and at least one other acting-lessons term reveals a number of citations. All of them, because they are announced in ERIC, have applications to education settings.

An ERIC search for the term "classroom management" with a variety of acting-lessons terms reveals the following number of citations: "classroom management" plus "role-playing": 4,730; plus "humor": 356; plus "props": 1,350; plus "suspense and surprise": 19; plus "suspense" (alone): 493; plus "surprise" (alone): 3,370; plus "teacher voice" (animation in voice): 245; plus "teacher movement" (animation in body): 104; plus "space utilization": 123; "plus "proxemics": 211; and plus "teacher enthusiasm": 84.

In addition to exploring ERIC, you should consider searching other databases as well for books, articles, and programs related to the effective use of humor in the classroom. You also are encouraged to search the Web using many of the ERIC descriptors from the previous paragraph.

CHAPTER

Enthusiastic Teaching: A Conversation with Friends

The mind is a fire to be ignited, not a vessel to be filled.

—Plutarch

INTRODUCTION

In the course of preparing this text, we have had occasion to chat with many other educators who share an appreciation for the value of acting lessons for teachers. Most not only share that perspective, but also have acted on it by writing on the topic, developing related teacher workshops, presenting conference papers, or serving as mentors. Each indicated such enthusiasm for this work that we asked if they would like to share some of their thoughts with our readers.

What follows is a selection of comments, observations, and experiences we received as a result of this invitation. Consider this an opportunity to "eavesdrop" on a conversation among experienced, enthusiastic educators who are dedicated to enhancing the teaching–learning experience for all of us who love the classroom.

Hopefully by now you have had your appetite whetted regarding the use of performance skills in the classroom. You have learned that using such skills is as essential to students' learning as is faculty competence in subject matter. Further, you understand that acting lessons used in the classroom do not undermine a teacher's professionalism; rather, they enhance it. You want to learn still more. Here is your chance.

FRIENDS WHO SHARE OUR ENTHUSIASM

We believe that what we have offered will help faculty build both the confidence and the competence to use performance skills more effectively in their teaching. But we also believe that no two authors and no single text can present it all.

Each author below was asked to write a brief essay about the parallel between acting and teaching. What they wrote specifically was their decision.

KAREN JOY AGNE
SUNY Plattsburgh

In my capacity as an educator, experience has allowed me to view the teaching–learning process from two perspectives. First, eighteen years as teacher of elementary children and director of gifted programs, a responsibility I have continued to this day, taught what it takes to reach young minds. This, followed by twenty years as an educator/trainer of teachers, has allowed me extensive observation of preservice and in-service teachers in the field. This perspective has allowed me to detect the most common deficits in beginning and/or less effective teachers. High on the list is personal presence.

At some point in my work with teachers I concluded that the most useful thing I could offer was lessons in acting. A good teacher wears many hats and wields many techniques, but all great teachers are performing artists. Acting is a natural for educators; drama, a form of critical pedagogy. Teachers, to be exceptionally effective, use props, pretend, change their voices, their expressions, their movements, their moods; indeed, they become the lesson. Teaching in role is a "must do" for the educator who aspires to perfection. Teachers could be taught how to develop historic or literary characters into dynamic, real, live personalities. Don't just teach physics. Become Einstein to explain physics.

In my two-week intensive graduate education course, Acting for Teachers, I invite students to complete two tasks. First, they must read or tell a story, during which "performance" they must use several props, change their voice and facial expressions to depict varied characters in their story, and be in costume. Next, after characterization write-ups, which include elements of name, occupation, theme, passion, foible, virtue, primary needs and primary activities, each student must then perform in the role of his character teaching a lesson. Students are required to perform on stage in full costume with voice change, special walk or movement, quirk, and props for a minimum of fifteen minutes per performance.

An amazing transformation occurs for most students of this course. In two weeks, or fifty-five to sixty intensive hours' time, introverted people become enthusiastic, self-confident performers. Teachers suddenly exude a "personal presence" which was heretofore absent from their demeanor. Students spend the first week participating in a multitude of impromptu theater games. During this time they get to know each other very quickly, learning to excel, mess up, laugh, trust, and play comfortably together. Only after this group's "coming together" occurs can they each successfully perform for each other. The intensive "group sync" is critical for the performance skills to become internalized. This is, finally, a happy, fun, and most popular course. Students commonly return, write, or e-mail to announce that they presented their performance to their own students with raving success and that they now realize the importance of acting in the classroom.

Acting has a powerful effect on the teacher and the learner. Teaching in role is not only a wonderful technique for making learning more in-depth for students, but it also has the distinct advantage of being adaptable to any subject area or age level of teaching. For example, I recall a wonderful performance by a local kindergarten teacher who became Mother Goose. Looking beautiful in her full skirts, apron, and bonnet, she carried her goose in a basket, the very real-looking goose being a perfectly constructed hand puppet, which interrupted to correct her each time she misquoted a rhyme. One could easily imagine how effectively this presentation would work for five-year-olds. Other popular examples include Bill Nye the Science Guy and Steve Irwin, the Crocodile Hunter, for chemistry and biology, as well as Marie Curie. Some characters portrayed for teaching history have included Ben Franklin, Henry Ford, Marie Antoinette, and even Johnny Appleseed. Many Shakespeare characters have also come to life in my course over the years. Einstein, of course, is a favorite for physics and math.

The use of acting in the classroom is unlimited in range of characterization. I have observed germs and amoebas doing their thing, as well as DNA molecules. My students and I deem acting to be perhaps the most versatile teaching technique available to the good teacher who seeks to become a great teacher.

LINC FISCH
Educational Consultant; Lexington, Kentucky

It was turning into a rotten morning. I had already trimmed my workshop, "The Classroom as a Dramatic Arena" (a.k.a. Confessions of a Closet Thespian), by over 25 percent in order to fit the conference format. I was told to expect an audience of about ninety; more than double that number showed up. The previous presenter ran overtime, robbing me of fifteen precious minutes of flextime and seriously impinging on my reserve for responding to participants' concerns. I couldn't exceed my time—lunch in a nearby building immediately followed the session, and it was raining like crazy. I had to seriously compress the Q-and-A segment. But how?

Somehow, inspiration struck. Perhaps Stanislavsky called from a century ago: "Improvise!" With about twenty minutes left in the session, I donned the bright red devil's advocate shirt that I hold back for dire emergencies. I proposed that the audience and I switch roles for a few minutes: I would ask the questions, and *they* would respond as though they collectively had been conducting the workshop. A palpable surge of interest seemed to spread through the room.

My first volley was piercing: "Why should I have to *pander* to students? I'm here to *teach*. The student is here to *learn*. We each have our responsibilities." (Note that a devil's advocate can get to the crux of matters more quickly and can be more provocative than usually polite audience members.) Instantly, several participants pounced on me: It's not pandering; it's *appealing* to them. You have to hold their attention in order to communicate with them. It's just plain sensible to use effective communication techniques. Only a little more effort is needed to accomplish a lot more. Teaching is more than just spewing out words for students to write in notebooks. Our students have become conditioned to fast-paced and lively presentations.

Ever the curmudgeon, I seized an opportunity to launch a second salvo: "You want me to *entertain* students? If they want inane comedy, they can watch Leno.

My role is to *teach*, not *entertain*." The return barrage intensified: You're equating good communication with entertainment; it's not. And it's not comedy, either. Consider things only because they enhance learning goals. Why wouldn't you want to use any techniques you can to promote learning?

Participants were still trying to gain the floor when I switched to a different tack: "The fact of the matter is that I don't have *time* for all that non-, er, stuff. I've got to *cover material*." They jumped on that, too: A lot of good ideas that actors employ aren't even seen on the stage—like voice control and warming up and sequencing scenes. What good is covering material if students don't comprehend? Is "covering material" what you should be doing? Shouldn't you be generating learning in students?

Finally, I resorted to self-effacement: "I hear what you're saying, but *I* couldn't do that. You can come in here and play the hotdog for an hour or so, but that's just not *me*." They didn't let up: It's not playing a hotdog—it's using good techniques to improve communication. A lot of what you can do is just simple, ordinary, sensible activity—like preparing your voice. Some of it is just considering your stage presence and how you might easily improve it. You don't have to do everything we talked about; you can select what fits a particular situation; you can adapt these ideas to your personal style and comfort level.

Thus, in a matter of less than ten minutes, I dealt with the major concerns many teachers have about transferring and applying ideas from the theater to the classroom. Even more important, the participants themselves generated the responses to these concerns and had ownership of them. And responses coming spontaneously from peers likely were more acceptable and less tainted than stock remedies offered by a traveling medicine man.

We now were about ten minutes from closure, and I sensed a slight stirring in the room. I brought the Q & A period to an abrupt end by the ringing of a telephone (another handy rabbit to pull out when necessary). I answered loudly so that all could hear: "Hello. Hey, Chef. Yes, I know lunch begins in twenty minutes. I know I have to finish by 11:50. But my concluding scene is the most important part of the entire session, and I can do it quickly. Just give me eight minutes and I'll have them on their way. Thanks, Chef. I appreciate your concern and your understanding."

I kept my promise to the mythical chef, and not a person left the room before 11:50! You see, a few lessons learned from Life upon the Wicked Stage—when used wisely, strategically, appropriately, and creatively—can enhance teaching immensely. Go for it as much as your persona can accommodate!

ALAN C. FRIEDMAN
Southwestern Illinois College

Teachers can improve the quality of their teaching by using acting skills. They repeatedly enter classrooms, face audiences, and must capture and maintain student attention, relying, like actors, on their voices, bodies, and emotions to do so. Like it or not, teachers face students used to MTV videos and movies with dazzling special effects. Teachers must fight fire with fire, making their teaching captivating, interesting, and entertaining. Actors, for 2000 years, have developed a body of techniques for capturing and maintaining audience interest. Teachers should become aware of, and adept in, some of these skills.

Acting and teaching should be physical as well as vocal. Actors vary their facial expressions, gestures, and movements to physicalize the ideas they express. Many teachers see their job as the transmission of words only and ignore the potential for physical action to animate their ideas. Walk down any hall in any college and you'll see teachers draped over their lecterns. You rarely see a teacher moving amongst his or her students, painting pictures through gestures, or standing on a chair, for example, to illustrate narrator omniscience in a literature class.

One reason many teachers cling to their lecterns is that they have stage fright when they perform. Like all actors, teachers need to learn relaxation techniques to stay loose in front of their students. Most lists of man's greatest fears put public speaking at or near the top. How are teachers exempt from stage fright? They are not. Opening day of classes is just as scary for teachers as opening night is for actors. Actors know they get stage fright and routinely do relaxation exercises, such as shaking and stretching, before they perform. Teachers often do little or nothing to relax since they are probably unaware they have stage fright in the first place.

Actors and teachers need to produce emotion to perform effectively. Actors need to replicate all human emotions as their scripts demand. Teachers have to produce only one main emotion—enthusiasm. Teachers cannot, however, always be excited about what they are teaching. There are days when they, like all workers, just don't feel like doing the job. Teachers need to develop, as actors do, ways to manufacture enthusiasm when needed.

Many teachers develop teaching routines over the years, using the same examples to explain the same points every semester. Effective teaching, like effective acting, requires that the performer continually create the illusion of spontaneity, of making the planned seem unplanned. Actors in plays repeat the same lines night after night. Yet, for each audience, they make their words appear to be just thought of, rather than carefully rehearsed. Likewise, a teacher's job is not to always say new things to students, but rather to make everything he or she says seem fresh and new to each class.

Many teachers do not accept the teacher-as-actor metaphor, refusing to believe that teachers are performers. They view performers as circus jugglers or vaudeville clowns, unworthy of the noble profession of teaching. But teachers are performers. Simply put, performers communicate material to audiences, engaging their attention and maintaining their interest. Is this not a teacher's job? If teachers embrace the inherent theatricality of teaching, they can extend their careers, viewing each day as the joyous opportunity to perform their material better than they ever have before. (See Friedman 2005.)

CARLA LIST-HANDLEY
Emerita, SUNY Plattsburgh

There are three basic components of any performance: a performer, an audience, and the material conveyed in the presentation. They translate readily into teacher, classroom of students, and lesson. The material being performed, the content of the lesson, we'll leave to the dictates of the teacher and/or the official school curriculum.

An actor/performer is playing a role, with the goal of convincing the audience that she is someone other than herself. A teacher plays a role as well, that of the *teacher*. Consider the behavior of a teacher in a grocery store. Is that person being the *teacher* while searching for the perfect bunch of celery? Probably not (unless, of course, there are students with the teacher who are learning about perfect bunches of celery). If the teacher encounters a student in the grocery store, he may well assume the *teacher* role for that conversation, but for the rest of the shopping trip he is most likely "playing his role" of grocery shopper. The teacher becomes a "regular person" when away from school, or perhaps when just out of the classroom. The regular person is therefore playing a role just as actors do; that role is the *teacher*.

The "audience" of students does something all audiences do with performers: they enter into an implicit contract with the performer. This contract is an agreement that the audience will allow the performer to be the performer while the audience remains the audience and does not attempt to carry out the performer's job. It is an interesting concept. A classroom teacher who is confident in his role as teacher is able to renegotiate the contract when he asks his students to become "active learners" who do some of their own teaching.

A teacher/performer should be aware that a component of the contract with the audience is a willingness to follow the dictates of the performer. The audience is malleable. Think of performances by groups such as the *Cirque du Soleil* in which the performers snatch a "volunteer" from the audience up onto the stage to perform with them. The "volunteer" invariably agrees, even though overwhelmingly embarrassed. The teacher has a similar power to command her students into action. An example would be a teacher asking members of a class to "go to the blackboard" and work out problems. Another example is a class performing an ad hoc debate; the teacher splits the room and throws out the topic and the students argue it aloud in class.

New teachers may fear the loss of control of the classroom that active learning approaches seem to exhibit. But control comes from confidence. Confidence is a component of the contract and is also closely tied to the enthusiasm that is discussed in this book. It is possible to create a confident persona in the early stages of teaching—that period when confidence is not yet built on positive experiences. A performer/teacher can, as Laurence Olivier has said, "hid[e] behind the disguise of the role" (Bernard 1992). This translates for the teacher into using, at the very least, clothing selected to create the *teacher* role, to give the teacher a feeling of confidence. The first impression students get from the teacher's entrance into the classroom (the performance space) will influence the tone for the class period or the class day. A non-teacher casual wardrobe does little to foster respect for the teacher and may make classroom control more difficult to establish and maintain. The teacher/performer knows the wisdom of dressing the part.

In short, the teacher has tools to use to become a confident classroom "performer." Since one of the dictionary definitions of *performance* is "a public presentation or exhibition" (Performance 2005), the teacher can look to "performance-enhancing" tools (that have nothing to do with drugs!) used by actors to improve his confidence in himself as a performer and his abilities as a teacher.

ROD HART

University of Massachusetts–Amherst

Everything I needed to know about teaching I learned in the theater. If this is an exaggeration, it is only slightly so. Thus, I created an acting class designed explicitly for teachers, which I have taught at the UMASS Amherst School of Education for the past several years. Following are five parallels between teaching and acting that form the basis of my curriculum.

Comfort. I lead my students through acting exercises and improvisations designed to help them become more aware of how their voices and bodies may demonstrate discomfort and anxiety. We practice warm-up techniques that performers use to relax and prepare vocally, physically, mentally, and emotionally. Students work through any performing anxieties by preparing a focused yet relaxed performance of a theatrical monologue.

Presence. Presence, in theater parlance, is the ability to be here now. Teachers who hide behind note cards and PowerPoint shows, who have taught the same lesson so many times they recite it without variation, or who are still emotionally worked up over something that happened with their previous class are not *present*. To be fully present teachers must first have their lessons prepared and rehearsed, their materials readied, their time-management strategies set, their mental and emotional faculties centered, and their focus outward into the classroom space. Acting exercises emphasize observation, concentration, and the outward focusing of energy necessary to be present.

Authenticity. Acting is not impersonating. Sadly, in my experience working with student teachers, I have observed many novices ape their cooperating teacher by "borrowing" her lesson plans, her classroom-management techniques, and even her style of dress. New teachers deserve an opportunity to explore their own unique way of speaking, moving, seeing and responding *as a teacher*. An actor would never go onstage without rehearsing her role, nor should a new teacher enter the classroom without proper rehearsal time and preparation.

Availability. Being available requires a commitment on the part of the teacher to *stay in the moment* and to *respond authentically*. As teachers, we find ourselves delivering the same lesson repeatedly and responding to the same cues (Can I go to the bathroom? Is this going to be on the test? Why did she get an A and I didn't?) ad nauseum. It is so easy simply to tune out. However, when we stop listening and start responding automatically (or defensively), we commit the same sin as the actor who sleepwalks through his role.

Connection. How can we simultaneously connect with our voices and bodies, our texts, our audiences, our environment, our emotions, and the ever-changing reality of the classroom moment? New teachers may take lessons not only from the actor but also from other theater professionals. The artist-teacher wears many hats including those of actor, director, dramaturge, stage manager, or acting coach. My students learn not only to script and perform their lessons but also to stage, costume, and light them to maximum effect.

Recognizing that teaching is indeed a performing art makes studying the arts an essential part of any teacher's professional development. I highly endorse teachers enrolling in an acting class and studying alongside other performing artists. No doubt they will discover for themselves more connections between acting and teaching than can be described here.

ROBERT KEIPER
Western Washington University

There is much parallelism between the daily routines and actions of a good teacher and those of a good actor. A major difference, however, is that the actor plays one role at a time while the best teachers play many roles throughout the day.

One of the first things the teacher/actor must do is learn the lines. In preparation for each class the teacher has to consider three sources for his/her text: (1) the actual "lines" from a text, handout, PowerPoint presentation, etc.; (2) the text from his/her professional training—instructional strategies, multiple-intelligences, motivation, discipline techniques, etc.; and (3) the text from one's life experiences, which enriches dialogue in the classroom.

Second, the teacher must look about the "stage"—the room in which the lesson will unfold. Can anything be done to arrange the room so that the teaching and learning are enhanced and made more memorable for a particular lesson? Are there any "props" which can visually accent the information? Consider using a physical mnemonic if the content has three to four main ideas. For instance, if the subject is the three Greek tragedian playwrights, move to a certain spot when discussing Aeschylus, to another place for Sophocles, and another for Euripides. Then, whenever referring to Aeschylus, always "visit" his place when providing more information about Aeschylus. This also gives motivation to one's movement and eliminates pacing. Finally, teach to the back row first.

Third, listen to how effectively the voice is used. Use pause and silence as effective "markers" of what is important; let it "soak" in. Vocally punch something that needs to be remembered; think of which word(s) are important and give them a little more volume. Listen for variance in pitch. Most adults utilize only two to three different pitches when talking, yet the average human voice is capable of producing sixteen tones. Use your voice to let students know that you are passionate about what you are teaching and that you truly enjoy being with them.

Last, all acting involves risk-taking, and there is no exception in a classroom which is "alive." The International Thespian Society's motto is wise to follow: "Act well your part for therein the honor lies." (See Keiper 1991.)

RICHARD W. LEBLANC
York University; Toronto, Canada

In teaching, if knowledge transfer occurs from teacher to student in a meaningful, credible, and memorable manner, the teacher has excelled. In acting, if the audience identifies with the actor's character, experiences, and circumstances, made real and resonating by the actor's performance, the actor has excelled.

A good teacher is not simply one who teaches, nor is a good actor simply one who acts. Good teachers inspire and motivate students. Great actors move their audiences and indeed, on rare occasions, forever change them. And that is the parallel. It is this higher-level emotive value beyond content that distinguishes "goodness" from "greatness," not only in the teaching and acting professions, but in others as well (e.g., business and politics). Great leaders inspire and move us to become better people, as part of our overall human condition.

Just as great barristers and trial attorneys are "actors" for the jury in their courtroom, teachers "act" for their students. The teacher's stage is his or her classroom. The teacher's "acting" is the medium by which knowledge is "transferred."

If we accept the proposition that there exists parallels between teaching and acting, then the range of techniques and practices that teachers use to practice and perfect their craft includes, among other things, impersonations, storytelling, role-playing, the soliloquy, incident, scenario and case analysis, experimentation, the creative use of imagination, props, and the use of humor and entertainment.

All of these techniques that use acting skills in the classroom require teachers to overcome anxiety and continuously experiment with approaches with which they are comfortable personally and which resonate with their students. Two techniques in particular are important: the use of humor and entertainment. These two are part of the actor/teacher's arsenal, or personal style "tool kit," and in no way suggest a lack of content or substance. Teachers do not need to be entertainers or comedians, only learn from them.

For example, humor may be self-deprecating and reflect an attitude of not taking situations, one's field, or oneself too seriously. Innocuous or insightful jokes may be made, often at one's own expense, to "break the ice" with an audience so that learning occurs in a more relaxed and informal environment. Good teachers use humor appropriately and strategically.

Similarly, good teaching should be highly entertaining. Lectures should not occur with hands glued to a podium, with the teacher droning on, but should be inspiring, passionate, and, yes, entertaining—aligned with the instructor's personal style and comfort level.

PROFESSOR PADDY MILLER
University of Navarra; Barcelona, Spain

I'm hooked on the case method class. As a basic theatrical forum it has all the essential elements—a well-chosen script, some basic props like blackboards and flipcharts, and an audience ready to participate. Nobody should try to conduct a case discussion at arms length as if it were entirely an intellectual affair. It is not.

I had colleagues once who would dress up for their cases—if it was Club Med, they'd turn up in a bright flowery shirt and sip rum from a coconut (it may have been a soda), and if it was Virgin Airlines, they'd turn up as either an air steward or a virgin. I forget which, but you get the idea. The point is that the case allows the teachers to immerse themselves in the detail and internalize some of its core images or themes essential for capturing the imagination of an audience. The teacher during the performance of the case should be inseparable from the case content, the teaching tools or props, and the physical environment of the performance. This calls for a complete command of the material, one's self, and the classroom.

But classroom performances are in decline because of technology creep, especially the all-pervasive PowerPoint. It is killing great performances. It's as if every play you go to has the same prop. Imagine how you'd react if the one thing that *Macbeth* and *Chicago* had in common was a huge double bed in every scene!

What makes it worse is that many people use PowerPoint as an *aide-mémoire*, getting their thoughts in a logical sequence and recorded in hard copy the night before. Their sessions are painfully boring because they insist on taking all of the surprise out of the script. It's like having the prompter on center stage in a double bed and allowing the audience to scan the script ahead of the actors.

Stage performances like classroom sessions belong in the category of re-creative art. During visits to the Guggenheim to see a Rembrandt, you are not asked to grab a set of brushes and a pallet and get to work on creating the master's images. But in a stage performance, as in the classroom, this is exactly what happens—as a student, you are asked to suspend judgment for a while in order to allow the instructor to re-create a scene which maybe he or she has done many times before. You are asked to participate in that process and eventually to conclude subjectively whether the performance achieved its objectives or not.

This is what makes PowerPoint such a dangerous prop in any performance—the assumption that the re-creative process can be short-circuited by preparing the script and sharing it with the audience is false. I think that PowerPoint has put presentation skills back many years. The problem is that the technology itself is difficult to integrate and internalize in a spontaneous dynamic session. It is a challenge for the teacher to blend the technology in a way that it becomes an extension of the total pedagogic production. The traditional stick of chalk was a piece of cake in comparison.

Many great teachers use chalk in the hand as an extension of the brain. Much as finger or a hand is used to create drama, chalk can be used to point, to juggle, to record, to shatter dramatically, and, when finally placed on the desk, to terminate the session. There is no prop less innocuous and more powerful.

The advantage of chalk as a prop is that nobody would start a classroom performance with the line "I've brought 24 pieces of chalk with me today." But PowerPoint players do. No teacher would assume that a spontaneously scrawled word on the blackboard could be improved by a bullet-pointed phrase. It is dynamic spontaneous theatre in the round compared to reading a train timetable.

SHEILA NEWBERRY
St. John's River Community College

One of Shakespeare's most famous speeches comes from *As You Like It*. "All the world's a stage, and all the men and women merely players." It is a metaphor that describes life as a stage and all people as actors. It is a concept that has been viewed through many different perspectives. As an educator, I propose a similar metaphor for the world of education. Teaching is a performing art, and all who serve as educators are front and center on their own personal stage every single school day. With over twenty-five years of teaching experience, I have had a great deal of time to consider this comparison of teaching to the arts. I believe that there are many similarities between the theater and the classroom. Let me explain:

Stage/Set: A pleasant classroom environment, conducive to learning

Props: Equipment that makes the teaching appropriate and effective

Curtain: Covers the stage (or props) and adds to audience anticipation

Director: The instructor who molds the actors into better, more gifted performers

Leading Actors: Class leaders who set the stage

Supporting Cast: The quiet or the disruptive student who often gets lost in the scene

Playwright: Represented by your curriculum

Script: Your syllabus, lesson plans, and class schedule

Audience/Critics: Students, peers, and administrators important to the success of the performance

Act I: Clarifying the Roles
Good actors on Broadway must study their script, learn to use props, and become comfortable on stage—all components necessary to present an outstanding performance. Teachers also must accomplish these skills. The teachers we remember most vividly are those who knew their subjects best *and* transmitted them with the greatest intensity and love (Banner and Cannon 1997). It was this conviction and love for learning that got me started teaching the way I do.

Act II: Presenting the Show
The first step to promote active learning in your classroom is to begin with low-risk strategies. They are typically of short duration, structured and planned, focused on subject matter that is neither too abstract nor too controversial, and

familiar to both the instructor and the students (Bonwell and Eison 1991). Faculty can get over their "stage fright" by gradually introducing new teaching techniques, such as humor, drama, music, role-playing, simulations, cooperative learning, computer-based instruction, questioning, writing, peer teaching, and games.

Act III: Reading the Reviews

Just like actors, teachers risk failure or success. Some will feel quite comfortable with the new teaching format, whereas others will protest kicking and screaming. Many feel that they will lose control of their class, not have enough time to cover all their course content, or not have the needed equipment or materials or that using active learning will take too much preparation time. Solution: Focus interest on the students and what will be best for them. A faculty member's ability to relinquish control and share power in the classroom can enable students to become actors playing major roles in their own education rather than simply being an audience listening and learning from a great performer on center stage (Bonwell and Eison 1991). Take the challenge and become the STAR that you can be!

ROGER SOENKSEN
James Madison University

My experience as an actor began in a junior college production and has continued ever since. Principles of acting carry over to classroom experiences, and this testimonial will demonstrate how I use some key concepts of acting in my teaching of undergraduates.

My directors over the years have consistently emphasized preparation. The investment of time spent repeating stage blocking and practicing lines pays off in a quality performance. In teaching, I have also found that preparation prevents poor performances. Time spent planning lectures, anticipating multimedia needs, and practicing delivery results in quality instruction.

Just as an actor must adjust to the size of the theater, the number of people in the audience, and the tone of the dialogue on stage, a teacher must adjust nonverbal delivery of the content being taught. I teach classes ranging from 22 to 222 students. This requires that I vary my vocal inflections according to the size of the room, as well as the number of students I am addressing. Students who can't easily hear you will daydream, text message on cell phones, etc. My voice must create the appropriate tone for a particular lecture, and it must be used as yet another tool to hold the attention and interest of my students.

Another lesson I learned from acting was that the job is not over once the curtain falls. I never deliver the same lecture twice. During acting class, my professors stressed the need to "package the scene," meaning that all the key elements of drama had to be performed in concert. Students in my class demand the same kind of packaging, so I am perpetually revising my content and delivery. I ask myself, "Where did the lecture drag?" "Are the multimedia aids helpful?" "Can the students relate to the illustrations I used?" I make quick notes at the conclusion of each class to recall areas of the lecture that require fine-tuning.

Perhaps the most important skill necessary to transfer from the stage to the podium is enthusiasm. No matter how many times an actor delivers the same lines, each delivery must be as good as the first because each audience is hearing them for the first time. You never want to send an audience home disappointed because of a lackluster performance. Teaching also requires that "old" content be kept fresh. I rewrite all my lectures each year, updating information and experimenting with instructional approaches. Sharing new research or trying a new delivery style helps keep my enthusiasm high. If students leave a lecture disappointed because of my lackluster performance, I haven't done my job well.

The use of these acting principles has enhanced my teaching. However, there is no sure formula or quick and easy way to become a good teacher. The key to success is hard work and a passion for the profession.

RICK THORN
Educational Consultant, UK

At its best, inspired teaching is a tool for transformation, inspiration, creativity, change, healing, and growth. At its worst, teaching is a tool for control, to discourage individuality, and to stifle creativity and ensure that ambitions are quashed. Successful teaching is an art in itself, and once the art is grasped, both the teacher and the student benefit enormously.

Truly inspired teaching is a performance, but it is not just any performance. It needs to be a performance that transforms the students, a performance that so engages and challenges them that they just have to respond—the ultimate response, of course, is that they engage with their own learning. Unfortunately, much teacher training, and so-called good practice, has reduced the art and performance of teaching to a few manageable, observable, and assessable techniques.

Teaching that sets out to inspire others should begin with passion. It must be a passion about what we teach, as well as the act of teaching itself. To just be passionate about a subject is not enough to teach it; we also have to be passionate about communicating what we know and inspiring the next generation of students. Indeed, we may be a little scared of showing and using our passion for fear of ridicule—by students and/or colleagues! But in my experience, the students who remember us as teachers years later very rarely remember the exact details of what we taught them. Rather, they remember our passion that inspired them.

Inspired teaching gives people new opportunities and shows them new possibilities. This is a healing act, for it is often what we learn that gets us out of the problems we have. Inspired teaching can help people transform themselves, give them new ways of earning an inspired living, and give them a new self-esteem.

To teach is a gift in itself, but when we teach in an inspired way, we give our gift to others, and that is both the gift of ourselves and the gift of what we know. This gift can truly transform the lives of others.

I know that in the middle of a busy term with piles of marking on our desks, it is easy to forget why we teach and why teaching is so critically important to society. But if we forget just what a potent and transformatory act teaching is, we will lose our power and passion to inspire others.

CHAPTER

Conclusion

The shrewd guess, the fertile hypothesis, the courageous leap to a tentative
conclusion—these are the most valuable coin of the thinker at work.

—Bruner

INTRODUCTION

There you have it. The more enthusiastic a teacher is about the material taught, the more effective the lesson. Students learn more and retain it longer. Students find the teacher more credible and are, therefore, more willing to listen and behave. Teachers should be able to let their natural enthusiasm show; but if they are having difficulty with that, they can take some lessons from the theater. By *acting* enthusiastic, the teacher becomes more confident and is soon perceived as credible and interesting. In this book, we have presented many specific lessons from the acting world that can help you achieve this goal. Bottom line: they work! Students testify to their success, and award-winning teachers sing their praise

SPEARHEADING PROFESSIONAL DEVELOPMENT AT YOUR INSTITUTION

The authors have yet to meet an audience of educators that seriously challenges the argument that a parallel exists between acting and teaching. Further, most teachers agree that they could become more engaging and interesting teachers by using acting skills in their classrooms. The question now becomes, where are teachers to go to learn these skills? One would hope that all teacher-education programs, and journals that represent them, would provide instruction in, and practice with, these acting skills prior to graduation. If your program has not provided such resources already, there are several steps you can take to spearhead professional development at your institution.

So, what can you do to spearhead professional development at your school or school district? Here are some suggestions. They fall into four categories: Research and Reading, Workshops and Seminars, Partnership and Practice, and Willingness and Courage.

Research and Reading

You have already made a move in the right direction by reading this book. And, of course, there are many other good articles and books out there on the parallel between acting and teaching. Many of them have been highlighted throughout this text. Still more can be located and accessed by using ERIC and other information-retrieval systems, as well as by entering key descriptors (i.e., "teaching and enthusiasm," "using humor in the classroom," or "using body language to motivate") into Internet search engines. We hope that you will secure some of the more interesting and useful resources, read them, and share them with colleagues. We also hope that you will carefully review what other informed authors had to say in the previous chapter, as well as reread the testimonials from award-winning faculty that appear in Appendix 2.

Teachers can find help in books on practical tips such as those offered by Magnan (1989). He advocates, among other tips, "Think of it as 'show' business (more 'show' and maybe a little less 'tell')." "Think BIG" (the value of eye contact, projecting the voice, using gestures larger than life), "people your ideas," and "claim your territory" (deliver points loud and clear from the front; move out among students to elaborate or illustrate points). Timpson et al. (2002) offer still more good ideas for energizing classrooms.

Consider starting a "professional library" in your school or department of *Acting Lessons for Teachers*–type resources. If you find particular readings and resources interesting and useful to you, chances are your colleagues will find them equally helpful and appealing. Be sure to pass some of these resources on to your superiors. With their support, something useful is more likely to happen in your school or department.

We even hope that you will be a contributor—yes, a contributor—to our shared goal of using acting/performance skills in the classroom. When you do something of an acting nature in your classroom that seems to interest and engage your students, consider writing up what you have done and submitting it for inclusion at a professional conference or for publication in a journal. This way, the word gets out to others. Encourage your colleagues to do the same thing.

Workshops and Seminars

He who does not research has nothing to teach.

—Proverbs

All teachers say that education is a lifelong endeavor. Well, teachers should practice what they preach. Although reading and research are valuable tools to the informed educator, these tasks too often are done alone and done without constructive guidance. Given that acting lessons for teachers entail them actually doing something that can be seen or heard by students, such skill development can profit from informed feedback. Therefore, we recommend that teachers join colleagues and participate in workshops and seminars that address the parallel between acting and teaching. When this training is obtained off-site at the educator's own expense, it may be tax-deductible, given that it is an effort to improve one's skills in his or her trade.

Sometimes the only workshops and seminars that teachers get a chance to attend are those in-service programs imposed on them by central administration. In this case, we suggest that teachers get themselves on committees that play a role in advising the program planners. If no such professional advisory committees exist, then individual teachers can be a missionary of one. Teachers can contact various central-administration personnel and share with them their proposal for acting/teaching workshops and seminars. Be sure to include some selected readings, some possible workshop/seminar providers, and some "evidence" that these in-service programs make a real difference in creating more engaging and motivating teachers. As a point in fact, the authors conduct such workshops and seminars. Of course, there are others, too, who could be tapped to provide stimulating and useful programs.

Another resource often overlooked is the local community theater personnel who could be contacted to see if they would be willing to deliver a workshop. Who knows, some of you may get "hooked" on drama and become weekend thespians. Wouldn't that be great? This experience would serve you well when you return to your classroom on Monday mornings.

Partnership and Practice

An idle mind is the devil's workshop.

—English Proverb

The first tentative attempts at incorporating acting lessons into one's classroom can feel scary, be risky, and offer no guarantee of complete success. Few teachers are willing to go out on a limb to try something this new unless they feel supported by both colleagues and administration. Who can blame them? Schools need to establish supportive partnerships between and among teachers so that when the going gets tough, and it will on occasion, there is somebody there to help. Those first trained can be called upon as acting mentors for those new to using acting lessons in the classroom.

At the college or university level, form a partnership between the school of education and the theater department. There is enough precedence for this working arrangement so that the task ought not to be insurmountable. For instance, all teaching-bound students at the Dutchess Community College (SUNY) fulfill their "arts" requirement by scheduling a Performing Skills for the Classroom course designed by Joe Cosentino, a professor of speech and theater.

And education majors at UMASS–School of Education line up to schedule Teaching as a Performing Art, a course designed by Rod Hart. If your schedule permits, you might consider "auditing" one of these courses, or at least one of your campus's Acting 101 classes.

You also could offer your own course. Robert Keiper offers a course, Dynamics of Teaching, at Woodring College of Education, Western Washington University, that is required of all secondary education students. Cathy Mester, one of the authors of this text, offers a drama-based teaching course titled Communication for Teachers. This elective course is scheduled by students seeking teacher certification.

At the K–12 level, initiate a partnership between subject-matter teachers and the theater arts faculty. In the latter case, the theater arts faculty are right there in the same junior high or high school. For elementary schools, they are at least in the same school district. Most, if not all, of these theater people themselves have had the typical Acting 101, or Introduction to Acting, courses. The majority of these people now play some role in training others to become actors and actresses. With some central-administration support, fueled by informed teacher input, acting lessons for teachers can become a reality.

If practice is supposed to make perfect, then teachers must have opportunities to practice their newly acquired acting lessons. In most cases this will take some time and probably some administrative reorganization to make such time, as well as mentor support, available. When the time comes for a teacher to put his or her skills into practice in the classroom, perhaps he or she can deliver it as a team— even a team as small as two. Because nothing breeds success like success, these first efforts at using acting lessons simply must be successful. We need to pull out all of the stops in order to ensure success.

What you want from any workshop or partnership, what we tried to make clear at the beginning of Chapter 1, is for it to support the acting–teaching parallel presented in this text and to present specific lessons from the acting world that can be used by teachers in their classrooms to engage and motivate students. Don't settle for anything less.

Willingness and Courage

Knowledge is of no value unless you put it into practice.
—Anton Chekhov

What we are asking teachers to undertake may not be for the faint of heart. It takes willingness, perhaps even courage, to step into the shoes of thespians. We not only have to step into their shoes, we also have to apply these newly acquired acting skills in front of an audience that can, at times, be cruel, unpredictable, and unforgiving. Further, we have to "live with" this audience of young people for the rest of the school year. Actors and actresses, at least in a play, do not have to face the same audience time after time. Yes, this takes courage; it takes heart!

It may be scary for new teachers to learn and begin to incorporate these acting skills into their teaching. It can even be frightening for seasoned teachers to do the same thing. But "true teaching takes courage because we must constantly be reinventing ourselves . . . we must change, else how can we ask students to change?" (Searle 2001, 6). Palmer (1998) explores this same idea in his book *The Courage to Teach*. Shouldn't teachers lead by example? Haven't we all watched an anxious student squirm, sweat, and render excuses before having to deliver his or her first speech? Haven't we all watched a child look with fright and claim that he or she can't possibly climb the knotted rope in gym? In fact, haven't some of us actually been that person who was sweating, squirming, rendering excuses, and looking frightened?

As a parent, teacher, or supportive friend, how have we responded? Haven't we all said something to the effect, "I know that it will be tough, but why don't you give it a try? I will help you prepare to carry out the task before you!" We hope that you view this text, as well as the suggestions described in this chapter, as useful ways to help you prepare.

A TEACHER'S MANNER AND METHOD

Courage is doing what you're afraid to do.
There can be no courage unless you're scared.

—Edward Vernon Rick

As the authors of this book, we want to acknowledge that we are teachers first and scholars second. Teaching is taken very seriously at our institution—so much so that every teacher has every class evaluated every semester. Merit pay, tenure, and promotion all are influenced by these results. Our sense of accomplishment, too, is influenced by these results. When our students report, in anecdotal form, that "the professor was able to make an otherwise boring subject interesting," we are torn between competing reactions. One part of us wants to grab the students, shake them, and announce in no uncertain terms that, in fact, all subject matter is inherently interesting. Another side of us recognizes that perhaps we have accomplished just what we have set out to do—we have begun to turn students on to our subject areas. Time will tell.

"When we look back on our schooling, we remember teachers rather than courses—we remember their manner and method, their enthusiasm and intellectual excitement, and their capacity to arouse delight in, or curiosity about, the subject taught" (Hook 1981, 24). This "manner and method" reflects many of the acting strategies presented in this book that can, and should, be used by teachers. "If you display enthusiasm and energy in the delivery of your lecture, students will be convinced that this is a lecturer who is in command of not only their subject matter but also their teaching" (TEDI 2002, 2).

Of all dramatic elements, say Klein and Fitch (1990), characters and their dramatic actions are recalled more strongly and frequently than dialogue. We remember more about what people do than what they say. Axtell

(1997) concurs. He claims that students may forget the details presented in their courses, but few forget the enthusiasm and passion with which inspirational teachers teach day after day. "Even more so than an actor, a teacher is a sculptor in snow" (Hook 1981, 24). Like the snow sculpture that will melt in the warming sun, the memories of a great teacher are preserved only by those who have *seen* him or her in action. The strategies presented in this book, then, may be even more important to a teacher than they are to an actor!

Robinson (1993), in her course, Dramatic Arts for Teachers, asserts that teachers' success in the classroom is dependent on "performance, performance, performance." We hope that reading this book will help teachers develop their own stage presence by performing, performing, performing—in the very best sense. We hope they will begin developing their unique, yet effective, "manner and method" acting skills.

THE CURTAIN COMES DOWN

Sarason (1999) argues that theater audiences do not expect to be bored, unmoved, and sorry they came. Students feel the same way. Let's not disappoint them. Good teaching practice is out there. As we have argued throughout this book, part and parcel of this "good practice" is making better use of acting skills in the classroom.

Now that you have read this book and are ready to put what you have learned into practice, it is time for you to leave and get on with it. Why haven't you left yet? Recall what Matthew Broderick, in his housecoat, said at the end of the 1986 film *Ferris Bueller's Day Off*. He turned and faced the audience directly, as if he were there with them live, and said, "You're still here? It's over. Go home. Go." Our version would be "Go to class. Act. Teach!"

APPENDIX

Education Resources Information Center (ERIC)

http://www.eric.ed.gov
Toll-free 800-LET-ERIC (800-538-3742)
Hours: Monday–Friday, 8:00 a.m.–8:00 p.m. ET

A PROFESSIONAL

One definition of a professional is that it is someone who regularly turns to a recognized body of knowledge in order to make decisions. Since the mid-1960s, one recognized body of knowledge for busy practitioners has been ERIC. Make use of this incredible resource for teachers and professors.

ERIC DESCRIPTION

The Education Resources Information Center (ERIC), sponsored by the Institute of Education Sciences (IES) of the U.S. Department of Education, produces the world's premier database of journal and nonjournal education literature. Practitioners should note that the "R" in ERIC stands for "Resources"—something that all educators can make use of.

The ERIC online system provides the public with a centralized ERIC Web site for searching the ERIC bibliographic database (1996–present) of more than 1.1 million citations to a broad collection of education-related resources, from government reports to journal articles. More than 107,000 full-text nonjournal documents (issued 1993–2004), previously available through fee-based services only, are now available for free.

ERIC's mission is to provide a comprehensive, easy-to-use, searchable, Internet-based bibliographic and full-text database of education research and information. A fundamental goal for ERIC's future is to increase the availability and quality of research and information for educators, researchers, and the general public. ERIC is "one of the most important, if not the most important, resource that has helped educators bridge the gap between practice and theory" (Barron 1990, 47).

CONDUCTING AN ERIC SEARCH

Conducting an ERIC search has never been easier. Simply go to a computer and type in "www.eric.ed.gov" in an Internet browser's address line. Up will come a screen that prompts you to choose whether you want your search to locate specific words in the document's title or body. You will then be prompted to enter a descriptor. Enter the descriptor(s) of your choice. If you want to enter several descriptors, do so. Remember, though, that if you enter separate descriptors (i.e., humor English classrooms) your search will locate all documents that contain these separate words. The number of documents located could be overwhelming. Sometimes you may wish to limit your search by grouping two or more descriptors. That is done by placing the descriptors in quotations marks (i.e., "humor in English classrooms"). This way, only documents that include the exact four words, together in that order, will be found. You may also phone ERIC directly, toll-free, at 800-538-3742.

TWO VERSIONS OF ERIC CITATIONS

ERIC searches typically locate documents that fall into one of two categories. Documents are either journal articles, with an EJ six-digit ERIC number, or a form of "fugitive" literature, with an ED six-digit ERIC number. Journal citations are obvious; they are articles from approximately 800 journals published worldwide. "Fugitive" literature citations are a bit less obvious; they are nonjournal documents such as conference proceedings, speeches, position papers, curriculum guides, and project reports. Both types of documents can be extremely useful to classroom teachers. An example of both types of document citations follows.

Resources in Education

ERIC Title: *The Power of Humor in the College Classroom.*
ERIC #: ED346535
Author: Edwards, Celeste M.; Gibboney, Elizabeth R.
Publication Date: 1992-02-00
Publication Type: Speeches/Meeting Papers; Information Analyses; Guides—Classroom—Teacher
Descriptors: Classroom Environment; Classroom Research; College Instruction; Higher Education; Humor; Student Attitudes; Teacher Effectiveness; Teacher Evaluation; Teacher-Student Relationship; Teaching Skills; Teaching Styles.
Abstract: Humor is an important tool for the teacher in college classrooms. Generally, laughter is a great benefit in anyone's life, having even physiological influence. Laughter reduces stress and may facilitate creativity. However, the use of humor can both enhance and hinder the learning process. Various researchers have tried to identify structures, types, and categories of humor.

Current Index to Journals in Education

> **ERIC TITLE:** Humor, Learning and Socialization in Middle Level Classrooms
> **ERIC #:** EJ545808
> **Author:** Pollack, Judy P.; Freda, Paul D.
> **Publication Date:** 1997-00-00
> **Journal Name:** *The Clearing House*
> **Journal Citation:** v70 n4 p176-78 Mar-Apr 1997
> **Descriptors:** Classroom Environment; Creative Thinking; Humor; Junior High Schools; Middle Schools; Self-Esteem; Socialization; Student Empowerment; Teacher-Student Relationships.
> **Abstract:** The article examines uses of humor in middle level classrooms and relationships between humor and effective teaching. Suggests that, with the incorporation of humor into the classroom to facilitate rapport building, student empowerment, creative thinking, attention, self-esteem, and socialization, middle-level teachers have the power to become the genesis for real education and a life-long love of learning.

Because the ERIC Web site, www.eric.ed.gov, is a U.S. Government site and in the public domain, one is free to use its wording. Some of that Web site wording has been included in this Appendix.

APPENDIX

Testimonials from Award-Winning K–12 Teachers and College Professors

TESTIMONIAL 1

Kimberly Austin, Patricia Lefford, and Melissa Yost*
Disney Interdisciplinary Teachers of the Year, 2005
Washington Middle School
Jamestown, New York 14701

In order for children of all ability levels to experience success, teachers must be creative and energetic. We team-teach fifth graders, teaching all subject areas, differentiating the instruction as appropriate for various projects and the breadth of learning styles represented by our students. This requires a great deal of cooperative planning and fundamental respect for our co-teachers' special strengths and skills. We are fortunate that each of us has a talent for particular performance skills.

We call this good fortune because our experience has shown us that today's children are motivated by visual stimuli more than anything else. The education system is competing against all kinds of entertainment for the children's attention. They need teachers to be physically and vocally expressive, to play roles, to make full use of technology, to use props—all day long. The whole day must be motivating, not just the beginning. The curriculum demands their full effort, and we have to be the ones to trigger that effort by the way we present the material.

An example of our approach would be the mammals' unit we do in science. Students must correctly categorize mammals as herbivores, carnivores, or omnivores by studying the mammal's teeth, skull, and scat (among other things). We introduce the different types of scat by donning surgical masks, gowns, and gloves, presenting the sample scat on trays held at arm's length. Just to make sure the students are tuned in, we have composed a "scat rap" that we perform together at the end of the explanation. As you can imagine, we have the students' unflagging attention! The most important result of this lesson, however, is that they **learn**. Young adults who took our class years ago report that they still remember how to differentiate the different classes of mammals!

While we are talking about results, let's talk discipline problems! In a word, we have few. With the creative style of teaching that we rely on and our highly organized and orchestrated approach to the curriculum, students are too busy learning and having fun to have time to be disruptive.

The final piece of our teaching philosophy relevant to performance skills would be our belief that good teachers are naturally driven to evolve. That is, we have to become trained in new technology and educated in new theories on a continuing basis. We value the new technology as a resource that can widen the world of all students, making them competitive for the future, regardless of their individual economic circumstances. Further, we value the opportunities to share ideas and interact with other successful teachers that are provided by programs like the Disney Teaching Awards.

In sum, we believe that a teacher's use of performance skills is necessary for motivating students, contributes to students' ability to retain information, and is a resource for constantly evolving teaching.

* Kimberly Austin and Patricia Lefford were interviewed by Cathy S. Mester, who paraphrased their ideas here.

TESTIMONIAL 2

Gregory J. Baleja
Department of Business and Social Sciences
Alma College
Alma, Michigan 48801

I have been involved in higher education for the past twenty-four years, and during that time, I have often pondered why my teaching style has been so effective and well received by my students. I have taught at a variety of schools, ranging from large research-based universities to small liberal arts colleges. The schools' policies have varied from "open admissions" to "highly selective" admissions criteria. Since my evaluations have been consistent across the institutions, I am therefore forced to conclude that the success of my teaching style is *not* contingent on any one particular category of student.

The question remains, why the success? Are there any common themes or practices that may account for this? In reviewing the comments sections of previous Instructor Evaluation Forms, and after a thorough self-evaluation, three areas are consistently noted: Voice Animation (Enthusiasm), Body Animation, and Subject Mastery. Each of these areas is expanded on below.

First, the most consistent theme centers on the use of voice animation. This is especially true when it comes to the importance of "Enthusiasm." The following are some selected student (audience) comments regarding the importance of enthusiasm:

a. "—attacked this course with vigor and a sense of enthusiasm that is a necessity when dealing with the material presented in the course."

b. "—is an enthusiastic teacher. I have learned so much in this course. He is very good with the students. Teaches in an interesting and fair manner and it is obvious that he enjoys his work."

c. "Instructor was very enthusiastic and kept the attention of the class members well. Even when I was in my most exhausted state, he still had the ability to keep my attention."

d. "The Professor is enthusiastic and teaches in a manner which keeps the student's interest and encourages class participation. He is extremely well prepared for his lectures."

In order for the students to show enthusiasm for the subject matter, it is imperative for the instructor to do the same. In this day and age of entertainment, it is crucial for the professor to use a variety of vocal variation techniques. Just as a performer will use inflection in his/her voice to draw attention to a particular point in the narration, it is critical for professors to do the same. Inflections can be used to draw attention to a particular key point, or to reinforce various aspects of the lecture.

Second, the use of body animation is important in gaining and then maintaining the attention of the audience (students). A professor standing in front of a podium or next to an overhead projector for an entire class period, creates a static environment that can lead to boredom and daydreaming, no matter how exciting the topic. Pacing the floor, talking with your hands, and the use of visual aids, for example, all lead to a dynamic environment within the classroom that prevents or at least minimizes the possibility of boredom. In addition, the professor needs to dress in a manner appropriate for the type of learning environment desired. Professional attire (two-piece suits, buttoned collar) creates an atmosphere of formality and superiority that may reduce interaction. Less formal attire (shirt and tie with open collar) may enhance the amount of interaction. Some student comments on this subject are listed below:

a. "Without the fear of an overpowering authority figure, I think we felt more comfortable in expressing our opinions."

b. "The open forum when discussing cases was very effective for it allowed *us* to think, and *you* to guide, instead of being *told* what to do."

Communication and learning cannot take place if the receiver of the information either refuses to accept it or is unaware of its existence because of staring at the ceiling, daydreaming about some outside activity, or being put off by the formality of the class and professor.

Finally, the professor needs to demonstrate mastery in the subject matter. This includes not only the normal knowledge associated with subject mastery, but also the ability to communicate the information in a manner that the students are able to comprehend. The information must be presented in terminology the audience is familiar with. Also, the use of *current* real world examples will reinforce the importance of the concept and will help the student in retaining the information. The following are examples of students' comments concerning this area:

a. "Examples used in class are very good and helped to illustrate points that could be boring and mundane."

b. "The instructor *always* shows enthusiasm with every lecture. He has the distinct ability to explain material with good examples that relate current aspects and learning in other classes."

Subject mastery is more than just theories and concepts. It also includes the ability to communicate the information in a manner that the audience understands and retains!

In summary, many of the practices that have contributed to my success in the classroom can be directly correlated to some of the basic concepts and tenets of acting (subject mastery, voice, and body animation). In this TV age, it seems to be beneficial, if not a requirement, for a professor to be part entertainer (actor), in order to disseminate knowledge effectively and efficiently to the student population.

TESTIMONIAL 3

Stephen R. Borecky
Division of Natural Sciences
Carlow College
Pittsburgh, Pennsylvania 15213

As I reviewed the draft of the table of contents for this book and tried to select the one or two specific areas to be addressed in this essay, I was reminded of a common question that is raised in my anatomy classes. Not a semester passes without one of my students asking, "What do you consider to be the most important organ system in the body?" My usual response centers on the concept of interrelatedness, since the survival of the organism as a whole depends upon the combined functions of all organs. I believe that the concept of interrelatedness also applies to the skills necessary for effective teaching. I am not suggesting that a weakness in or lack of one or more of the specific skills discussed in this book automatically makes one an ineffective teacher, but I do feel that teaching effectiveness is greatly enhanced as new skills are acquired and others are modified and developed.

I consider the development of teaching skills to be a gradual evolutionary process. Fish did not become amphibians and amphibians did not become reptiles in quantum leaps of anatomical and physiological changes, but rather evolved though a series of gradual changes influenced by the environment in which they lived. A similar pattern is observed in the evolution of teaching skills. However, unlike the random mutations associated with the evolution of animals, teachers can select and develop those traits that improve their performance within their own specific educational environments. Just as some traits are essential to the survival of organisms in any environment and others are unique specializations, there are teaching skills that must be mastered before entering any classroom setting and those that will slowly evolve to fit the teacher's personality and specific discipline. Subject mastery is one of those essential traits, but it has been my experience that this trait can produce conflicts in the development of other skills.

Although familiarity with one's subject area is a vital component of quality teaching, it is equally important to develop those skills that separate the teacher from the lecturer. A lecture can be compared to reading a play, while teaching is the equivalent of viewing a stage performance. Both experiences provide the same information, but the performance makes the characters and plot come alive, and, if the actors have polished their skills, the audience comes away with a visual and auditory experience that they will remember. Teachers must avoid becoming so involved in learning the "lines" that the skills necessary for delivering them are neglected and a potentially dynamic learning experience becomes another "boring lecture" to the students.

Familiarity with the subject can also result in a decline in enthusiasm as the same content material is presented year after year. At this time it is important to identify with the students in the class and remember that to them the information represents a totally new experience. I have heard actors state that they strive to generate the same level of enthusiasm for a role in their one-hundredth performance as they did in their first. Even though the scenes and dialogue have been rehearsed and performed many times before, they recognize that it is a new event for the members of the audience. It is the same in teaching. The humor, animation, and enthusiasm displayed by the teacher provide the framework for an enjoyable learning experience.

When actors can no longer generate enthusiasm for a role, they can move on to assume other roles in new productions. Unfortunately, teachers are not afforded this luxury, but the teacher does have an advantage over the actor. An actor who tires of a role is limited in the adjustments that can be made in the portrayal of the character while still maintaining the continuity of the performance. Iago portrayed as a comic hero would definitely upset the balance of Othello. On the other hand, a teacher can assume many characters and utilize many techniques and still present the same content material to the students. If a topic begins to appear dry and uninteresting to you as a teacher, you can imagine how the students in your class will respond to your presentation. As teachers, our audiences pay a high price for admission to our performances, and I firmly believe that at the conclusion of the course they should feel that they have received their money's worth.

TESTIMONIAL 4

Virginia Schaefer Carroll
English Department
Kent State University
East Liverpool, Ohio 43920

Because I teach composition and literature to non-majors who usually resist—if not detest—the subject matter of all English courses, one of my objectives in each course is to make the subject more interesting and accessible. Many of the acting skills described in this book can be useful in engaging students in the course and focusing their attention on the major ideas or problems of a discipline. The technique that I find most useful, however, is the dramatic aside.

In the pedagogical context, an aside means a turning away from the "text" of the class lecture or outline for the day and a turning toward the students themselves. To be dramatic, the aside must be seen as a clear interruption of the text, probably achieved by such stage techniques as changing the voice, physical space, expression, and pacing of delivery. As on the stage, an effective aside should be a well-integrated surprise, performed naturally and spontaneously in response to the audience. Also, no matter how entertaining the aside may be, the professor must achieve a smooth transition back to the text.

My own use of such a technique began with my first teaching at the university level. I learned quickly that a well-timed, slightly prolonged pause riveted the students' attention, and that I could use that space effectively with an aside. Sometimes these asides were as startling as an actor's movements toward the audience in experimental theater: for example, during a particularly dry, but essential, review of argumentative structure, I might suddenly change face and place, make direct eye contact, and say, "I know what you're thinking." I then glance around the classroom, and in exaggerated parody of my and their voices, guess the random thoughts and complaints of a range of students. Their surprised laughter suggests that my guesses about their responses are fairly accurate and that they are relieved to know I understand their difficulty with the subject matter.

In recent years, I have been relying on this technique much more unobtrusively, but students come to recognize and enjoy the moments when I drop the script. One of the skills of composition is the development of an argument through specific examples—a challenge to those who want to fill their essays with platitudes and lovely abstractions. The literature in many courses, such as Great Books, seems remote and inaccessible to the students. So I frequently pepper the lectures with asides as examples; these are usually spontaneous responses to something in the room, to an NPR report I heard on the drive to campus, to an issue facing the university or community, to some event from my own life, or even to an occurrence out the window (the Ohio River is conveniently located as a visual aid). Sometimes these asides take on the proportions of true digressions, lasting a few moments and conveyed dramatically. But often I deliver them at high speeds or mumbling audibly; students learn to pay attention or they miss most of the jokes.

Such a technique is especially effective at the campus where I teach. Many of my students seek a connection to what they are learning and struggle to see an intersection of English courses and their career paths. The technique of using asides seems to put students at ease with what they are hearing and what they are thinking; the students become more animated, spontaneous, and enthusiastic in their responses; they seem to trust themselves more in drawing conclusions from their own experiences, responses, and observations (an essential skill in critical thinking); and they overcome some of their resistance to the subject matter. It's also fun.

TESTIMONIAL 5

Raymond J. Clough
Department of Modern Languages
Canisius College
Buffalo, New York 14208

In the mid-60s, as a young college teacher, I had the good luck one evening to hear the actor Vincent Price do a dramatic reading of Edgar Allan Poe's "The Tell-Tale Heart." It was a large auditorium, and Price was sitting in an overstuffed armchair, a table at his side and a large book on his lap—no other decor. Bathed in the soft glow of a spotlight, he proceeded to enthrall the audience of perhaps one thousand people with a flawless and moving reading of Poe's classic story. No one budged; few coughed. Price held his audience spellbound for the entire reading. He used all the tricks of his trade—dramatic pauses, voice modulation and projection, crisp articulation. He scanned the audience, seemed to be speaking directly to each one of us. The effect was verbal alchemy.

This was a great epiphany for me. That night I relearned the importance of something I had been taught in grammar school—elocution—which, as every actor knows, is essential to the theater. A teacher must likewise pay attention to training the voice, learning to project it and to develop a comfortable, natural delivery style. The effort will pay enormous dividends in the classroom where it is critical to communicate clearly with your audience.

Price's performance that night also drove home to me the necessity of knowing materials cold, of having a sense of stage presence, and the importance of gestures. His glances at the book on his lap were merely for calculated effect. He knew the tale by heart, and, as the story built to its inexorable climax, he put the book aside to rise and slowly move forward to his audience, beating his breast rhythmically as he described *basso profundo* the heart pounding ever-louder under the floorboards. He was clearly feeding off our rapt attention, and we, in turn, were responding to his transcendence. Effective teaching is performance art also. Every class can and should be a dramatic event, and, if you are very lucky, every now and then when you and the audience are one, you will know why it is a very special calling.

Good teaching is natural. It flows. It requires a sense of timing. It is very useful to move around the room, make your students follow you as you approach them, invade their space conspiratorially, confidentially, as if to share something special with them and then draw back, pulling their attention toward you. A class can, in a sense, be choreographed, and the effect can be dramatic. You have to know how, as the comics say, to work a room. This, of course, can be taught theoretically, but the skill is best learned and honed by trial and error.

An effective teacher knows instinctively how to hold a class. He or she has great flexibility and can adjust teaching techniques to the situation at hand. When things go flat, a little self-deprecating humor, improvisation, or a set routine can save the day.

It is a truism that people learn in different ways. As far as possible, classes must be multisensorial—a shotgun approach. We sometimes forget, however, that people also learn at different rates. Just as there are many rehearsals before opening night in the theater, classroom material must be reviewed, the message highlighted, and repeated before the students are asked to "perform publicly" on an exam.

Good teaching must constantly question and renew itself, otherwise, as Ionesco taught us in *La LeÁon*, learning can become fatal to the learner.

TESTIMONIAL 6

Karin A. Grimnes
Department of Biology
Alma College
Alma, Michigan 48801

Although I have had no formal training in acting techniques, I have become increasingly aware of their importance to the quality and effectiveness of my teaching. As my teaching style has evolved, I have paid special attention to the use of my body and the use of space in the classroom. I am not afraid to use these techniques in a humorous or self-deprecating mode if needed. My primary goal is to increase student motivation, learning, and attentiveness in any way that works.

In the classroom, I am in continual motion. I frequently find myself pacing while I talk, and often gesture toward the board for emphasis. I write notes in outline form, and write very fast. Consequently, I spend little time with my back to the class. I enjoy sweeping gestures and dramatic pauses. Sometimes I cheer for correct answers or make victory gestures. I maintain eye contact with most members of the class, and therefore I can often tell when a point is not understood.

I teach courses in biology, and one (developmental biology) involves an appreciation of three-dimensional structures in development. I describe the events of development using myself as the embryo, twisting and turning my upper body as needed. Then I am able to ask students which side of the embryo is on the yolk and other questions about the relationship of embryonic parts. I encourage them to do the same motions and will often grab a student and make them bend, and then describe the events going on around them. I warn them at the beginning of the term that I may get physical with them. As I am a short person, this statement amuses them, and they usually allow me this privilege.

Another helpful technique to illustrate moving layers involves putting on two jackets and demonstrating how some layers must fuse before others. By asking them to explain what I have done, I can quickly determine their level of understanding. I may ask them to repeat the demonstration. Most of these techniques I use in the lab where I might be talking with three students at a time since I do not wish to embarrass students by forcing them to act the motions out in front of the entire class.

Another class I teach is invertebrate biology. I illustrate crab foraging behavior, spider orientation, and scorpion attacks by waving arms and leaping or lunging. I may ask students to demonstrate prey escape behavior while I play predator. I have found that the behavior demonstrations help solidify concepts and create an "episode" that is remembered intact for a long period of time.

When I have a major point to emphasize, or I can tell that student interest is flagging, I invade their space. Students are immediately more attentive when their space is compromised, but I try not to overuse this technique. When I am presenting an argument, I may present one side at one end of the classroom and the other view some distance away. I then ask questions and run to the side which the answers support. When I bring up contradictory information, it may be accompanied by a melodramatic gesture of despair.

I believe in the skills I have listed above; these skills have been added slowly to my repertoire. I am always searching for new ideas, but have discovered that not all techniques are suitable for my teaching style. I can usually identify inappropriate techniques, but if I have any doubt I use a few students as victims. They let me know when I am off base.

TESTIMONIAL 7

Roger A. Hall
Department of Theater and Dance
James Madison University
Harrisonburg, Virginia 22807

One of the courses I teach to my undergraduates is playwriting, and I am struck by the ways in which constructing a lecture or a classroom exercise is similar to writing a scene or a short play. Plays are but human will striving to attain goals and confronted by opposition and obstacles. Teachers can use that same scheme to present information that induces questions and creates suspense.

One of the lessons that playwriting has taught me is to pose questions for the characters and for the audience in the very first lines of a play. The same is true for a class, where the audience is the students. A teacher needs to structure material in order to pose questions at the start of a class. When I'm talking about tragedy, I'll ask, "Why for 2,500 years have audiences gone to see plays about awful things happening to decent people?" But the questions don't have to be direct. If I hang up five different kinds of masks before the class begins, the questions about what those different faces represent, how they might have been used, and how I intend to use them in the class are inherent in the props before I've said a word. Asking questions and getting the "audience" to formulate questions leads to problem-solving, and problem-solving leads to critical thinking.

Conflict is another lesson of playwriting applicable to teaching. We teachers forget sometimes that the factual information and the standard opinions we impart were not always so concrete. Evolution, the shape of the earth, and the center of the solar system once sparked dangerous clashes of opinion. History, science, even art and culture are rife with conflict and obstacles. Conflicts not only make subject matter exciting, but also reveal to students the human character of the material. I encourage teachers to see learning as a series of conflicts and obstacles rather than an inevitable narrative of "this and then this and then this."

Another lesson common to playwriting and to other forms of writing is to write about what you know best. Similarly, teachers should use what they know best. I still recall the stories of my eighth grade American history teacher. He made us feel the sensations of a war by telling us about his experiences in World War II. He made the battle of Gettysburg come alive by describing the terrain he'd walked himself. All of us, no matter how mundane our lives, have personal memories and experiences to draw upon, and whatever personal references we can use to connect solidly to the material will linger in our students' minds.

"Climax" is another playwriting element that can help teachers structure a good class. Whether I'm working with playwrights or performers, I'll always ask, "What's the climax of this scene or play?" Teachers should ask themselves the same question. Students won't remember everything, so a good teacher must determine the most important part. If a student will only remember one thing from today's class or lecture, what should it be? Then build to that. Emphasize that. Make it the climax of the class.

The use of these playwriting techniques—inducing questions, identifying conflicts and obstacles, using personal connections to material, and developing material to a climax—will help a teacher create classes with drama: classes that generate interest, sustain suspense, and leave students with a feeling that something important has been achieved.

TESTIMONIAL 8

Carol L. Harrison (retired)
Department of Humanities
Medaille College
Buffalo, New York 14214

After using acting skills and techniques in the classroom in varied courses over the span of twenty years, I can readily attest to their aid in maintaining both the vibrancy and quality of learning taking place. So often, professors looking for ways to improve upon the traditional pedagogy of lecture-discussion overlook the simple and simply fun aspect of incorporating acting and simulation principles into teaching.

I have often heard from beleaguered, burned-out colleagues, "I can't act" or "You can't be sure students are learning anything" to "It's a waste of good time better spent." Not so. For classroom freshness, student vitality, and assessable student learning outcomes, nothing beats enhancing a lecture or reiterating a difficult theoretical concept like acting.

Whether it is a literature or writing class, I always follow three cardinal rules of acting in the class. First, keep the activity relevant to the concept to be learned. For example, in a simulation technique I use in an argumentation and persuasion writing class geared to pre-law majors, I bring to class the usual old briefcase, plus my coat and purse. I intentionally leave the lecture hall door open. No one seems to notice these slight changes. I begin the lecture as usual on the topic of observation, detail, and description. After a few minutes and with my back to the class, I write the class objectives for the day on the board. At a pre-arranged verbal signal, a student from another class runs into the lecture hall and furtively snatches my purse left purposely on the front desk.

The class objective is now open for discussion. As in the real world, I ask the class to give an accurate description of the thief in every detail—the same question witnesses are asked to answer after a surprise event. Of course, no one gives an accurate description, which opens up the relevant but tangential topic of adjectives and accuracy. How tall is tall? Exactly what color of blue? I then request the "thief" to return so that the class may have a good look.

The second rule is to use props. As in the previously cited example, the purse and coat were considered props. Props enhance the "reality" of acting. They make the involvement of the imagination immediate and visual. Props may be complex or simple. I try to keep the props simple mainly because it takes up less class preparation time and less set up time. It also permits handling of simple props by students when called for and allows more class time for discussion.

A doctor's bag, a feather boa, and a briefcase and newspaper serve as simple props in a basic college-level writing course discussing the importance of active voice with verbs. Pre-chosen student volunteers from the class are picked to demonstrate the variety of ways to dress up the rather simple verb "to walk." Our first example is the harassed businessman late for an important appointment. The student picks up the briefcase and the newspaper and in front of the class (space has been blocked out for this activity before class begins) shows how Mr. X would walk to his appointment. Surprise! "To walk" now becomes "walked briskly," "hurried," "scurried," and "raced."

Dr. Y on call with his doctor's bag now demonstrates "marching." "Walking proudly" down the hospital corridors. Finally, Miss Z with her feather boa elicits a different kind of walk. "To walk" now becomes "strutting," "sauntering," "sashaying" down the street. What we find in terms of learning outcomes is that students in this class indeed know the other terms for the simple word "walk," but never used them. Our little acting activity accompanied by the use of simple props set fire to vocabulary building and encouraged the usage of other less familiar words. The lesson ends with an introduction to Roget's *Thesaurus* and a class eager and willing to try new words in writing.

The third cardinal principle in use of acting activities is perhaps the most obvious—involve the students. It is often the temptation of a professor who is a natural "ham" to hog the stage. Let the students become the principals, for active involvement encourages active learning and successful retention.

In the freshman writing course, teaching the basic rhetorical modes can be anything but exciting. They are standard and unvaried; however, through acting even the most static mode can become an exciting and valuable exercise.

In one exercise, I come to class five minutes late. I am dressed in the costume of a fashionable young woman. My class has been told that they are counselors who must get to the root or cause of this young woman's problem by the end of the period. They may, in turn, ask her any questions they like. As the "patient," I will exhibit all of the "effects" of her illness or problem. During the course of the period, I take out of my purse the picture of a young man and sigh. I chew gum; I act distracted. I act morose and depressed. I cough and cry into my Kleenex. I answer questions laconically. Gradually, they build up a list of "effects" from which they can deduce a probable "cause"—she's heartbroken because she's been jilted! On an examination, they surely remember cause and effect!

Thus any instructor with a little imagination and initiative can become an actor in the classroom. It is not only challenging, but it provides the life and vitality, the spark to the traditional pedagogy of lecture discussion. However, a word of caution: acting and simulation activities are not a replacement or cover-up for inadequacy of content or preparation. Students are quick to spot a quack. Following the cardinal rules of relevancy to topical content, use of simple props, and student involvement will guarantee a successful acting activity and student learning outcomes, no matter what the subject matter.

TESTIMONIAL 9
James Kurre
Penn State Teaching Fellow
Penn State Behrend
Erie, PA 16563

In one of my Economics classes, I have a visit from a pseudo-guest. The class before, I tell the students that we'll be having a visitor who is running for County Executive, and he's campaigning on some of the very issues that we're discussing in class. I warn them that he's a little eccentric, but well-meaning, and they should be prepared to discuss/debate these issues with him. I assign them to read about the concepts we'll be discussing before the next class, and tell them to be prepared since they'll be representing the college to an outside visitor. The topics of this particular assignment deal with the mutual benefits from trade, variations in resource endowments from place to place, economies of large-scale production, and comparative advantage.

On the day of the class, our visitor is not there as class starts (I'm a little distressed about that) but then I see him outside the door and go out to welcome him. In fact, the visitor is me in a different persona. Out in the hall I quickly put on an appropriate (or inappropriate!) t-shirt or jacket, a ball cap, and maybe one or two other easy props, and come back in the room and introduce myself as Jim-Bob Springnoni.

Jim-Bob is too loud and demonstrative, has a bit of a (bad) accent, is very outgoing, waves his hands and arms a lot as he talks, and shakes hands all the way up the aisle to the front of the room. He's the worst kind of pushy, opinionated politician. Jim-Bob's a likable guy. He sometimes uses home-spun phrases or strange examples such as, "That's as obvious as a cat at a funeral," or "Even a city councilman can see that." He's sure he has the common-sense answer to all problems. He spouts popular, but clearly wrong, ideas about what we should do with economic policy related to trade and protectionism.

The kids are typically taken aback by Jim-Bob's whirlwind appearance, and are reluctant to talk at first. After all, this is very different from our usual class! But I stay in the Jim-Bob character and he manages to wheedle or goad them into a discussion of the first key issue that I'm trying to get across. Jim-Bob starts off with an argument that virtually anyone can see through. That encourages the students to speak up and point out the error in his logic. If no one speaks up, he addresses one or two individuals. ("Say there, young fella, you look like an intelligent one. *You* agree with me, don't you?") He provokes them to either agree to a clearly wrong idea, or to begin to say what's wrong with it. That gets us into the discussion. Then he moves to less obvious fallacies. The kids understand pretty quickly that each of Jim-Bob's arguments is wrong, but it challenges them to figure out for themselves where the flaw is in the logic for each case. The later ones are much less obvious, of course. It's a little like solving a puzzle or a mystery.

Along the way, sometimes I need to step out of character for a second to make a point. In that case, I take off the hat and speak in my normal voice. After I'm done, I put the hat back on and am Jim-Bob again. When the hat's on, I'm Jim-Bob and the students have to deal with him; they can't turn to their professor for help. (Asking the professor questions is a way to avoid having to come up with the answers themselves.) If they try, Jim-Bob points out that Dr. Kurre left the room and will be back later, and they have to deal with Jim-Bob on their own just now.

It's a fun change from our regular class. It's a little scary to walk in that room as Jim-Bob each time I do this, but by staying in character and being outrageous, Jim-Bob wins them over and they typically wind up participating enthusiastically once they get what we're trying to do. It's a memorable class for them, and helps them see the crucial points in a very different way. You don't have to be a good actor to do this—I'm certainly not! It just takes an over-the-top attitude and a commitment to stay in character until the students get into it, too. And Jim-Bob's just the guy to get them to do that! Remember, it's not *you* saying all this outrageous stuff—it's Jim-Bob. Helping Jim-Bob see the light can be a very effective teaching technique.

Aside from learning the material in a different way, no matter how the class goes, the students appreciate the fact that I've tried to do something a little different from the ordinary, and keep class interesting.

TESTIMONIAL 10

Douglas Light
Department of Biology
Ripon College
Ripon, Wisconsin 54971

The lights dim. The curtain rises. A man appears on the screen; he is reading a letter. The camera closes in on his face, and a tear can be seen emerging from his right eye. Soon there are tears streaming from both eyes. His expression of sadness is filled with such torment the audience begins to cry. Although the audience is cognizant that they are watching a celluloid fantasy, they still cry. Why? Good acting sweeps people away and involves them in the mood of the acting production. It is the ability to involve an audience that a teacher must master if he/she is to be completely successful at teaching.

The best way I know to involve students and persuade them to learn is to show unbridled enthusiasm. I express enthusiasm through excitement and animation of my voice, hands, face, and body, and by my words. I lecture with the exuberance of a football announcer describing a 96-yard touchdown run. The response from students to this enthusiasm has been very rewarding. For example, one student wrote on a course evaluation, "How can the professor get so enthusiastic about osmosis? His enthusiasm did convince me that there must be something interesting about it, so I listened and learned." Another student commented, "How can the professor be so energetic at 8:00 AM; it's absolutely revolting, however, it does keep me interested."

Although essential, I have found that enthusiasm alone is not sufficient to be a good teacher. The difference between a good actor and a great one is that the latter not only memorizes the script but also "becomes" the character portrayed by knowing all there is to know about that character. By analogy, it is absolutely essential that a teacher be completely (within reason) knowledgeable about his/her subject matter. This does not mean just memorizing the lecture material but also being familiar with pertinent background information. To help keep command of the subjects I teach, I read all assignments in the textbooks and pertinent journals and books on a regular basis. A good command of the subject also permits me to include suspense and surprise in my teaching. For example, I will often pose a series of questions at the beginning of class and answer them during the lecture. Like an old "cliff-hanger," I will leave some questions unanswered until the next class meeting. I believe this helps foster critical thinking. Rewards for long hours of preparation are plentiful. Student evaluations have commented that a knowledgeable teacher is much more interesting than one appearing to grope for answers.

For an actor, control of voice expression is important for indicating emotion; for a teacher it is used for emphasis. I stress important points by speaking loudly and in an animated manner, whereas tangential points are presented in a more relaxed manner. I have found that my change in voice intensity and expression has helped students distinguish more easily between important points and ancillary ones. Further, I have found that addition of humor helps break the intensity of a lecture and recharge the students' energy level.

In conclusion, I incorporate enthusiasm, animation, suspense, surprise, voice control, and humor in my lectures. Further, I work hard at being knowledgeable about the subjects I teach. Because all of this requires a tremendous expenditure of energy, an immediate litmus test for my success is leaving a classroom or laboratory feeling physically and emotionally drained.

TESTIMONIAL 11

Anthony J. Lisska
Department of Philosophy
Denison University
Granville, Ohio 43023

I have found that using humor at an appropriate time in a class is an effective way both to make a point and to keep student interest alive. Of course, humor cannot take the place of instruction, but it can help to develop the instructional process. When I taught the Philosophy of Education, I customarily sent my students to the theater department to enroll in acting classes. The students considering secondary school teaching needed to become very outgoing and spontaneous in their delivery. While instruction is never coextensive with entertainment, nonetheless to learn how to work an audience should not be downplayed.

One example of humor in teaching philosophy comes from a consideration of Aristotelian ethics. In his *Nicomachean Ethics*, Aristotle goes to great lengths to indicate that specific circumstances and the particular situation are extremely important in determining the correctness of a moral judgment. Hence the particular context of a situation is morally relevant in determining the moral appropriateness of an action.

The example I use is both humorous and experiential. I build the scene from my experience as a freshly minted sixteen-year-old driver. The scene goes like this: My two brothers and I had the family car out for a spin. I am the oldest, and I was introducing my brothers to the thrills of 1950s drag racing. We took our parents' car (a 1953 Chrysler with fluid drive—that means you had a clutch with an automatic shift). One can embellish the story by thinking of *Happy Days* or *Grease*. I tell the students that my brothers and I got the car out on a country road about 9 o'clock on a cool summer night. We decided to see what it would do as a potential dragster. I put the car in low gear, floored the accelerator as much as I could with the clutch in. The engine revved up, then I popped that clutch to see if this Chrysler sedan would accelerate quickly enough to be a potentially fine dragster. As soon as I popped the clutch, all we could hear was "crash, bang, ping, ping, ping, thump," and then the car would not go forward. [slight pause] And then I mention, "Of course, I tore the transmission out of the car!"

Here we were, my brothers and I, stranded on a country road. My younger brother kept telling me I had really made a mess and our father was going to have me drawn and quartered and then tarred and feathered. I got home paralyzed with fear. I thought my father would certainly banish me from the family after taking me to the woodshed. I climbed the stairs to our apartment, shaking, knees quivering, heart fluttering. I had just torn the transmission out of the family car. I didn't use my own car for that, but the family car! He certainly would have the justification to punish me with gusto.

I found my father and told him what I had done. I was expecting to get cracked across the face with the back of his hand. My dad looked at me, straight in the eyes, and said slowly and earnestly, "Son, you can't treat a car that way!"

That statement of my father's, I tell my students, had more of a profound effect on me than had he punished me with an old-fashioned whipping and grounded me for six months.

Of course, the Chrysler was fixed. The mechanic gave my father the two gears which I had stripped. Well past my graduate school days, I kept those gears on my desk as a reminder *not* to do stupid things.

I tell my students that this was an example of a person seizing upon a particular situation and acting in a certain way which had a profound effect. The buildup of the story is humorous—the students laugh and they can relate to it. And then they do see the final punch line concerning a wise father who knew how to react to a prodigal son.

TESTIMONIAL 12

William M. Mahoney
Department of History
West Virginia Wesleyan College
Buckhannon, West Virginia 2620

As a history professor at a small liberal arts college, I have spent a decade learning my craft in an environment conducive to the development of educational acting skills and the awareness of the classroom as a stage upon which the instructor may combine aspects of the lecturer and the performer.

In my view, the important first step in creating a comfortable classroom environment is a process of self-disclosure, whereby the instructor breaks down some of the more formalized elements of the teacher–student relationship in favor of a more personalized approach. From the instructor's standpoint, this means knowing students' names and engaging them in conversation before and after class as a means of converting strangers into a receptive audience. In addition, it is helpful if the students view the instructor as a real person with a personality and interests that extend beyond the boundaries of the classroom and the course. The key to all of this is accessibility, and it has been especially important for me to develop a less formal relationship with students so that I am more comfortable in "performing" as a lecturer and discussion leader. The more comfortable I am with a class, the more spontaneous and creative I try to become in explaining history to majors and non-majors alike.

Personally, a successful process of self-disclosure affects my actual teaching in two distinct ways. First of all, it allows me to overcome my own reticence about addressing an audience and therefore to utilize humor, personal touches, and even performance techniques in attempting to make history more than just a collection of names and dates. Second, the creation of a comfortable classroom environment allows me to abandon class notes in favor of greater use of physical space and a more spontaneous and impressionistic style of lecturing. The notes remain available for consultation during a lecture, but freedom of movement and the element of spontaneity take the instructor a step closer to utilizing acting skills without sacrificing narrative continuity or depth of detail in a lecture.

When discussing the performance aspects of lecturing, one can mean a number of things, from knowing one's lines to utilizing movement and gestures to draw a student's attention to the story lurking behind the facts. Given the wealth of dramatic events and fascinating individuals in history, the study of the past lends itself to storytelling techniques and to role-playing on the part of both teacher and student. In addition to using novels and plays as auxiliary readings in some courses, I often rely on storytelling techniques in an attempt to bring characters and events to life or to recreate a setting or environment to help students visualize the material. For instance, relating an "eyewitness" account of life in the trenches during the First World War or the fall of the Bastille during the French Revolution can create a storyline and characters for historical facts found in the textbook.

Finally, a degree of role-playing can also enhance the performance aspects of classroom teaching by personalizing the material from the perspective of a recognizable individual. By having Louis XIV describe his own achievements or Hitler and Mussolini explain why the voters must choose between them or chaos, the instructor can personalize history by luring students out of their own perspectives and presenting historical events at the level of individual experience.

TESTIMONIAL 13

Daniel J. McBrayer
Department of Education and Psychology
Berry College
Mount Berry, Georgia 30149-5019

As a teacher of psychology I find that my subject matter is quite easy to apply to "everyday" situations in the lives of undergraduate students. This process involves actively demonstrating the concept being taught, much like the actress would demonstrate the feelings and nuances in her role on stage. This demonstration is accomplished through acting out, sometimes in role-play, the concept in ways that are personal, dramatic, and/or humorous.

Just as an actress in an intimate theater will move close to her audience to grab their attention, a teacher can use proxemics to drive home a point. I spend considerable time "in the audience." I always have two to five empty chairs around the room and use these chairs to sit next to a student I am questioning or challenging. When seated I am at eye level and engage in a conversation, while the other students witness—sometimes in awe! At times I will role-play with the student, and at other times I will role-play with an imaginary student in my empty chair. The power of this strategy is remembered and discussed among the students for weeks and months. Using movement, proximity, and demonstration in class can actually be more powerful than acting on stage because of the interaction it affords.

There are times when I create a preplanned, written scenario to be acted out with preselected students. This modification of a script gets the students directly involved in the teaching of the concept. At other times I have a colleague in my department enter my classroom at a prearranged time to share news, attack, embrace, and so on. This strategy will "bring to life" a concept we are discussing (e.g., eyewitness testimony, perception, emotion). In each case, we (as actors) are using voice, emotion, proximity, and reality as teaching techniques.

As a method of creating suspense in the audience, I frequently use two strategies. A strategy that works at my institution is to share with them some developing administrative thought or policy that will impact their lives. These situations are, in the end, clearly communicated as fictitious. However, while I am sharing the potential policy with them, it is very real. Numerous concepts from a psychology textbook can be tied to the thinking and behavior of administrators. This process involves them, forces them to see alternatives to their thinking, and causes them to crystallize their thoughts on the topic. In a sense this is manipulating an audience as we would in acting—yet not in a pejorative manner.

The second strategy to create interest and suspense in the audience is the use of my imaginary family. We have unusual names like Vachael, Oral, Alred, Orval, Bertha, Bobby Jack, and so on. We also have unusual occupations and live in cities with very unique names. This uses humor and serves in being "catchy." Students will notice how Vachael seems to be living, using, or misunderstanding the concept being taught, but may not pay as much attention if it was my sister Allison.

The [previous] techniques clearly involve acting in teaching. I use them because I enjoy going to class and choose to make the learning environment fit my personality style—and that is to enjoy the subject matter, make it come alive, and make it last beyond the next test! My acting experience, outside the classroom, has been somewhat limited. I have learned how to act, and how to teach, on the same stage! I believe, given the experience base of the current undergraduate student population, we need to meet them part way—which suggests that they have been accustomed to being "entertained." These strategies do not "limit" my responsibility to teach content; they simply enhance the content; and make it a part of the student's reality.

TESTIMONIAL 14

Scott Richardson
Department of Modern and Classical Languages
St. John's University
Collegeville, Minnesota 56321

As a classics professor I regularly feel on the defensive in non-major courses. To those oriented toward practicality and "relevance" (a word generally used with a baiting tone in my presence), I must make a special effort to earn their interest by showing that works written in a dead language by people who lived before 1960 actually do have a strong bearing on their own lives and world. Besides directly addressing this issue as we approach the texts, I very often make use of a couple routines.

Every college student in the country watches the David Letterman show. Once a week he starts the program with the Viewer Mail segment, which involves facetious replies to usually facetious letters, a parody of the "Sixty Minutes" bit. Toward the end of every semester in all of my courses, including language courses, I start the class with my own Viewer Mail. I write the letters myself, of course, and prepare the replies, which I deliver from memory as though talking to a TV audience. Some of the letters have to do with the worth of studying dead languages or the literature and culture of dead civilizations; some deal with the worth of education in general; some poke fun at my own interests or pedagogical habits. I try to make most of the letters sound almost (but not quite) like letters that people would write who had no understanding of what a liberal arts education entails or why I am teaching what and how I do. My implicit mockery of those who would think this way brings out in the open some of the doubts actually felt by many and at the same time makes the students feel superior to the morons who would so bluntly call attention to their own philistinism. I pretend to take the letters seriously and to give an off-the-wall reply that tacitly (but clearly) hints at the true value of a classical education. This routine is always well received and involves spontaneous group participation stemming from everyone's acquaintance with the TV show. The surprise factor is important, I think, so I would recommend it as a one-shot gimmick. It works best with more than half of the term over, since it depends on the students' familiarity with the subject matter and with the professor's attitude toward the field.

Greek tragedy and mythology, foreign as they seem, have a great deal of "relevance" to everyone's life, and a classics professor would have little trouble luring the students to see their own lives and societies in light of the grand stories and dramas of the Greeks. My favorite routine comes with the discussion of the god Dionysus, which I usually center around Euripides' *The Bacchae*, his play about Dionysus' revenge on his blasphemous relatives. Dionysus is the god of the irrational element of the universe and in human nature, a force we neglect or repress at our peril, yet to follow it blindly leads to catastrophe. How to handle the Dionysian vis-á-vis the Apollonian in ourselves is one of our biggest struggles; how should we respect Dionysus' power yet not become devotees? To bring this character to life, I invoke the cult film *The Rocky Horror Picture Show*, whose main character is a stunning avatar of Dionysus: he is effeminate and virile, gentle and vicious, hedonistic and vengeful, soft and powerful; his philosophical tenet is "give yourself over to absolute pleasure," and he is unmerciful toward anyone who stands in his way. He introduces himself with a rousing rock 'n' roll song, "Sweet Transvestite," whose tune I have stolen for my own song, following closely the original lyrics, about Dionysus, in which I present the central features of the god's character, the main plot elements of the play, and several of the technical terms of Bacchic worship. I pass around the lyrics, get out my guitar, make sure they are familiar with the film song (either tape, videotape, or my own performance), and then lead them all through this Dionysian hymn. Everyone—even those who are shy— joins in uninhibited. They come away with a vivid picture of this bit of Greek culture.

TESTIMONIAL 15

Betsy Rogers
National Teacher of the Year
Elementary 1-2
Birmingham, Alabama 35020

The essence of my philosophy and the climate of my classroom are best described by the poem that is on the door of my classroom which begins, "You are entering the world of a child." I believe that children need to learn in a safe, caring and intellectually engaging environment with a teacher who is responsive to the needs of the children.

From the beginning of my teaching career, I have drawn on my dramatic instincts to engage students. As a teacher of young children, I realized this was an essential quality to be an effective classroom teacher. Through the years, I collected props and outfits to create the type of dramatic classroom that would motivate students and create a memory.

One of the most humorous teaching moments in my career came when I was dressed as Betsy Ross telling the story of our flag. I had a wonderful Colonial outfit that was given to me by a member of The American Federation of Women's Clubs. I powdered my hair, wore my great grandmother's wire rim glasses and demonstrated with an old flag and sewing basket. At the time, I was teaching first grade and these students were at the age where they really knew who I was, but had just enough doubt to think I might be the real Betsy Ross. During the presentation, the school intercom came on and called my name. I froze not knowing what to do. Finally after calling my name several times, I had to answer. The class burst into laughter. To this day, one of the students in this class, who is now in graduate school at Oklahoma State University, still laughs about this incident. My point being, by using drama and the unexpected, this lesson made a lasting impression on my students. This is what drama can do to make lessons come alive in the classroom.

Understanding that it is important for students to be actively involved in lessons, I used a theme-based curriculum that provided the opportunity for the students to be involved in dramatic situations. By the conclusion of the theme, our classroom environment completely reflected the study. For example, when we completed a Middle East/Desert theme, our room displayed desert sunsets and magic carpet art, an animal desert center, desert mural, Middle East countries center, flags and maps of the countries, charts about special places, an Egyptian computer program, and a nomad tent called our Aladdin Tent. Our "stage" had been set! The theme concluded with all students, including myself, dressing in Middle Eastern costumes and having a Middle Eastern feast.

Creating the type of exciting and engaging classroom often can happen by acting on the teachable moment. However, I believe to sustain this type of environment it must be intentional. This takes a lot of planning and gathering of resources. It took me years to collect props and items to match my teaching themes. Garage sales can often be a great resource for props and costumes. I also used a variety of puppets and masks for Readers' Theater. As I looked at each lesson, I would always ask myself, "How can I make a memory out of this lesson for my students?" This takes intentional planning and often lots of time. However, it always paid off in big dividends as I continually run into former students or their parents and they recall their favorite lesson in my class.

TESTIMONIAL 16

Martha Rogers
Department of Telecommunications
Bowling Green State University
Bowling Green, Ohio 43402

It's my belief that good teaching is 25 percent education and 75 percent inspiration. The most valuable lesson a student can learn in the classroom is that the subject is fascinating, exploring it is meaningful and worthwhile, and learning is fun.

To me, the best way to generate excitement in students is to generate it myself. Good actors who receive positive reviews are often described as exhibiting a high energy level. That energy is contagious. Of course, my job is to walk into the classroom well prepared with my material, thorough, refreshed and updated, and well organized. That's the 25 percent education part. But the real challenge is to teach that material each time as if it's the first time. Every "performance" must retain the excitement of opening night. For every member of the audience, after all, it is just that.

Every professor has her or his own style. What seems to work for me includes lots of eye contact, voice modulation, and poignant pauses. (I sometimes hear a southern Baptist preacher in the room and realize it's only myself.) But however dramatic the hand gestures or however careful and clear the diction (I'm trying to improve this), the one most important element to me, the one that cannot be faked, is enthusiasm—sheer, delighted *exuberance* with the topic and the audience. I hope to give the impression that I can't wait to hear what I'm going to say next. If my goal is to educate my students a little and inspire them a lot, it's as important that I raise my eyebrows as much as review questions, that I pace the classroom as well as the material, that I look over the rim of my eyeglasses as carefully as I look over student term papers.

The effect is everything. Whatever my students may think of *me* when they leave the classroom doesn't matter. What *does* matter is what they think of *themselves*. If they are challenged to do the job better, to learn more, to know more, do more, be more, I can see it in their eyes. It's worth it to wave my arms, pound a desk, shout, use funny voices—whatever it takes to get a point across and watch for laughing, for looks of concern, for incredulity, for thoughtfulness, and ultimately for the look that says "I've never thought of that before!"

TESTIMONIAL 17

Charlotte Rotkin (retired)
Professor of English
Pace University
Pelham Manor, New York 10803

I teach literature to a diverse population of undergraduates at a large urban university in New York, and have found that the thespian's technique lends itself to success in the classroom. I use theatrics as an efficient and pedagogically sound method of presenting information in an entertaining manner. A dramatic delivery and self-deprecating irony can be extremely effective in engaging students' attention. When I rely on humor as a teaching tool, I notice that some of the usual antipathy to literature is allayed. I therefore open every semester with the following remarks: "I know you didn't register for this course because you love English! You're here because it's required. So try to make the best of it. Pretend you've turned on your television set and the channel selector got stuck on me!"

Responsive smiles and the relaxation of body postures result in a change in the electrical charge in the room. From a negative atmosphere of uncertainty, animosity, and fear, the electrical current has become, to some extent, a positive one. I've captured some members of the audience. But I'll be on stage another forty minutes and I can't afford to lose them. So I present my regulations regarding decorum in an institution of higher learning. I say, in a semi-authoritarian tone, "I have two rules in this class. There will be no hitting and no vulgarity!" The ensuing explosion of laughter is occasionally interspersed with the query, "What's vulgarity?"

In addition to being exposed to the literary element of irony, by the time the first session is over, the class will have touched upon vocabulary enhancement via the definitions of irony, tone, and vulgarity. They will have been apprised of appropriate classroom behavior for college students, and they will have become aware of my demand for their active participation in the learning process, all painlessly presented through wit.

Our shared laughter creates a temporary bond between us. In order not to lose that precarious sense of identification between the student-audience and me, I, as instructor-performer, try to bring into being a theatrical use of available space, and I do that by envisioning the area separating my lectern from the first row of seats as the imagined apron of a stage. The space separating audience and performer can be bridged by stepping in front of the lectern and inclining the upper portion of the body over the imagined apron in responsive attention to a student's question or comment.

Most students are receptive to and gratified by the personal attention and eye contact I make as I move through the class-audience and attend (like a talk-show host) to the student whose hand is raised. When a point of view which I may not have considered is brought forth, I pause and indicate by my ruminating manner that I hadn't thought of that. I then take time to absorb it out loud, with an occasional assist from the originator of the idea, or from a similarly inclined other student. When I reach the perspective from which the students are coming, I generally nod in agreement and bowing slightly will say, "That's a very valid point you've got there. If I were wearing a hat, I'd take it off to you." Periodically a cap is proffered, and my gesture of a sweeping bow is well received. Although some students have difficulty analyzing irony, most recognize its intended wit in word, tone, or gesture and are responsive to its gentle humor.

TESTIMONIAL 18

James L. Smith
New Mexico Teacher of the Year
History
Las Cruces, New Mexico 88005

Kurt Vonnegut's statement, "You are what you pretend to be," serves as a good maxim for teachers. Every teacher needs to play a role and, when natural ability might fail, it may require the ability to pretend—pretend to be a person who can inspire students and bring a joy of learning into the classroom.

It has been thirty-five years since I sat in an algebra class, and I have long forgotten the process of solving algebraic equations. However, I have never forgotten the other lessons that I learned from my math teacher.

Mr. Dooley, my math teacher, did not tolerate foolishness. His class was designed to help students learn, and he used class time productively. He had a sense of humor, but his humor was always geared to the task of learning algebra. He could tell good stories with students hanging on every word, but the stories always led to a math problem that needed solving. He was relaxed, but his students never wasted time. I always knew to show up in his class ready to learn. I always felt compelled to do my best, because I knew Mr. Dooley would never accept a second-rate effort.

When I was in high school, I saw Mr. Dooley as a mythical figure, a character larger than life. I now realize something I could not have imagined then—he was also a human being with a variety of flaws that I am sure we could find in any human being. I now understand that the mythical character I thought of as "Mr. Dooley" was simply a role assumed by a man who understood the responsibilities of his profession. Teachers, like actors on a stage, assume a role to play. Mr. Dooley played his role well and, in the process, helped a lot of students.

Success in the classroom depends, in large part, on the role the teacher plays in front of students. Can the teacher inspire students and ignite flames of curiosity? Is the teacher the type of person who challenges students to do their best? Like good actors, good teachers know they must create a clearly-defined character for an audience. They know that if they want to inspire their audience they must create a character with which the audience can identify.

Good teachers also know that teaching demands full immersion in the role. After creating a role to assume in the classroom, the teacher must continue to play that role in the hallways between classes, at the Saturday night basketball game, and when running into students at the mall. After all, it may not be what a teacher does in the classroom that has the most impact on a student's life.

Success as a teacher demands that the character a teacher develops must seem authentic to students. In the same way that a moviegoer can spot a bad actor in the first reel, students can detect a fraudulent teacher on the first day of school. Teachers must therefore utilize the imagination of an actor to capture a sense of authenticity in the role they play. Students know whether their teacher is dedicated to the profession or is just marking time until the bell rings at the end of the day.

Teachers, like actors, must find elements of their own personality in the role they are playing. They must find the part of their spirit that wants to help students and then bring that spirit into the classroom. They must accentuate the part of their personality that is honest, caring, and full of love. And, they must shine a spotlight on the part of their soul that wants to give students a bright future and make the world a better place.

Like anyone else, a teacher might not always be the person he or she would like to be. Every teacher should try, however, to pretend to be the person who motivates students. Each teacher should try to act the part. Even if a teacher has played the part for several years, he or she can assume the attitude of a good actor and know that this year's audience—the students—has never before seen the performance. Each teacher must play the part well.

TESTIMONIAL 19

Trudy Steuernagel
Coordinator of Women's Studies
Political Science Department
Kent State University
Kent, Ohio 44242

I never thought of myself as an actor or the classroom as a stage, but clearly there are techniques I use that are shared with fellow performers. For me, the single most important thing I do in my political theory courses, aside from knowing the texts, is to position myself in respect to my students. My entire teaching career has been spent in a large state university. Most of the classrooms are, at best, impersonal. What I strive to do is create a sense of intimacy in the classroom.

It is not unusual for me to have fifty students in an introduction to political theory class. Since I emphasize class discussion, the creation of a sense of intimacy is particularly important, especially to those students who are uncomfortable speaking in front of a large number of people. I have found the following techniques useful. I am the only audio-visual aid. I remain firmly committed to a minimalist approach to teaching, and despite my recognition that many of this generation of students expect some kind of electronic enhancement, I make no concessions, no excuses (although it is true I am unable to operate a film projector, overhead projector, video or audio cassette recorder. I am somewhat more skilled at unrolling maps, and occasionally I will attempt to indicate the location of Thrace), and no apologies.

I use a podium resting on a table to hold some notes. I try to refer to them as infrequently as possible. This frees me to roam the room. I always do this during the lecture part of the class. I will often, if the room is long and shallow, position myself at one corner or the other for some extended periods of time. This directs student attention to me. I also try to match my pacing speed to my vocal speed. If, for example, I am setting the stage for a discussion of Plato's allegory of the cave, I will speak in hushed tones and pace very deliberately, attempting to create a mood for the students to place themselves in the cave, to imagine the flickering firelight and the macabre puppet show. As our discussion moves to the movement from the cave to the sunlight, I will all but run across the room, arms uplifted, and voice soaring. This works *only* if you are confident of your knowledge of the text. If you have to sneak a peek at your notes, the spell is broken.

When I am interested in greater student involvement during the discussion part of the class, I try to make myself as unobtrusive as possible. This is not too difficult since I am anything but a compelling physical presence. I will often sit on the table, pull my legs under me, and lean forward. At this stage I want to listen and be a part of the group. I try not to do anything that would distract attention from the student who is speaking.

I use variations of these techniques in all of my classes and, for the most part, have been rewarded with an exciting classroom atmosphere. A word of caution, however. I have also fallen over wastebaskets, knocked a map stand into a window, and bumped my shins on any number of inanimate offenders. The use of classroom space to enhance teaching has its dark side.

REFERENCES

Abrami, P. C., Leventhal, L., and Perry, R. P. 1982. Educational seduction. *Review of Educational Research* 52: 446–64.

Adams, P. 1992. *Gesundheit!: Bringing good health to you, the medical system, and society through physician service, complementary therapies, humor, and joy.* Rochester, VT: Healing Arts Press.

Adams, P. 1998. *House calls: How we can all heal the world one visit at a time.* San Francisco: Robert D. Reed.

Ambady, N., and Rosenthal, R. (1993). Half a minute: Predicting teacher evaluations from thin slices of nonverbal behavior and physical attractiveness. *Journal of Personality and Social Psychology,* 64(3): 431–41.

Andersen, J. F. 1986. Instructor nonverbal communication: Listening to our silent messages. *New Directions for Teaching and Learning* 26: 41–49.

Andersen, J., and Withrow, J. 1987. The impact of lecturer nonverbal expressiveness on improving mediated instruction. *Communication Education* 30(4): 242–53.

Anderson, V. 1977. *Training the speaking voice.* New York: Oxford University Press.

Armour, R. 1975. Humor in the classroom. *Independent School District* 35(1): 61.

Arnold, G. B. 1990. The teacher and nonverbal communication. *The Political Science Teacher* 3(3): 3–5.

Arterberry, T., and Sawatzky, B. (2006). *Meaning through motion: A study guide.* http://performingarts.net/Trent/study.html

Axtell, J. 1997. Twenty-five reasons to publish. *Journal of Scholarly Publishing* 29(1).

Bain, K. 2004. *What the best college teachers do.* Cambridge, MA: Harvard University Press.

Bandura, A. 1986. *Social foundations of thought and action.* Englewood Cliffs, NJ: Prentice Hall.

Banner, J., and Cannon, H. 1997. *The elements of teaching.* New Haven, CT: Yale University Press.

Barcinas, S. J., and Gozer, M. D. 1986. Dramatization as a teaching technique in work orientation. *Passages* 2(1): 54–57.

Barron, D. D. 1990. ERIC, research and online update. *School Library Media Activities Monthly* 7(3): 46–50.

Bartlett, T. 2003. Did you hear the one about the professor? *Chronicle of Higher Education* 49(46): A8.

Barto, D. 1986. *Teacher as actor—Henry David Thoreau: From room one-eleven to Walden Pond and beyond.* Paper presented at the meeting of the National Council of Teachers of English, Philadelphia.

Baughman, M. D. 1979. Teaching with humor: A performing art. *Contemporary Education* 51(1): 26–30.

Beebe, S. 1980. "The role of nonverbal communication in education: Research and theoretical perspectives." Paper presented at the National Communication Association, New York.

Bergen, D. 1992. Using humor to facilitate learning. *Childhood Education* 62(2): 105–106.

Bernard, A. 1992. Laurence Olivier: A biography. *American Theatre* 8(12): 32–35.

Bettencourt, E., Gillett, M., and Hull, J. 1983. Effects of teacher enthusiasm training on student on-task behavior and achievement. *American Educational Research Journal* 20(3): 435–50.

Billson, J. M., and Tiberius, R. G. 1991. Effectual social arrangements for teaching and learning. In R. J. Menges and M. D. Svinicki, eds., *College teaching: From theory to practice*, pp. 87–109. San Francisco: Jossey-Bass.

Boerman-Cornell, W. 1999. The five humors. *English Journal* 88(4): 66–69.

Bonwell, C., and Eison, J. 1991. *Active learning: Creating excitement in the classroom.* ERIC Accession Number ED 340-272.

Bradley, B. E. 1981. *Fundamentals of speech communication.* Dubuque, IA: Wm. C. Brown.

Brigham, F. J. 1991. *Generating excitement: Teacher enthusiasm and students with learning difficulties.* Paper presented at the Annual Meeting of the Council for Learning Disabilities, Minneapolis.

Brigham, F. J., Scruggs, T. E., and Mastropieri, M. A. 1992. Teacher enthusiasm in learning disabilities classrooms: Effects on learning and behavior. *Learning Disabilities Research and Practice* 7: 68–73.

Brookfield, S. D., and Preskill, S. (1999). *Discussion as a way of teaching: Tools and techniques for democratic classrooms.* San Francisco: Jossey-Bass.

Brooks, S., and Bylo, B. 2004. Using PowerPoint. *Internet4Classrooms.* www.internet4classrooms.com.

Brophy, J., and Good, T. 1986. Teacher behavior and student achievement. In M. Wittrock, ed., *Handbook of research on teaching*, pp. 328–75. New York: Macmillan.

Brown, S. L. 2004. *High school students' perceptions of teacher effectiveness: Student ratings and teacher reflections.* Dissertation. The University of New Mexico AAT 3144067.

Browne, M. N., and Keeley, S. M. 1985. Achieving excellence: Advice to new teachers. *College Teaching* 33(2): 78–83.

Bruner, J. S. 1960. *The process of education.* Cambridge, MA: Harvard University Press.

Bryant, J., Comisky, P., Crane, J., and Zillmann, D. 1980. Relationship between college teachers' use of humour in the classroom and students' evaluations of their teachers. *Journal of Educational Psychology* 72(4): 511–19.

Bryant, J., and Zillmann, D. 1988. Using humor to promote learning in the classroom. *Journal of Children in Contemporary Society* 20(1–2): 49–78.

Buchowski, M. 2005. No joke: Laughing helps burn calories. *Vanderbilt Magazine* Summer: 16.

Burns, M. U., and Woods, P. S. 1992. *Teacher as actor.* Dubuque, IA: Kendall/Hunt.

Burts, C. C., et al. 1985. Effects of teacher enthusiasm on three- and four-year-old children's acquisition of four concepts. *Theory and Research in Social Education* 13(1): 19–29.

Butler, L., Miezitis, S., Friedman, R., and Cole, E. 1980. The effect of two school-based intervention programs on depressive symptoms in preadolescents. *American Educational Research Journal* 17(1): 111–19.

Campbell, C. P. 1981. Characteristics of effective vocational instructors. *Canadian Vocational Journal* 16(4): 24–28.

Carroll, J. 1991, March 24. Teacher's personality swings from likable to arrogant, testy. *Erie Times-News*, p. N-1.

Carroll, J. 2002, April 15. Getting good teaching evaluations without stand-up comedy. *Chronicle of Higher Education: Chronicle Careers.*

Chekhov, M. 1991. *On the techniques of acting.* New York: HarperCollins.

Chirpich, T. P. 1977. Ideal and non-ideal gases: An experiment with surprise value. *Journal of Chemical Education* 54(1): 378–79.

Civikly, J. M. 1986. *Communicating in college classrooms. New Directions for Teaching and Learning,* no. 26. San Francisco: Jossey-Bass.

Clark, R. W. 2005. The physics teacher: Sliders, staircases, and seduction. *Journal of Chemical Education* 82(2): 200.

Clayton, M., and Fortin, M. 2001. *Classroom spaces that work.* Turners Falls, MA: Northeast Foundation for Children.

Collins, M. L. 1981. *PHI DELTA KAPPAN Newsletter* (June).

Comisky, P., and Bryant, J. 1982. Factors involved in generating suspense. *Human Communication Research* 9(1): 49–58.

Conquergood, D. 1983. Storied worlds and the work of teaching. *Communication Education* 42(4): 337–48.

Cooper, P., and Simonds, C. 2003. *Communication for the classroom teacher.* Boston: Allyn and Bacon.

Cornett, C. E. 1986. *Learning through laughter: Humor in the classroom. Fastback 241.* Bloomington, IN: Phi Delta Kappan Foundation.

Creed, T. 1997. PowerPoint no, cyberspace yes. *National Teaching and Learning Forum* 6(4): 1–4.

Day, C. 2004. *A passion for teaching.* New York: RoutledgeFalmer.

Dead Poets' Society. 1989. Touchstone Pictures.

Dembo, M. H. 1988. *Applying educational psychology in the classroom.* New York: Longman.

Demetrulias, D.A.M. 1982. Gags, giggles, guffaws: Using cartoons in the classroom. *Journal of Reading* 26(1): 66–68.

Dinkmeyer, S. G. 1993. *Humor as an instructional practice: A longitudinal content analysis of humor use in the classroom.* ERIC Accession Number ED 359 587.

Dinkmeyer, D., McKay, G. D., and Dinkmeyer, D., Jr. 1980. *Systematic training for effective teaching (STET).* Circle Pines, MN: American Guidance Services.

Dolle, D., and Willems, G. M. 1984. The communicative approach to foreign language teaching. In G. M. Willems, ed., *Communicative foreign language teaching and the training of foreign language teachers,* pp. 85–102. Bloomington, IN: Viewpoints.

Donald, J. G., and Sullivan, A. M. 1985. *Using research to improve teaching.* San Francisco: Jossey-Bass.

Duncombe, S., and Heikkinen, M. 1988. Role-playing for different viewpoints. *English Journal* 36 (1): 3–5.

Eggleston, T. J., and Smith, G. E. 2002. Parting ways: Ending your course. Teaching Tips. *APA Observer* (15) 3.

Eison, J. 1990. Confidence in the classroom. *College Teaching* 38(1): 21–25.

Enerson, D. M., Johnson, R. N., Milner, S., and Plank, K. M. 1997. *The Penn State Teacher II.*

Enerson, D. M., and Plank, K. M. 1993. *The Penn State Teacher.* University Park: Pennsylvania State University.

Festinger, L. A. 1957. *A theory of cognitive dissonance.* Evanston, IL: Row, Peterson.

Fisch, L. 1991. Further confessions of a closet thespian. *Connexions* (Fall): 1.

French, J., Jr., and Raven, B. 1960. The bases for social power. In D. Cartwright and J. Zander, eds., *Group dynamics: Research and theory.* Evanston, IL: Row, Peterson.

Fried, R. L. 2001. *The passionate learner: How teachers and parents can help children reclaim the joy of discovery.* Boston: Beacon Press.

Friedman, A. 1995. The teacher as actor. *The National Teaching & Learning.* FORUM 4(2):1–3.

Frymier, A. B., and Thompson, C. A. 1992. Perceived teacher affinity-seeking in relation to perceived teacher credibility. *Communication Education* 41(4): 388–99.

Geske, J. 1992. Overcoming the drawbacks of the large lecture class. *College Teaching* 40(4): 151–54.

Gillett, M. 1980. *The effects of teacher enthusiasm on the at-task behavior of students in elementary grades.* ERIC Accession Number ED 202 823.

Glasser, W. 1998. *Choice theory in the classroom.* New York: HarperCollins.

Glover, J. A., and Bruning, R. H. 1990. *Educational psychology.* Boston: Little, Brown.

Goor, M. 1989. *Humor in the classroom: Options for enhancing learning.* Paper presented at the National Conference of the Council for Exceptional Children/Council for Children with Behavior Disorders, September, Charlotte, NC.

Gorham, J., and Christophel, D. M. 1990. The relationship of teachers' use of humor in the classroom to immediacy and student learning. *Communication Education* 39(1): 46–62.

Goulden, N. R. 1991. *Improving instructors' speaking skills.* Idea Paper no. 24, Center for Faculty Evaluation and Development, Kansas State University, Manhattan.

Graham, P. 1999. Roundtable discussion. Cited in A. Nguyen. 2000. Class act: The drama of good teaching. *Washington Monthly* 32(5): 7 pages.

Graham, P. 2005, December 19. Personal communication with authors.

Grant, B. M., and Hennings, D. G. 1971. *The teacher moves: An analysis of nonverbal activity.* New York: Teachers College Press.

Gravois, J. 2005. Investigation begets investigation in the wake of Ward Churchill. *Chronicle of Higher Education* 51(32): A10.

Greenberg, E., and Miller, P. 1991. The player and the professor: Theatrical techniques in teaching. *Journal of Management Education* 15(4): 428–46.

Grobe, R. P., Pettibone, T. J., and Martin, D. W. 1973. Effects of lecturer pace on noise level in a university classroom. *The Journal of Educational Research* 67(2): 73–75.

Guilford, P. 1959. The structure of the intellect. *Psychological Bulletin* 53(4): 267–93.

Hall, E. T. 1966. *The hidden dimension.* New York: Doubleday.

Hanning, R. W. 1984. The classroom as theater of self: Some observations for beginning teachers. *ADE Bulletin* 77: 33–37.

Hanning, R. W. 2005, September 23. Personal communication with authors.

Hativa, N. 2000. Teaching for effective learning in higher education. Boston: Kluwer.

Herbert, P. J. 1991. *Humor in the classroom: Theories, functions, and guidelines.* Paper presented at the Annual Meeting of the Central States Communication Association, April, Chicago.

Highet, G. 1950. *The art of teaching.* New York: Random House (Vintage).

Holloway, G., Abbott-Chapman, J., and Hughes, P. 1992. *Identifying the qualities and characteristics of the effective teacher, Report 2, Normative dimensions of teacher/student interaction.* Hobart, Tasmania: Youth Education Studies Centre, University of Tasmania.

Hook, S. 1981. Morris R. Cohen—Fifty years later. In J. Epstein Jr., ed., *Masters: Portraits of great teachers.* New York: Basic Books.

House, P. A. 1988. Components of success in mathematics and science. *School Science and Mathematics* 88(8): 632–41.

Humphreys, B. R. 1990. *A cheerful heart is good medicine: The emotional and physical benefits of humor.* Doctoral research paper. Viola University, California. ERIC Accession Number ED 317 892.

Hunsaker, J. S. 1988. It's no joke: Using humor in the classroom. *The Clearing House* 61(6): 285.

Hurt, H. R., Scott, M. D., and McCroskey, J. C. 1978. *Communication in the classroom.* Reading, MA: Knopf.

Jackson, L., and Murray, M. 1997. *What students really think of professors.* Lewiston, NY: Edwin Mellon Press.

Javidi, M., Downs, V. C., and Nussbaum, J. F. 1988. A comparative analysis of teachers' use of dramatic style behaviors at higher and secondary education levels. *Communication Education* 37(4): 278–88.

Johnson, B. D. 1991. Great teachers. *Maclean's* 104(42): 34–35.

Johnson, D. R. 1973. The element of surprise: An effective classroom technique. *Mathematics Teacher* 66(1): 13–16.

Jones, F. H. 1987. *Positive classroom discipline.* New York: McGraw-Hill.

Jones, F. H. 2000. *Tools of teaching.* Santa Cruz, CA: Fredric H. Jones & Associates.

Jordan, J. R. 1982. The professor as communicator. *Improving College and University Teaching* 30(3): 120–24.

Jose, P. E., and Brewer, W. F. 1990. Early grade school children's liking of script and suspense story structures. *Journal of Reading Behavior* 22(4): 355–72.

Justen, E. F. 1984. The missing link in ESL teacher training. *MEXTESOL Journal* 8(2): 49–62.

Kapoun, J. 2003. The use of PowerPoint in the library classroom: An experiment in learning outcomes. *Library Philosophy and Practice* 6(1): 10–17.

Keane, B. 2005, December 14. Family Circus, *Times,* p.7D.

Kher, N., Molstad, S., and Donahue, R. 1999. Using humor in the college classroom to enhance teaching effectiveness in "dread courses." *The College Student Journal* 33(3): 400–406.

Keiper, R. W. 1991. *The teacher as actor.* Paper presented at the 71st Annual Meeting of the Association of Teacher Educators, New Orleans.

Kelly, N., and Kelly, B. 1982. *Backgrounds, education, and teaching styles of award-winning professors.* Annual Meeting of the Rocky Mountain Educational Research Association, Albuquerque, NM. ERIC Accession Number ED 230 080.

Kin, K. W. 1995, January 3. In a nation of readers, manga popularity jumps. *The Japan Times,* p. 17

Klein, J., and Fitch, M. 1990. First grade children's comprehension of "noodle doodle box." *Youth Theatre Journal* 5(2): 7–13.

Knapp, M. L. 1971. The role of non-verbal communication in the classroom. *Theory into Practice* 10(4): 243–49.

Knapp, M., and Hall, J. 1992. *Nonverbal communication in human interaction*. Fort Worth, TX: Holt, Rinehart, and Winston.

Korobkin, D. 1988. Humor in the classroom: Considerations and strategies. *College Teaching* 36(4): 154–58.

Kougl, K. 1997. *Communicating in the classroom*. Long Grove, IL: Waveland Press.

Kounin, J. 1970. *Discipline and group management*. New York: Holt, Rinehart, and Winston.

Krathwohl, D. R., Bloom, B. S., and Masia, B. B. 1956. *Taxonomy of educational objectives. Handbook II: Affective domain*. New York: David McKay.

Kress, G. C., and Ehrlichs, M. A. 1990. Development of confidence in child behavior management through role-playing. *Journal of Dental Education* 54(10): 619–22.

Kurre, J. 1993. "The art of teaching." Speech presented to Penn State-Behrend faculty, Erie, Pennsylvania.

Lai, J. 2005, February. Passionate teaching. *Linkage* 236: 1.

Larson, G. 1982. Humorous teaching makes serious learning. *TETYC* 8(3): 197–99.

Loomans, D., and Kohlberg, K. 1993. *The laughing classroom: Everyone's guide to teaching with humor & play*. Tiburon, CA: H. J. Kramer.

Lowe, D. W. 1991. *Using cartoons in psychology lectures: The "far side" of psychology*. Paper presented at the Thirteenth Annual National Institute on the Teaching of Psychology Conference, Tampa.

Lowman, J. 1984. *Mastering the techniques of teaching*. San Francisco: Jossey-Bass.

Lubawy, W. C. 2003. Evaluating teaching using the Best Practices Model. *American Journal of Pharmaceutical Education*. 67(3): 1–3.

Lundberg, E. M., and Thurston, C. M. 2002. *If they're laughing, they just might be listening*. Fort Collins, CO: Cottonwood Press.

MacAdam, B. 1985. Humor in the classroom: Implications for the bibliographic instruction librarian. *College & Research Libraries* 46(4): 327–33.

MacLaren, R., and Olson, D. 1993. Trick or treat: Children's understanding of surprise. *Cognitive Development* 8(1): 27–46.

Magnan, B. 1989. *147 practical tips for teaching professors*. Madison, WI: Magna.

Maier, M. H., and Panitz, T. 1996. End on a high note: Better endings for classes and courses. *College Teaching* 44(4): 145–47.

McHugh, J. 2005. Synching up with iKid. *Edutopia* 1(7): 33–35.

McKay, J. 2000. *Generation of idiom-based witticisms to aid second language learning*. Edinburgh, Scotland: University of Edinburgh.

McKeachie, W. J. 1986. *Teaching tips: A guidebook for the beginning college teacher*. Lexington, MA: D. C. Heath.

McTaggart, J. 2003. *From the teacher's desk*. Bangor, ME: Booklocker.

McTaggart, J. 2005, December 12. Personal communication with authors.

Meier, R. S., and Feldhusen, J. F. 1979. Another look at Dr. Fox: Effect of stated purpose on evaluation, lecturer expressiveness, and density of lecture content on student ratings. *Journal of Educational Psychology* 71(3): 339–45.

Meyer, W. U., Niepel, M., Rudolph, U., and Schutzwohl, A. 1991. An experimental analysis of surprise. *Cognition and Emotion* 5(4): 295–311.

Murphy, C. A., and Walls, R. T. 1994. *Concurrent and sequential occurrences of teacher enthusiasm behaviors*. Paper presented at the Annual Meeting of the AERA, New Orleans, April 4–9.

Murray, D. M. 1984. Writing and teaching for surprise. *College English* 46(1): 1–7.

Murray, H. G. 1985. Classroom teaching behaviors related to college teaching effectiveness. In J. G. Donald and A. M. Sullivan, eds., *Using research to improve teaching,* pp. 21–34. San Francisco: Jossey-Bass.

Murray, H. G. 1997. Effective teaching behaviours in the college classroom. In R.P. Perry and J.C. Smart, eds., *Effective teaching in higher education: Research and practice.* New York: Agathon Press.

Naftulin, D. H., Ware, J. E., Jr., and Donnelly, F. A. 1973. The Doctor Fox lecture: A paradigm of educational seduction. *Journal of Medical Education* 48: 630–35.

Neilsen, D. L. F. 1993. *Humor scholarship: A research bibliography.* Westport, CT: Greenwood Press.

Neuliep, J. W. 1991. An examination of the content of high school teachers' humor in the classroom and the development of an inductively derived taxonomy of classroom humor. *Communication Education* 40(4): 343–55.

Nguyen, A. 2000. Class act: The drama of good teaching. *Washington Monthly* 32(5): 7 pages.

Norris, A., and O'Bannon, B. 2001. Technology and teacher preparation: Creating learning environments for increasing student involvement and creativity. *SMARTer Kids Foundation.* http://www.smarterkids.org/research/paper11.asp

Not so rich, or famous. 1993. *NEA Today* 12(4): 25.

Nussbaum, J. F. 1992. Effective teacher behaviors. *Communication Education* 41(2): 167–80.

Nussbaum, J. F., Comadena, M. E., and Holladay, S. J. 1987. Classroom verbal behavior of highly effective teachers. *Journal of Thought* 22: 73–80.

Oldenburg, D. 2005, May 1. Laugh yourself skinny. *The Washington Post.*

Oppenheimer, T. 2005. Technology made easy. *Edutopia* 1(7): 42–44.

Ostrand, J., and Creaser, J. 1978. Development of counselor candidate dominance in three learning conditions. *The Journal of Psychology* 99: 199–202.

Our readers write. 1982. *English Journal* 71(2): 68–76.

Palmer, P. J. 1990. Good teaching: A matter of living the mystery. *Change* 22(1): 11–15.

Palmer, P. J. 1998. *The courage to teach: Exploring the inner landscapes of a teacher's life.* San Francisco: Jossey-Bass.

Patrick, B. C., Hisley, J., and Kempler, T. 2000. "What's everybody so excited about?": The effects of teacher enthusiasm on student intrinsic motivation and vitality. *The Journal of Experimental Education* 68(3): 217–36.

Penner, J. G. 1984. *Why many college teachers cannot lecture.* Springfield, IL: Charles C. Thomas.

Performance. 2005. http://www.merriamwebster.com.

Perry, R. P. 1985. Instructor expressiveness: Implications for improving teaching. In J. G. Donald and A. M. Sullivan, eds., *Using research to improve teaching* (pp. 35–49). San Francisco: Jossey-Bass.

Peterson, I. 1980. Humor in the physics classroom. *The Physics Teacher* 18(9): 646–49.

Phi Delta Kappan. 1991. 72(7): 501.

Pickering, S. 2004. *Letters to a teacher.* New York: Atlantic Monthly Press.

Pilla, R. S. 1997. *The Penn State teacher II.* 171–72.

Pollack, J. P., and Freda, P. D. 1997. Humor, learning, and socialization in middle level classrooms. *The Clearing House* 70(4): 176–78.

Powell, J. P., and Anderson, L. W. 1985. Humour and teaching in higher education. *Studies in Higher Education* 10(1): 79–90.

Powers, T. 2005. Engaging students with humor. *aps Observer* 18(12): 1–6.

Puckett, M. J., and Shaw, J. M. 1988. The storytime exchange: Ways to enhance it. *Childhood Education* 64(5): 293–98.

Ramsell, B. 1978. The poetic experience of surprise and the art of teaching. *The English Journal* 67(5): 22–25.

Richmond, V. 1992. *Nonverbal communication in the classroom*. Edina, MN: Burgess.

Richmond, V. P., Gorham, J. S., and McCroskey, J. C. 1987. The relationship between selected immediacy behaviors and cognitive learning. In M. McLaughlin, ed., *Communication yearbook 10*, pp. 574–90. Beverly Hills: Sage.

Rist, R. 1970. Student social class and teacher expectations: The self-fulfilling prophecy in ghetto education. *Harvard Educational Review* 40(3): 411–451.

Robinson, W. K. 1993. Dramatic arts for teachers: Preparing prospective teachers to take center stage. Paper presented at the National Association of Teacher Educators meeting, Los Angeles.

Rosenshine, B., and Furst, R. 1973. The use of direct observation to study teaching. In R. Travers, ed., *Second handbook on research on teaching*. Chicago: Rand McNally.

Ross, E. 2005, June 4. A good laugh may help shed extra weight. *Associated Press*.

Rubin, L. J. 1985. *Artistry in teaching*. New York: Random House.

"Sage Advice." 2005. *Edutopia* 1(7): 42–43.

Sallinen-Kuparinen, A., Marttinen, P., Permamaki, P., and Porhola, M. 1987. In A. Sallinen-Kuparinen, ed., *Perspectives on instructional communication*, pp. 97–111. Jyvaskyla, Finland: University of Jyvaskyla, Publication of the Department of Communication 5.

Sandler, T. M. 2006. Personal communication.

Sarason, S. 1999. *Teaching as a performing art*. New York: Teachers College Press.

Schibsted, E. 2005. Rearrange the desks: Move the chairs to open their minds. *Edutopia* 1(5): 29.

Schwartz, L. L. 1980. Criteria for effective university teaching. *Improving College and University Teaching* 28(3): 120–23.

Searle, B. 2001. The spirit of teaching. *NEFDC Exchange* 12(2): 6.

Sev'er, A., and Ungar, S. 1997. No laughing matter: Boundaries of gender-based humour in the classroom. *Journal of Higher Education* 68(1): 87–105.

Shade, R. A. 1996. *License to laugh: Humor in the classroom*. Englewood, CO: Teacher Ideas Press.

Shedlock, M. L. 1951. *The art of the story-teller*. New York: Dover.

Showalter, E. 2003. *Teaching literature*. Malden, MA: Blackwell.

Smith, H. A. 1979. Nonverbal communication in teaching. *Review of Educational Research* 49(4): 631–72.

Soenksen, R. 1992. *Confessions of a professor, nee actor*. Paper presented at the National Communication Association Convention, Chicago.

Sprague, J. 1993. Why teaching works: The transformative power of pedagogical communication. *Communication Education* 42(4): 349–66.

Stanislavski, K. 1936. *An actor prepares*. Translated by Elizabeth Reynolds Hapwood. New York: Theatre Arts Books.

Starratt, R. J. 1990. *The drama of schooling/The schooling of drama*. New York: The Falmer Press.

Streeter, B. B. 1986. The effects of training experienced teachers in enthusiasm on students' attitudes toward reading. *Reading Psychology* 7(4): 249–59.

Strine, M. S. 1993. Of boundaries, borders, and contact zones: Author(iz)ing pedagogical practices. *Communication Education* 42(4): 367–76.

Sukow, W. W. 1990. Physical science workshops for teachers using interactive science exhibits. *School Science and Mathematics* 90(1): 42–47.

Sullivan, R. L. 1992. It's a H.I.T. *Vocational Education Journal* 67(3): 36–38.

Sultanoff, S. M. 2002. Integrating humor into psychotherapy. In Charles Schaefer, ed., *Play therapy with adults*. New York: Wiley.

Tamborini, R., and Zillmann, D. 1981. College students' perceptions of lectures using humor. *Perceptual and Motor Skills* 52(2): 417–32.

Tauber, R. T. 1999. *Classroom management: Sound theory and effective practice*. Westport, CT: Greenwood.

TEDI (Teaching and Educational Development Institute) 2002. *Teaching Anxiety*. Queensland, Australia: The University of Queensland.

The Teacher Institute. 2005. Keep your students in suspense. *Better Teaching* 19(2): 1–4.

Timpson, W. M. 1982. *Teaching as performing*. Englewood Cliffs, NJ: Prentice-Hall.

Timpson, W., Burgoine, S., Jones, C., and Jones, W. 2002. *Teaching and performing: Ideas for energizing your classes*. Madison, WI: Atwood.

Tobin, K. 1986. Effects of teacher wait-time on discourse characteristics in mathematics and language arts classes. *American Educational Research Journal* 23(2): 191–200.

Tompkins, J. 1996. *A life in school: What the teacher learned*. New York: Addison-Wesley.

Torok, S. E., McMorris, R. F., and Lin, W. 2004. Is humor an appreciated teaching tool? Perceptions of professors' teaching styles and use of humor. *College Teaching* 52(1): 14–20.

Travers, R. M. 1979. Training the teacher as a performing artist. *Contemporary Education* 51(1): 14–18.

Travers, R. M., and Dillon, J. 1975. *The making of a teacher: A plan for professional self-development*. New York: Macmillan.

Tufte, E. 2003. PowerPoint is Evil. *Wired* 11(9): 2–4.

Vidler, D. C., and Levine, J. 1981. Curiosity, magic, and the teacher. *Education* 101(3): 273–75.

Vizmuller, J. 1980. Psychological reasons for using humor in a pedagogical setting. *Canadian Modern Language Review* 36(2): 266–71.

Wallinger, L. M. 1997. Don't smile before Christmas: The role of humor in education. *NASSP Bulletin*, 81(589): 27–34.

Walter, G. 1990. Laugh, teacher, laugh. *Teaching for Excellence* 9(8): 28–29.

Walz, J. C. 1986. Increasing student talk time in the foreign language classroom. *Canadian Modern Language Review* 42(5): 952–67.

Wandersee, J. H. 1982. Humor as a teaching strategy. *American Biology Teacher* 44(4): 212–18.

Warnock, P. 1989. Humor as a didactic tool in adult education. *Lifelong Learning* 12(8): 22–24.

Weaver, R. L. 1981. Effective lecturing techniques. *The Clearing House* 55: 20–23.

Webster's seventh new collegiate dictionary (1972). Springfield, MA: Merriam.

Weimer, M. 1993. *Improving your classroom teaching*, Survival Skills for Scholars Series. Newbury Park, CA: Sage.

Wells, E. F. 1979. Bewitched, dazzled, and delighted. *Teacher* 96(9): 53–54.

Welsz, E. 1990. Energizing the classroom. *College Teaching* 38(2): 74–76.

Winter, J. 2004. She who laughs, lasts. *Principal* 83(4): 38–40.

Witty, P. 1950. Some characteristics of the effective teacher. *Educational Administration and Supervision* 36: 193–208.

Wlodkowski, R. J. 1985. *Enhancing adult motivation to learn*. San Francisco: Jossey-Bass.

Woods, P. 1983. Coping at school through humour. *British Journal of Education* 4(2): 111–24.

Woolfolk, A. E. 1993. *Educational psychology,* 5th ed. Englewood Cliffs, NJ: Prentice-Hall.

Wulff, D. H. 1993. Tales of transformation: Applying a teaching effectiveness perspective to stories about teaching. *Communication Education* 42(4): 377–97.

Ziegler, J. 1998. Use of humour in medical training. *Medical Teacher* 20(4). 341–48.

Zillmann, D., and Hay, T. A. 1975. The effect of suspense and its resolutions on the appreciation of dramatic presentations. *Journal of Research in Personality* 9(4): 307–23.

Ziv, A. 1989. Using humor to develop creative thinking. *Journal of Children in Contemporary Society* 20(1–2): 99–116.

SUBJECT AND NAME INDEX

About the Authors

ROBERT T. TAUBER is Professor Emeritus, School of Humanities and Social Sciences, Penn State–Erie, The Behrend College. He has taught and counseled in K–12, and has taught at the university level for 35 years. While at Behrend College he taught a variety of education courses, supervised students on field experience, and served as Dean's Representative for the College of Education. After retiring from Penn State University as Professor Emeritus, Dr. Tauber continues to teach graduate courses as an Adjunct Professor at Gannon University, Erie, PA, and an Adjunct Professor at the University of Florida, Gainesville, FL. He is well published, both nationally and internationally, and has served two sabbaticals, one at Durham University (UK) and one at the University of Melbourne (Australia).

CATHY SARGENT MESTER is Senior Lecturer in Communication, School of Humanities and Social Sciences, Penn State–Erie, The Behrend College. Mester is a 35-year member of the faculty in Communication and Media Studies at Penn State–Erie, where she also currently serves as Program Chair. She has created a specialized course in instructional communication for pre-service teachers and frequently leads workshops for inservice teachers as well as business and community leaders. Co-author of three books and numerous conference papers and articles, Mester has taught at all grade levels, served as a school board president, a faculty organization president, and is listed in *Who's Who Among American Teachers*.